A Philosophical Defense of Culture

SUNY series in Chinese Philosophy and Culture

Roger T. Ames, editor

A Philosophical Defense of Culture

Perspectives from Confucianism and Cassirer

SHUCHEN XIANG

Cover image of Ernst Cassirer from Wikimedia Commons.

Published by State University of New York Press, Albany

For information, contact State University of New York Press, Albany, NY
www.sunypress.edu

Library of Congress Cataloging-in-Publication Data

Names: Xiang, Shuchen, author.
Title: A philosophical defense of culture : perspectives from Confucianism and
    Cassirer / Shuchen Xiang.
Description: Albany : State University of New York Press, [2021] | Series:
    SUNY series in Chinese Philosophy and Culture | Includes bibliographical
    references and index.
Identifiers: ISBN 9781438483191 (hardcover : alk. paper) | ISBN 9781438483207
    (pbk. : alk. paper) | ISBN 9781438483214 (ebook)
Further information is available at the Library of Congress.

10 9 8 7 6 5 4 3 2 1

Dedicated to my mother

Contents

Acknowledgments

This project has been long in gestation; I first conceived the project around 2012–13. The various people, to whom I am indebted draws a map of the journey I have made for its materialization. From my time at Pennsylvania State University, I would like to thank my mentor Erica Fox Brindley for having always encouraged my intellectual independence. I am also grateful to Courtney Rong Fu for her great kindness to me then. From Princeton, I would like to thank Jessica Xiaomin Zu, for many things. From my time at the University of Hawai'i, I would like to thank Professor Chung-ying Cheng for introducing me to the *Yijing*. I am furthermore extremely grateful to Professor Cheng for having provided me with the many opportunities to present and develop my work. I am grateful for having received guidance from Professor David McCraw, whose infectious enthusiasm for the classics has inspired a whole generation of scholars educated at Hawai'i; I feel privileged to count myself among them. Finally, I am very lucky to have received the kind attention of Professor Roger Ames during his last year there and his support throughout the gestation of this project. From the APA Eastern Division 2016, I would like to thank Professors Huaiyu Wang and Aaron Creller for their helpful comments on my work. From Aarhus University, I would like to thank Professor Guido Kreis for his personal guidance on this project; his help has been invaluable to me. I have gained enormously from his own work on Cassirer. I would like to thank Professor Michael Forster, from the University of Bonn, for providing me with the much needed platforms for developing my work. From the University of York, I would like to thank professors Peter Lamarque and Catherine Wilson for their kind attention to me during the earlier phases of this project. From Nanyang Technological University, I would like to thank Lili Zhang for the conversations that helped refine my ideas, and

Professor Brook Ziporyn for talking me through some ideas while he was a visiting professor there. I would like to thank Professor Karyn Lai for reading the first draft of this project and providing such helpful feedback. Similarly, my thanks to Professor Geir Sigurðsson both for his comments at a conference where I presented an early iteration of this project and for his later comments on the first draft. From the Humboldt University of Berlin, I would like to thank Professor Christian Möckel for helping me find my feet among all the Cassirer literature; my interpretation of Cassirer is also indebted to his own work on Cassirer. I would also like to thank Professor Donald Phillip Verene for reading this manuscript and for his advice. I would also like to thank Professor Xinzhong Yao for supporting this project and giving me valuable feedback on it. I am most grateful, however, to Michael Beaney for having believed in this project from the beginning and for having continuously supported me throughout its gestation. His help came at a crucial moment, and I would have been lost without him. I hope that the final product does not fall too much short of his earliest expectations. From Peking University, I would like to thank Zhang Yan for her calligraphy, which is on the front cover. I would also like to thank Zhang Yixuan and Wang Rouzhu, both of whom looked over appendix 3 for me. Any mistakes are of course my own.

From SUNY Press, I would like to thank the two anonymous reviewers whose feedback helped me to gain some much needed perspective on the project and helped give it its final finish. I would also like to thank Mr. James Peltz for all his help in the submission process and in preparing the manuscript. I would also like to thank the copyeditor Gordon Marce for his grammatical expertise and the detailed attention he paid to my manuscript. Parts of the introduction have been previously published in "Orientalism and Enlightenment Positivism: A Critique of Anglophone Sinology, Comparative Literature, and Philosophy," *Pluralist* 13, no. 2. Parts of chapter 2 have been previously published in "Freedom and Culture: The Cassirerian and Confucian Account of Symbolic Formation," *Idealistic Studies* 47, no. 3, as well as "The Symbolic Construction of Reality: The *Xici* and Ernst Cassirer's Philosophy of Symbolic Forms," *Journal of Chinese Humanities* 4, no. 2. Parts of chapter 6 have been previously published in "Organic Harmony and Ernst Cassirer's Pluralism," *Idealistic Studies* 49, no. 3. I thank all these journals for permission to reuse these articles.

Finally, my thanks to Jacob Bender for having made so much possible, for making it all so much easier, and everything that much more enjoyable; and to my mother, who gave me everything. In some ways she is the inspiration for this project, for she embodies the living tradition that I find so much beauty in.

Abbreviations

I have abbreviated the major works of Cassirer's that I have most copiously used, so that it is easier for the reader to see where I am citing from. These are listed below, along with the date that links each to the main reference list. I have used the author-date system for Cassirer's other works.

DI   *Determinism and Indeterminism in Modern Physics: Historical and Systematic Studies of the Problem of Causality* (1956)

EM   *An Essay on Man* (1944)

FF   *Freiheit und Form* (Freedom and Form; 2001a)

KEH   "The Kantian Element in Wilhelm von Humboldt's Philosophy of Language" (2013c)

KLT   *Kant's Life and Thought* (1981)

LCS   *The Logic of the Cultural Sciences* (2000)

LM   *Language and Myth* (1946a)

MS   *The Myth of the State* (1946b)

NHPC   "Naturalistic and Humanistic Philosophies of Culture" (1961)

PSF 1   *Philosophy of Symbolic Forms*, vol. 1, *Language* (1955a)

PSF 2   *Philosophy of Symbolic Forms*, vol. 2, *Mythical Thought* (1955b)

PSF 3   *Philosophy of Symbolic Forms*, vol. 3, *The Phenomenology of Knowledge* (1957)

PSF 4   *Philosophy of Symbolic Forms*, vol. 4, *The Metaphysics of Symbolic Forms* (1996)

SF   *Substance and Function, and Einstein's Theory of Relativity* (1923)

SMC   *Symbol, Myth, and Culture: Essays and Lectures of Ernst Cassirer, 1935–1945* (1979)

PE   *The Philosophy of the Enlightenment* (1951)

PK   *The Problem of Knowledge: Philosophy, Science, and History since Hegel* (1950)

Introduction

Wen (文) is a term whose sophistication and significance for the Chinese tradition parallels that of *Dao* (道) and *Qi* (气). It is a term that designates everything from natural patterns to the individual units that make up Chinese writing, to literature, to human culture itself.[1] I argue that *wen* became such an important term to Chinese civilization because embedded in the term is the Chinese philosophy of culture and humanism. As Wing-tsit Chan writes, "If one word could characterize the entire history of Chinese philosophy, that word would be humanism—not the humanism that denies or slights a Supreme Power, but one that professes the unity of man and Heaven. In this sense, humanism has dominated Chinese thought from the dawn of its history" (Chan 1963, 3). It is because of a profound and dominant humanism in the Chinese tradition that the term *wen* became so ubiquitous. *Wen* embodied the ideal of Confucianism: attaining humanity through culture while recognizing that we are part of a natural continuum. It embodies the Confucian vision of harmony between humans, human culture, and the natural world. Whereas the philosophy of culture originated in the eighteenth century with thinkers such as Vico, Herder, Voltaire, and Rousseau, Chinese philosophy (notably the Confucian tradition), since the beginning of philosophical speculation, orientated itself around the question of culture. How culture was justified can be seen in a philosophical reconstruction of the etymology of the term *wen*. *Wen* is both humanism and the *form* of humanism—it is the totality of cultural forms through which we achieve our humanity.

There is pressing contemporary need to think about culture, especially culture under the Confucian-Cassirerian mode. The context for a philosophical defense of culture is the colonial world order that was so disastrously unable to accept the plurality of cultural orders and

1

the legitimate sovereignty and agency of human beings to create their own cultural forms. Through its "discovery" of the American continent, Europe encountered previously unimagined diversity. It was this confrontation with diversity that precipitated the first formulations of "international law," on the basis of which the Amerindians were robbed of their sovereignty.[2] The universalism of international law was claimed by the father of international law, Francisco de Vitoria, on the basis of two assumptions: one, that the cultural differences of the Amerindians were a sign of their deviance from international law (universalism); and, two, that international law (universalism) was Roman law writ large.[3] This stillborn, troubled first encounter with cultural diversity has left a lasting legacy; mainstream academic philosophy, in the Francisco de Vitorian mode, still assumes the fact of universalism and is worryingly insensitive to the empirical existence of diversity. For mainstream academic philosophy, culture is irrelevant to philosophy, just as the existence of cultural difference was of no consequence for the Spaniards' vision of universalism. What cultural difference that exists is parsed as either nonessential or deviant and so of no consequence to a putative essential sameness. (Cultural) diversity is not real, only sameness is. The inability to dignify cultural difference as real has led to the more worrying (historical) phenomenon of parsing difference in racial terms. Given the empirical fact of human diversity but the simultaneous refusal to attribute this diversity to a human agency capable of establishing its own terms of engagement with the world, diversity was parsed in ontological terms. During the heyday of empire, whole swathes of natural scientists and philosophers theorized the racial origins of human difference.[4] For these thinkers, the fact of (cultural) diversity can only mean that not all humans are equal on the great chain of being or the ladder of civilization. Due to this history, mainstream academic philosophy currently utilizes impoverished resources for understanding difference or pluralism. What this book offers is a way of thinking about human beings that emphasizes their agency to create different *cultures*, which then become, to a large degree, constitutive of their identities. There are no "ifs" in history: we cannot ask what the world might be like *if* we had preserved more of the civilizations and cultural forms that were erased due to their inability to conform to a putative "universal." What we can do, however, is strive not to repeat the same history. To do this, we need a systematic worldview in which human beings are defined by their culture. This is a better definition of the human being than either emphasizing our fundamental sameness (i.e., we are all rational animals) or ontological difference (i.e., we belong to different races of varying worth). Defining the human being in terms of culture assumes that (1) the existence of culture is a sign of the (creative, spontaneous) agency of that group of people, and (2) cultures are dynamic and can change. As "symbolic animals" (in Cassirerian terms) or people of *wen* (in Confucian terms), we are inherently *cultural* beings, and implicit in this definition is a way of thinking about personhood that gives an important role to pluralism in our identities while acknowledging a fundamental commensurability. As cultural beings, we differ because we have different cultures, but we are fundamentally commensurable because we are all symbolic animals. That we have culture is a sign of that fundamentally human capacity to create culture. Culture avoids the deceptive universalism of defining the human being in terms of rationality, as there are as many different reasons as there are different cultures. Culture also avoids the peril of reifying perceived differences into underlying substances. What difference exists between cultures is a creation of human spontaneity, as opposed to a sign of essential, ontological difference such as race. Culture avoids the pitfall of that imagined, dichotomous other beloved by defenders of universalism—a babelesque relativism in which there is no possibility of commensurability between cultures. The empirical fact is that there has *always* been a plurality of cultures and that cultures, through mutual engagement, absorb and transform each other. The very fact that different cultures adopt each other's characteristics is evidence of the possibility of cultural translation. Just as mutual understanding (translation) is possible between different languages, so is mutual understanding possible across different cultures.

Finally, the Confucian-Cassirerian conception of culture allocates human beings a position among the myriad things of the world that allows for both commensurability (or continuity) and uniqueness. We are continuous with all other living things in that we seek to express ourselves, but we are unique among all living things in that we have an especially sophisticated language. The Confucian-Cassirerian conception of culture reinstates the human being to an accurate position within the myriad things and so secures an ecologically sustainable self-identity for humanity. To defend the importance of culture as a philosophical para-digm, I draw on classical Confucianism and Ernst Cassirer's philosophy of symbolic forms. The classical Confucian conception of culture is one of the important elements in the longevity and success of the Chinese

civilization, while Ernst Cassirer is an heir to the spirit of Goethe, and
the golden age of German humanism.

Historical Reconstruction of *Wen*

It is Cassirer's and Confucianism's humanism on which I wish to focus
in this project. To do so, I will draw on a few related themes. Key to
both Confucianism's and Cassirer's humanism is the human creation of
"form": a dynamic, functional system for organizing experience,[5] which
is not derived from or modeled on a transcendent source but instead
constructed by humans in coherence with their natural and social milieus.
In the Cassirerian context, these forms include, but are not limited
to, language, myth, science, art, law, and religion. In the Confucian
context, these forms include, but are not limited to, the hexagrams
of the *Yijing*, language, literature, music, and ritual.[6] The metaphysical
foundation for, or transcendental element of, this humanistic form is the
inalienable expressivity of the phenomenal world to human beings. Via
this form, the social human being is harmonized with the nonsubjective
world. While the world is inherently expressive to human beings, it is
only through the human creation of form that we can go back to the
phenomenal world and order it in a way that enables meanings that
extend beyond momentary affectivity. Simultaneous with the creation
of form is thus an ordering of the phenomenal world that enables it to
gain a heretofore unavailable stability and meaning. The truth, stability,
and meaning of our world is thus dependent upon the forms of our own
creation. The forms themselves derive their truth, stability, and meaning
in relation to the (functional) law which in turn is derived from the
internal coherence of the totality of individual forms. This philosophy
of form is thus neither a realism nor an idealism: it is nondualistic.
Truth, stability, and meaning (or the conditions of possibility of our
humanity) are neither passively copied from an antecedently existing
reality nor imposed by the ego. A symbolic form is, furthermore, not
a *forma substantialis*; it is dynamic. This symbolic form is, lastly, not a
preexisting-determined fact of the world; it must be created (*tun*) by
the forming powers of the human spirit. We can only comprehend the
world and ourselves through our own creations (*Gebilde*), and so the
creation and maintenance of these creations is both descriptive of and
the prescriptive task of human culture.

With this metaphysical-epistemological model of the genesis of meaning is a stress on harmony and personal cultivation. Without an already integral, preexisting truth, stability, and meaning to be copied from an antecedently existing reality, these aspects of reality need to be created and maintained. The human agent thus becomes the maker and keeper of this harmony. We are only able to do this by embedding ourselves ever more deeply in these forms, so that we may participate more meaningfully, and thus be capable of increasing competence in the guardianship and creative innovation of the space of our cultural forms, hence the stress on personal cultivation.

Ernst Cassirer (1874–1945) is perhaps the European tradition's greatest philosopher of culture.[7] Against the previous tradition that defined man in terms of his rational capacities, Cassirer posited that the defining attribute of man was his capacity for symbol making. Instead of the capacity for truth being the defining feature of human beings, it is the capacity for meaning. Consequently, whereas previously any possibility for our attainment of freedom lay in the attainment of truth, now it lies in our capacity for meaning-making. Meaning is dynamic, evolving, cooperative (between peoples as well as between people and the *forms* of meaning-making) and pluralistic. It is these symbols, or forms, or symbolic forms that allow us to achieve a freedom from the natural world of determinism, and so be free for our humanity—free for those distinguishing aspects that set us apart from the rest of the natural world. In his last speech, Faust says the highest wisdom is to recognize that "[h]e only earns his freedom and existence, who daily conquers them anew." Cassirer comments that, while the meaning that life is endowed through this conquest might not constitute man's happiness, it does constitute "his distinctive dignity" (Cassirer 2007b, 527). Like the Confucian *ren* (仁), the epitome of humanity can never be reached, but our distinctive dignity lies in the actions that make us free for the infinite potentiality of our humanity.

Given the importance of culture for our ability to achieve humanity, the idea that *wen* enables or carries the Dao (*wen yi zai dao* 文以載道) became a dominant guiding principle for the Chinese literati throughout Chinese history. This mutual dependence on humanism (i.e., Dao) and the forms of humanism is expressed by Cassirer's own definition of humanism: " '*Humanitas*,' in the widest sense of the word, denotes that completely universal—and, in this very universality, unique—medium in which 'form,' as such, comes into being and in which it can develop and flourish" (*NHPC* 22). In both traditions, what most essentially defines humans is that there is no fixed essence: humans are defined by their ability to become human through cultural forms. What defines us is our capacity for civilization, and the enabling condition of civilization is the symbol. It is in this sense that Cassirer famously said that man is a symbolic animal, not a rational animal (*EM* 26). This project will focus on the classical Confucian texts[8] that employ the term *wen*: the *Analects* and the *Xunzi*. It will also focus on (Confucian) texts that center around aspects of refined human culture that the Confucians saw under the rubric of *wen*—texts on music (*Yue Ji* 乐记), literature (*Wenxin Diaolong* 文心雕龙), and poetry (*Maoshi Xu* 毛诗序); as well as the "Ten Wings" (十翼) and especially the *Xici* (系辞), which provides a philosophical justification for the beginning of writing and civilization. It will look to other key texts in the Confucian canon, which is particularly sophisticated in articulating the relationship between human beings and the wider cosmic order: the *Zhongyong* (中庸) and *Daxue* (大学). What we will see is that the same paradigmatic relationship applies in the hexagrams, poetry, language, and ethical forms. A humanly created *form* is needed to consummate what was already implicit in either the world or the self. Conversely, there is always an assumption that the innate tendencies of either things or the self, tend toward externalization and only fully exist after the various cultural forms have manifested their potentiality. The fact that it is only the cultural forms of civilization that consummate "nature," it is argued, is the Confucian understanding of *tian ren he yi*. The ideal of *tian ren he yi* that I refer to does not seek to make humans identical with *tian* and vice versa in order to unite them. It overcomes this dualism. I will show that *wen*, because it reconciled human culture with a natural continuum, because it is the *form* in which one realizes humanism, and because it embodies humanism *per se*, explains its omnipresence and privileged status in classical Chinese discourse.

This project is, in part, an exercise in philosophical translation. While it will be demonstrated that there are historical or metaphilosophical reasons for the comparability of the Confucian and Cassirerian project, the two intellectual traditions inevitably use different vocabularies. The translation of Confucianism and Cassirer into each other's discourses will be mutually complementary. Cassirer will provide a vocabulary of critical idealism that will better situate the Confucian project of culture within the map of Western philosophy. Conversely, the sophistication of Confucian humanism will better draw out the ethical undercurrent of the Cassirerian project that—as a German Jew in exile until the last days of his life—became central to his last writings. The ultimate aim of this project, however, is to transcend the national boundaries in which contemporary philosophy conceives itself. Aspiring to write *meaningful* philosophy for the entirety of humanity or from the perspective of humanity, from our point in history onwards, requires the philosopher to speak to the human experience at large. A truly universal philosophy, at the risk of stating the obvious, cannot be written from within the confines of one's own national tradition. We are no longer in a colonial situation, in which the traditions of others can be maligned and dismissed as non-"philosophy." Philosophy is an activity that characterizes all human beings, that is, a systematic attempt to think about the human being's relationship to the world. A truly "universal" philosophy needs to earn its name by actually seeking to include the totality of humanity. This project aspires to be philosophy written under such a cosmopolitan mode.

The Contemporary Relevance of Cassirer and Confucianism

In the opening chapter of *An Essay on Man: An Introduction to a Philosophy of Human Culture*, Cassirer talks about "the crisis in man's knowledge of himself." What Cassirer diagnoses as the crisis in man's knowledge of himself, is not dissimilar to Nietzsche's proclamation that "God is dead" (Nietzsche 2006, 5, 69; 2001, 120). One of the consequences of the Copernican overthrowing of the Aristotelian-Christian ontology was that there was no longer a meaningful way to approach the question of the nature of man. This crisis in man's knowledge of himself was not merely a theoretical problem needing the right solution, but an existential one that threatened the "whole extent of our ethical and cultural life" (*EM* 21–22). Cassirer sees much of philosophy from the Renaissance onwards as providing a new means for grounding our knowledge of ourselves. While this European existential crisis signaled the beginning of "modernism," the Chinese tradition has been secular from its formative beginnings. Cassirer's "modern"[9] solution for this metaphysical and existential vacuum, like Confucius and Confucianism, was culture. For both Cassirer and Confucianism, the twilight of the Gods is already actuality; but, instead of nihilism, this is, on the contrary, a reason for optimism: our fates are utterly in our own hands. For both Cassirer and Confucianism, the mark of our distinctive dignity—one can say freedom—is that the process of being human is never complete. Humanity is at once completely in our own hands and an asymptotic hypothetical that we will never reach. It is this infinite potentiality that is the source of our freedom.

China of the twentieth century suffered a comparable "crisis in man's knowledge of himself." By the middle of the nineteenth century, the Chinese people were compelled by the historical course of events to confront Western culture. The followers of radical scientism, a doctrine espoused by the leaders of the May Fourth Movement (1919) saw classical Chinese culture as that which had historically held back intellectual progress and was directly responsible for China's demise in the face of foreign aggressors. The May Fourth Movement is symptomatic of the profound intellectual malaise, urgent sense of cultural inferiority and panic about the fate of China that paralyzed the Middle Kingdom at the beginning of the century. This potent mix led the May Fourth Movement to a radical rejection of traditional Chinese learning and an almost visceral obsession with westernizing China. Right at this point, however, Liang Qichao, the leading scholar in China, returned from a research tour in Europe, and wrote a book about what he had seen at the end of the Great War of 1914–1918. Liang's pessimism about Western culture woke many Chinese intellectuals from their vision that westernization would be the panacea to cure all China's ills. New Confucianism arose as a response to the profound intellectual crisis that shook China to its core following the humiliations of colonialism in the late nineteenth and twentieth centuries. I think that the New Confucians were right that Confucianism, as a philosophical humanism, is not only a necessary philosophy for modern China but also of relevance for the modern world. The New Confucian's answer to the threat of westernization, which they identified with instrumentalization and utilitarianism (i.e., one side of Kantian freedom/determinism paradigm), was Confucianism. A large part of the Confucian project, which is relevant to our contemporary times, I argue, is the Confucian conception of culture.

History has remembered Cassirer as a philosopher of the exact sciences, and not as a political or spiritual leader. Nor has history been kind to him. Some of Cassirer's most successful students—Leo Strauss, Hans Blumenberg, Edgar Wind—reneged on Cassirer's vision. Rudolf Carnap characterized Cassirer as "rather pastoral." Isaiah Berlin judged him "serenely innocent," and Adorno called him "totally gaga." As Edward Skidelsky, the author of Cassirer's first English biography concludes, Cassirer's "thought remains, when all is said and done, a stranger to our age" (Skidelsky 2008, 7). Even if we "look back with nostalgia to a liberal such as Cassirer, whose interests were not confined solely, or even principally, to politics but spanned the breadth of human civ- ilization"; his "humane and happy dream," when all is said and done, "*was* only a dream" (237). Cassirer's vision for the harmony between the various fields of human endeavor and for philosophy as the keeper of this harmony is today dismissed as naively optimistic. In the symbolic encounter between Cassirer, Heidegger, and Carnap at Davos in 1929, the only loser was Cassirer. Carnap (along with other members of the Vienna Circle) later emigrated to the USA and lived long enough (1970) to see analytic philosophy established, while Heidegger, despite all the scandals, captured the imagination of postwar Europe[10] and became a seminal influence on the dominant intellectual trends of the twentieth century: post-existentialism, structuralism, postmodernism, and deconstruc- tionism. Cassirer died in 1945, after twelve years in exile, never having stayed in one place (England, Sweden, and the USA) long enough to establish his influence.

Confucianism is similarly looked upon as an innocent idealism or optimistic humanism too naive for the rigors of "modernity."[11] It is often seen as nothing other than a collection of utilitarian norms constituting a banal pragmatism, or it is understood as another "world religion."[12] Few people appreciate the humanism that lies at its heart. The Confu- cian-Cassirerian optimism in human beings and culture is not a naive one. The optimism that they share is one where we do not need to put own fates into the hands of some extra-human law, be that scientific, natural, legal, or religious. No scientific, natural, legal, or religious law can have the ultimate authority in determining what we *should* do.[13] Neither Cassirer nor Confucianism ever gave up the idea that we can become the best versions of ourselves through terms that we ourselves have made—culture; and therein lies their optimism. By placing Cassirer's philosophy of symbolic forms in dialogue with the Confucian philosophy of culture and vice versa, I hope that a stronger case will be made for a humanism conceived through a philosophical defense of culture. It is culture—the idea that we become what we are through forms of our own creation, and for which we are wholly responsible—that will help us to survive.

Cassirer felt a deep personal attachment to Goethe.[14] In her memoirs, his wife tells of his intense, lifelong devotion to Goethe.[15]

Toni Cassirer's assessment of Goethe's intellectual influence on Cassirer encapsulates many of the themes of this project. The ultimate goal of Cassirer's philosophy of symbolic forms is to give philosophical form to the feeling of liberation that Goethe's works inspired in him.[16] For me, it is as if Cassirer rewrote Goethe's life and works, or indeed Goethe's spirit in (systematic) philosophical, as opposed to literary, terms:

> His interpretation of history; his feeling for nature: his ongoing endeavour to broaden his outlook, to extend his knowledge to almost all areas in order to strengthen his judgement, and to protect it from one-sidedness, to keep it pure from influences of personal experiences, to dissociate it from current events—all this derived from Goethe. His firm belief in the values of the human personality, the longing for form and harmony, the abhorrence of violent destruction—of both his own and of the surrounding world—his abhorrence of ideological, political, or religious slogans—in short, the quintessence of his being, came from Goethe. I understood Goethe through Ernst and Ernst through Goethe. (T. Cassirer 1981, 87; my translation[17])

I think Cyril Connolly put it very beautifully when he wrote in *The Unquiet Grave,* "For me success in life means survival. I believe that a ripe old age is nature's reward to those who have grasped her secret. I do not wish to die young or mad. The true pattern of existence can best be studied in a long life like Goethe's" (Connolly 1951, 10). If we wish to die neither young nor old, then the philosophy of Cassirer—the Goethe of our times—as well as the philosophy of a tradition characterized by peace, longevity, and tolerance, bears study. As Leibniz observes in his preface to the *Novissima Sinica,* written during the period 1697–99—a century that saw the Thirty Years War, Second Northern War, and Nine Years' War—the Chinese tradition has excelled in civil philosophy in a way that exceeded the European tradition:

> But who would have believed that there is on earth a people who, though we are in our view so very advanced in every branch of behavior, still surpass us in comprehending the precepts of civil life? Yet now we find this to be so among the Chinese, as we learn to know them better. And so if we are their equals in the industrial arts, and ahead of them in contemplative sciences, certainly they surpass us (though it is

almost shameful to confess this) in practical philosophy, that is, in the precepts of ethics and politics adapted to the present life and use of mortals. Indeed, it is difficult to describe how beautifully all the laws of the Chinese, in contrast to those of other peoples, are directed to the achievement of public tranquility and the establishment of social order, so that men shall be disrupted in their relations as little as possible. (Leibniz 1994, 46–47)

I believe that what Leibniz saw as a laudable ability to adapt to the present life on the part of the Chinese can be accounted for through a reconstruction of their philosophy of culture. There was a comprehensive theoretical foundation that gave coherence and legitimacy to their practical philosophies, and it is an account of this theoretical foundation that I hope to provide.

For Cassirer, there are real consequences to our inability to conceive of philosophy as anything other than a contemplative science removed from culture, seeking only to understand transtemporal truths. Cassirer does not shy away from criticizing academic philosophy's failure to do its duty as the keeper of humane culture in the run-up to World War II. He saw the profession split down the middle between the antithetical extremes of Lebensphilosophie and logical positivism. It was no accident for Cassirer that logical positivism, which so easily led to mere technic and the mystical thrownness to our fates found in Lebensphilosophie, was so easily co-opted for the ends of political extremism. None of these philosophical schools took upon themselves the task of caring for the overall form of culture. They believed there was either one ultimate supracultural panacea, or an Archimedean point from which to objectively assess all human activity, and that was going to solve the problems of humanity. In their narrow focus on one domain, they became paralyzed in the face of the complexity of human culture as a whole. In Cassirer's eyes, both Lebensphilosophie and logical positivism gave way to the dogma that there is an a priori beyond the fact of culture itself. In Cassirer's view, and this is a view that I share, this is regression to the security of a God-principle as the ultimate explanation for all of human phenomena. It is fatalism as opposed to a humanism that holds that we make our own fates; and this fatalism infantilizes our human capacities.

This famous dualism which gripped German intellectual life is parodied in Thomas Mann's novel of ideas The Magic Mountain in the form of Naphta and Settembrini battling for the soul of Hans Castorp (who symbolically represents Germany). Hans Castorp was ultimately lost to humanity not because Castorp couldn't overcome Naphta and embrace Settembrini, but because Settembrini did not offer a truly compelling vision of humanity. His enlightenment rationalism was antinomistically opposed to the other dimension of humanity represented by Naphta. What was not presented in the novel was a figure like the Goethean Cassirer, someone who gave form to human experience in a way that reconciled these two positions.[18] Cassirer perhaps could have rescued Hans Castorp from his torpor, because Cassirer recognized the necessity and value of *all* human experience. In one dialogue between Hans Castorp and the sanatorium's director, Hofrat Behrens, Hans Castorp speaks of giving up the distinctively human dignity of conquering daily anew our freedom and existence:

> "And if one is interested in life, one must be particularly interested in death, mustn't one?"

> "Oh, well, after all, there is some sort of difference. Life is life which keeps the form through change of substance."

> "Why should the form remain?" said Hans Castorp.

> "Why? Young man, what you are saying now sounds far from humanistic."

> "Oh, but form is so finicky [ete-pe-tete]." (Mann 1955, 266–67; modified)

Form is indeed so finicky, and so for so many of Mann's Nietzschean and Schopenhauerian protagonists[19]—Hans Castorp, the Buddenbrooks, and Adrian Leverkühn—they could not achieve form and so freedom. It is through form that we achieve freedom, as the title of Cassirer's 1916 *Freiheit und Form: Studien zur Deutschen Geistesgeschichte* tells us. It is the human ability to give form to experience that rescues us from unfreedom (our biological determinacy) and makes us free to be a human being in the world. If I may borrow Toni Cassirer's elegant turn of phrase, I understood Confucianism through Cassirer, and Cassirer through Confucianism. In both, it is through (cultural) forms that we achieve our freedom and humanity.

Existing Literature on *Wen*

There is, so far as I know, no philosophical works in the English language specifically on "culture" in Chinese philosophy. There are significant reasons for this. By and large, comparative works in the English language tend to take philosophical themes of pertinence to the Western tradition as a point of comparative orientation. Until recently, however, culture has not been perceived as a domain proper to philosophical enquiry.[20] Traditionally, Western philosophy has been a quest for certainty, and culture, understood as mere *doxa*, was irrelevant to the discipline. It is because culture has been peripheral to the concerns of Western philosophy that there has also been correlatively little work on culture in Chinese philosophy.

The importance of *wen* or culture for the Chinese tradition has not gone unnoticed, however, in sinological scholarship. Despite this, there has been a significant inability to appraise why *wen* or culture was so significant for the Chinese tradition. The inability of existing scholarship to take seriously the Chinese philosophical ideas about culture, I argue, reflects a failing on the part of (Anglophone) philosophical discourse to give theoretical legitimacy to the concept of "culture" itself. The inability for sinological scholarship to take culture seriously betrays two related philosophical assumptions. (1) In sinology, as in philosophy, the operative assumption has been that culture is merely *doxa* and as such is closely allied with its political manipulation through rhetoric (as with the Sophists whom Plato attacks for this reason in *Gorgias*). (2) Sinology has labored under a positivism[21] that takes for granted the fact/value distinction. There is a realm of "facts" that can be empirically and universally understood through the methods of modern scholarship (i.e., the social "sciences"). Under this view, there is no originary spontaneity to "culture" for creating different values that differ across different cultures. Under the positivism embraced by mainstream sinology, human beings and national cultures are reduced to the common denominator of the social sciences. This inability to see culture as anything else than mere dogmatism/ideology cannot therefore see *wen* as anything other than merely ideology. In some ways, Cassirer's project of culture was conceived as a means of overcoming the reduction of culture through methodologies that pretended to be universal and value-free.[22] Cassirer's project of culture is thus important in that it can help dignify the plurality of different cultures.[23] We can see these assumptions in operation in the two examples below.

Mark Edward Lewis is evidently aware that the pervasiveness of *wen* in classical Chinese intellectual life is glaring for anyone familiar with Chinese culture. "Writing permeates our images of China." He informs us, "An urban scene distinguished by column upon column of graphs, visual arts defined by the brush and graphic line of the calligrapher-painter, a political order controlled by a mandarinate selected for textual mastery, a religious practice relying on written documents to communicate with the spirits: at every level of life script holds sway" (Lewis 1999, 4). How is it that we explain this reverence for literacy throughout the span of Chinese history? In his (empirically magisterial) study, Lewis is guided by the conclusion that *wen* gave the theoretical support for the vision of an empire in which all future members of the upper echelons were educated or indoctrinated. *Wen* thus became a self-perpetuating prophecy that was upheld by those with power. *Wen* as this "soft power" or the software of the state was more resilient than its hardware, and, together with the economic dependence of its adherents, secured its longevity. The "intellectual commitment of the local elites" (4) to *wen*, is reduced to a purely utilitarian calculus. The explanation for the importance of writing in Lewis's *Writing and Authority* thus redounds to the link between writing and state propaganda. The extent of the Chinese empire was greater than the central state had the physical means to govern, thus the centrality of writing lay in its ability to buttress "the vision of an empire" that could be spread across space ("between the imperial system and the localities") and time (survive "the collapse of each of its incarnations") (4). "The implanting of the imperial vision in local society in the form of the written language and its texts" (4) is thus the reason why writing came to define Chinese civilization. The extent of the meaning of writing in early China is thus ultimately exhausted by "the uses of writing to command assent and obedience," and through examining "the types of writing employed in state and society to generate and exercise power" (1). To stress so overwhelmingly that one of the defining elements of Chinese culture was a result of political-utilitarian motives is to deny that there is any objectivity to "spirit" (*Geist*).[24] This ends up playing into orientalizing stereotypes of the Chinese as unfree, passive, half-humans (because they were denied a crucial aspect of their humanity) who have always lived under oppressive regimes. Divorced from a vision of subjective agency in which the subject (in concert with others) spontaneously creates her own meanings, the Chinese tradition is reduced to the vision of man found in the deterministic half of the

Kantian dualism. By not conceding that the Chinese were makers of their own meaning (and therefore freedom), one is making the Kantian dualism between freedom-determinism into geographical fact.[25]

Likewise, in one of the most recent books to deal with Chinese writing, *Beyond Sinology: Chinese Writing and the Scripts of Culture*, Andrea Bachner (2014) "uses the sinograph to analyze what binds languages, scripts, and medial expressions to cultural and national identity" (14). Since the " 'value' of a script has always been determined by its potential to fulfill specific social and ideological functions" (3), the pride of Chinese culture—its writing—is reduced to a "script politics" (3), to "national language politics" (7). Any national pride in the sinograph is only a manifestation of "Chinese nationalism" tapping "into an age-old cultural tradition, reconstructed as a cultural whole, as a basis for political unity" (9).[26]

The problem with this kind of "hermeneutics of suspicion" about *wen* is that the Chinese tradition did not have a comparable (Platonic) divide between Truth/Doxa; and as such did not see culture as secondary upon Truth, and so see it as closely related to ideological control. We are at a loss to understand *why* the Chinese tradition took culture so seriously if we see it merely as an arm of the political. Another problem is that the "hermeneutics of suspicion" was a term coined by Paul Ricoeur to characterize the skeptical or critical attitude about tradition found in the likes of Marx, Freud, and Nietzsche. The great irony is that this hermeneutics of suspicion—used to critically assess one's *own* tradition—is used by a dominant strand in the Western tradition to critically assess the Chinese tradition. In this way, and under the context of colonialism and neocolonialism, the application of the hermeneutics of suspicion becomes a tool (on the part of many Western scholars) to delegitimize the cultural, intellectual, sociopolitical coherence of China as a historical entity. The application of the hermeneutics of suspicion to the Chinese tradition on the part of Western academe becomes a form of orientalism.

Another way of "explaining" why the Chinese took culture so seriously in the sinological literature on the subject is to say that a continuous historical reason for its importance cannot be given. Martin Kern for example argues that, "*Wen* is neither static nor universal; strenuous claims on its unwavering continuity beyond the realities of social and intellectual processes never escape the aporetic nature of any suprahistorical concept, i.e., being itself a child of its times and hence historically confined" (Kern 2001, 43–44). On this interpretation, *wen* is basically meaningless: each speech act involving *wen* is so unique that each use of *wen* is a private speech act. By so radically historicizing *wen*, Kern has reduced it to mere particularity, and we are prevented from seeing the *continuity* and thus meaning of the term. I think Kern's kind of historicism (i.e., empiricism) is well criticized by Cassirer when he writes that, "But our wealth of facts is not necessarily a wealth of thoughts. Unless we succeed in finding a clue of Ariadne to lead us out of this labyrinth, we can have no real insight into the general character of human culture; we shall remain lost in a mass of disconnected and disintegrated data which seem to lack all conceptual unity" (*EM* 22). By focusing on merely the "particular," Kern has not been able to offer a "universal," and the particular thus remains meaningless.[27] Kern is marking as off limits the possibility that there *is* an explanation for why the Chinese tradition took *wen* so seriously.

For Cassirer, once we give up on the (humanistic) idea that there is a creative spontaneity of spirit that makes the world meaningful for us, then the facta of culture, "necessarily amount to their history, which, according to its object, would define itself as history of language, history of religion and myth, history of art, etc." (*PSF* 1:84). The facta of culture would amount to a merely empirical description (of *disjecta membra*) that makes no claims to what these facts *mean*. Presciently, therefore, Cassirer has diagnosed the contemporary relationship between academic sinology, skepticism and positivism. For Cassirer, a necessary logical result of a naive realism (positivism) that regards the objects of reality as something directly and unequivocally given, is an attitude of skepticism. If cultural forms (language, art, history, etc.) are not understood as *organs* of reality, as possessing their own spontaneous law of generation, but as mere imitators of an already complete reality, then skepticism towards culture is inevitable. If we succumb to the ideology that meaning is objectively present in bare facts, then the meaning that different aspects of culture posit is merely a secondary addendum; and the reasons cultures posit these meanings will necessarily be understood as dogmatic and ideologically driven.

There is another problem with this radical historicism. Just as for Kant it is the transcendental unity of apperception that secures the reality of the self—otherwise the self would be merely an arbitrary succession of experiences and could not secure itself against (Humean) skepticism—it is the continuity of a tradition that secures the reality of that tradition. When we repudiate that there is an originary spontaneity to traditions that create their own meaning (and thus continuity), then we rob them of their status as subjects. This disenfranchisement, pari passu, plays into the hand of orientalizing stereotypes while we repudiate what Cassirer calls our "ethical task"—that of finding meaning among the welter of phenomena.

To the detriment of the Chinese tradition, therefore, there has so far been no account of why culture was treated with such reverence. The Chinese tradition is treated as a "particular" that can simply be understood through "universal" methodologies (which is of course, in reality, anything but). The Chinese reverence for *wen*, under this positivism, is either inexplicable—leading to the orientalizing view of China (and the "Rest") as a kind of Alice in Wonderland of pure whimsy that does not have a consistent logic, or this positivism explains this reverence through the methodologies of the social sciences. All peoples everywhere, under this assumption, are inherently selfish and all their actions only driven by a Hobbesian utilitarian calculus. The only plausible explanation for the reverence for *wen* is thus some nefarious, egoistic agenda. This lack of real explanation, while evidencing the governing assumptions of Western philosophy, is also a great shame for understanding the Chinese tradition. This is because culture goes to the heart of the Chinese philosophic worldview in the way that, for example, the appearance/reality distinction is a central characteristic of Western philosophy. In not giving an account of why and how culture was so crucial to the Chinese tradition, we have not really understood the tradition. This project will thus seek to redress this lacuna by (re)constructing a Confucian philosophy of culture through an imaginary conversation with an interlocutor—Ernst Cassirer—the greatest philosopher of culture in the Western tradition.

Outline of Chapters

Chapter 1 will lay out six characteristics of Cassirer's philosophy, as well his interpretation of Western intellectual history. It is these six characteristics that lead to a valorization of the humanly created symbol. These six characteristics, as will be shown throughout the following chapters, is shared by Confucian philosophy.

Chapter 2 will introduce the idea that, for the Confucians, the world is fundamentally expressive to people. Put differently, the "nature"—*qing*

(情) of the world tends towards manifestation in "patterns" (*wen* 文). The human creation of the sign is a *creative* consummation of the "nature" of things. The Cassirerian counterpart to this "expressiveness of the world" is his theory of "symbolic pregnancy": the world is *always* phenomenologically meaningful. For Cassirer, as for the Confucians, it is only once we stabilize this symbolic pregnancy in a symbol, however, that humans can attain to a higher level of meaning and thus achieve civilization.

Chapter 3 will show how this paradigm of sign creation also applies to Confucian poetics. The self, under the Confucian view, is both *inherently* emotional—has *qing* (情)—and *needs* to express/manifest these emotions. Poetry and music are creative consummations of the *qing* and pattern of the self in the same way that the sign is a creative consummation of the *qing* and patterns of the world. The *form* of poetry/music, however, can only arise in a social context. For Cassirer, art is a golden mean between the emotionality/sensuousness of myth and the abstraction of religion. Art is able to affirm our emotional nature without merely languishing in, or making us a slave of, the emotions. This is art's contribution to humanity.

Chapter 4 will show how this paradigm of culture as creative consummation is equally found in pre-Qin and Han theories of the origins of writing and literature. Humans manifest patterns (*wen*) appropriate to themselves, just as the myriad things in the phenomenal world manifest their own patterns. This chapter will also show that the "mutually participatory relationship between man and the cosmos" that underlies *xiang* is also to be found in the terms *wen* (文) and *li* (理)—two other key terms associated with meaning and representation.

Chapter 5 will show that, because, as shown in the previous chapters, external manifestation of an "inner" nature is inherent to the nature of all things, and the *wen* of humans (poetry, music, language) creatively consummate the self, culture becomes *necessary* for the fulfilment of the self. This understanding of subjectivity is termed a "functional" self, in the sense that the self is like a mathematical function that is dependent on the facta of culture (i.e., like the function depends on the mathematical series) for its existence. The self and the facta of culture become mutually dependent and determinative. The Cassirerian understanding of subjectivity, like Confucianism, is similarly "functional": the self *is* its potential to take on, and creatively partake of, culture. There is no "essence" to the self separate from its manifestation; or its "essence" *is* its tendency to manifest itself in, and creatively partake of, culture. Cassirer's "aesthetic individual," as just such a one who realizes her individuality through cultural traditions, is thus reminiscent of the Confucian understanding of self-realization. Carrying on the discussion from chapter 3, it will be seen once again how cultural forms arise from a social context and have fundamentally social telos.

Chapter 6 will pick up the discussion on pluralism outlined in chapter 1. It is *because* the myriad things have a latent order "within" them that they necessarily manifest that "order" is thus not *imposed externally*. Each thing manifests its own pattern or order, and so there are a *pluralism* of different orders. Acknowledging this pluralism did not, however, pose the intellectual threat of chaos to the Confucians. For the Confucians, the organic world is paradigmatic of a harmony among diversity. If each thing manifests its own order, then there are infinite orders in nature, but nature is harmonious; the flourishing of each individuality on its own terms need not impede the coherence of the whole. It is this paradigm of what I have termed an "organic harmony" on which Confucianism modeled its own thinking about "harmony in contrariety." Like Confucianism, Cassirer was also very serious about there being a plurality of orders, a "harmony in contrariety" among the symbolic forms. For Cassirer, the first historical figure who was able to reconcile individualism/individual liberty without conceding to the chaos of the whole, and so spearhead a paradigm shift, was Leibniz. Leibniz's *Monadology*—in Cassirer's eyes—came to have a profound influence on subsequent German thought. The stress on holism, becoming, and per-spectivism found in the thought of Goethe's natural science, Wilhelm von Humboldt's philosophy of language, and Herder's views on history and cosmopolitanism are all indebted to the philosophy of the organic initiated by Leibniz. The *Monadology's* resemblance to Chinese, organic thinking will be pointed to, and thus a key reason for the similarity between Cassirer's thought and Confucian philosophy gestured toward.

A pervasive theme throughout these chapters is the lack of dualism in the Confucian tradition between form and matter; be this between meaning and its mode of representation/manifestation, or between the self and its mode of representation/manifestation. There is, as a result of this absence, no comparable hermeneutics of suspicion about repre-sentation, as representation *does* lead to the truth about phenomena/the self. It is because things always already tend toward externalization, and their manifestation is *not* a distortion of their "natures" that there are no epistemological or ontological difficulties in suggesting that a cultural form completes these manifestations. In other words, there is an *inter-penetration* of form and matter. In both the Cassirerian and Confucian understanding of language and meaning and the self and the means of self-realization/self-manifestation, we see this mutual dependency of form and matter. One can interpret this lack of dualism in Cassirer as owing to an organic/biological model of growth that was best articulated, in the Western context, by Herder. Under this model, the material mani-festation of some inner élan helps define what is to be realized. The very manifesting of the thought, *Geist*, emotion, or human nature in cultural forms, helps *define* what was previously merely nebulous potential.

1

Humanism and Language

Cassirer and the *Xici* (系辞)

Both Cassirer and the Confucians converge on a particular understanding of humanism: that linguistic (or "symbolic") usage defines our humanity. Cassirer's definition of humans as "symbolic animals" mirrors the Confucian conviction that it is through culture (*wen* 文) that we become transformed (*hua* 化) into human beings. Related to this shared conception of the human being as a symbolic animal is another shared point of orientation: Cassirer and Confucianism's respective understandings of freedom. Freedom is understood here as made possible by meaning-making; meaning-making in turn enabling freedom *from* determinism, freedom *to* create an ideal world (through signs), and, in turn, freedom *for* a specifically human way of realizing oneself.[1] Cassirer and the Confucian tradition thus converge on this understanding of human beings, language, and freedom.[2]

This particular understanding of humanity and human freedom as enabled by the use of signs parallels the relationship between language and thought of the "linguistic turn," whereby thought is seen as dependent on and bounded by language and meaning consists in the use of words.[3] For Cassirer, this linguistic turn[4] is a result of the European tradition's overcoming of Aristotelian substance ontology. In other words, there is for Cassirer an inseparable relationship between naive realism or substance ontology and the copy theory of meaning, and conversely a relationship between a "functional" ontology (see the section "From Substance to Function" for a definition) and the linguistic turn, whereby language *creates* meaning. I will show that this same relationship between a functional ontology and the idea that language creates meaning is found in the *Xici*.

The Confucian tradition, as we will see in the *Xici*, *assumed* this relationship between humanism, language, and freedom. On the Cassirerian side, however, this understanding of human beings, language, and freedom *arose* in European intellectual history after the Copernican Revolution against a substance-based ontology. This chapter will tell the story of how Cassirer understood this transition to an understanding of human beings as defined by their symbol-making capacities in European intellectual history. The elements of this historical genesis will conversely, as a negative foil, also elucidate the philosophical characteristics of the *Xici*. There are six key pieces in this story. (1) Relationality: without an appeal to a substance, relations as opposed to substances become primary. (2) Holism: meaning is understood not through appeal to a "substance" but through the coherence between the part and the whole. (3) Relatedly, there is an emphasis on particularity, becoming, and pluralism. (4) Further, it is assumed that there is no dualism between the (universal) concept and the (sensuous) particular. (5) Concomitantly, there is a humanistic stress on the human being as the locus, or maker of these networks of relations and thus meaning. (6) Symbols are necessary for enabling human beings to make these networks of relations for understanding reality. These six characteristics, I argue, also describe the *Xici* and the *Yijing*.

The *Yijing* or *The Book of Changes*, as its name suggests, is based on a processual metaphysics that assumes the constancy of change and becoming. Its hexagrams operate, furthermore, through a structuralism in which the meaning of each hexagram is manifested by contrasting its own configuration (of *yao* lines) to all other possible configurations. Under the system of the *Yijing*, it is through relationality between the part and the whole, as opposed to the properties of substances, that meaning is derived. The *Xici* sees the human being as equal with heaven and earth, and as a cocreator in cosmic processes. This harmony, or nondualism between nature and culture is a marked characteristic of the *Xici*, as is evidenced by the key concept of the *Xici*—*xiang* (象)—which is both sensuous and conceptual. All these characteristics would imply that naive realism or "substance ontology" *cannot* be ascribed to the *Xici*—which, unfortunately, has been the dominant interpretation so far—and, because a copy theory of meaning describes the view of language of naive realism, the *Xici*'s view of language cannot be that of a copy theory of meaning.

What is at stake in my emphasis on the *Xici* as operating under a linguistic turn view of language and why I stress that it *cannot* be operating under a copy theory of meaning is that the former is simultaneous with humanism, and the latter is antithetical to humanism. My motive lies in defending the *Xici* as a humanist text.

Xici: Humanism and Language (*Wen* 文)

Confucianism is a humanism that understands the human creation of signs as that which enabled culture and thus humanity, and we will see this from a correct understanding of the *Xici* (系辞). The *Yijing*[5] started its life as a divination manual, which gradually acquired the status of a book of wisdom. For most of China's imperial history the *Yijing* was revered as the most important book in the Chinese philosophical tradition. The Ten Wings[6] is associated with the transformation of the *Yijing* from a divination manual[7] to a Confucian classic. To a large extent, the importance of the Ten Wings lay in the *Xici*, as, throughout the imperial era, the *Xici* "received more exegetical attention than any other single wing" (Smith 2008, 38), and so was considered the most important part of the Ten Wings. What is so important about the *Xici* is that it offered an account of the genesis of culture.

Throughout the Chinese tradition, the trigrams/hexagrams (*gua* 卦) of the *Yijing* were identified with writing[8] (*wen* 文); and the trigrams/hexagrams (and writing) synecdochally represented human culture (*wen* 文) itself.[9] The *Xici* (2.2), as the "most important account of Fu Xi [Baoxi], the origin of the hexagrams, and the beginning of writing"[10] (Lewis 1999, 197), is thus *the* canonical account of the origins of trigrams/hexagrams and written language. Accounts in the Warring States and early imperial texts of the origins of writing and the trigrams/hexagrams were thus often conflated with each other.[11] The *Xici*'s philosophical account of the origins of the trigrams/hexagrams is by implication the Chinese tradition's account of the origins of the written script, as well as human culture in general. Correctly understanding how the *Xici* rationalized the genesis of the trigrams/hexagrams will thus amount to an authoritative way of describing how the Chinese (Confucian) understood the genesis of culture.

The most common way that the *Xici* has been interpreted by Western sinologists has been under a metaphysical realism. What is at stake when we understand the *Xici* as operating under a metaphysical realism is that it *cannot* be a humanism. This metaphysical realism and the representationalist model of knowledge it entails, I argue, via Cassirer's insights into the genesis of European humanism, is at odds with the *Xici*'s other philosophical characteristics, and leads to a dualism between humans and the world. I argue, therefore, that the *Xici* is a humanist text that celebrates the creation of a system of human symbols that, due to its ability to harmonize the human and the natural, become the enabling condition for human freedom. The Confucian[12] strategy for appropriating the divinatory classic lies in their claim that the ability to prognosticate rests on the human ability to first meaningfully order the world. Meaning is thus antecedent to, and more important than, the ability to prognosticate. In enabling humans to meaningfully order the world, the hexagrams are the enablers of meaning, meaningful experience, freedom from determinacy, and, in turn, ethical conduct. The *Xici* as a post facto rationalization of the *Yijing* as a mantic text accounts for the divinatory powers of the hexagrams by explaining how the hexagrams create *meaning* (through a symbolic system).[13] Whereas freedom from determinacy is understood in the original mantic text through one's ability to make prognostications, the *Xici* understands freedom as coming from the human ability to create culture; because it is culture that is understood to be the enabler of meaningful experience, and thus freedom. In this "Confucian Enlightenment," a philosophy of language, as opposed to the power of divination, provides the explanation for the human ability to order the world. The same relationship between humanism and language can be found in Cassirer's own thought as well as his interpretation of European intellectual history.

Cassirer: Humanism and Language/Symbol-making

Ernst Cassirer is perhaps the European tradition's greatest philosopher of culture. He is also widely regarded as one of the greatest intellectual historians of the twentieth century (Friedman 2005, 71), and the derivation of his own philosophy of the symbolic forms is inextricable from his encyclopedic knowledge of European intellectual history.[14] His interpretation of European intellectual history is marked by the theme of the gradual replacement of the concept of substance, starting from the Renaissance, by the concept of function. This paradigm shift precipitated the victory of humanism[15] against medieval scholasticism and culminated in the high-tide of the German humanism of the *Goethezeit*.[16] There are thus two epicenters of humanism that influence Cassirer's work. The first is that of the Renaissance, which focuses on "human" achievements—the *studia humanitas*—as opposed to the God-centered knowledge of the *studia divinitas* that pervaded the Middle Ages. The second epicenter was found in the *Goethezeit*, in figures such as Goethe (1749–1832), Herder (1744–1803), and Wilhelm von Humboldt (1767–1835). They represent what has been called a "humanist" or "Romantic"[17] tradition in German philosophy, whose philosophies were premised on the Herderian idea of "rising oneself to humanity through culture [*Bildung*]" (quoted in Gadamer 2004, 9).

The culmination and endpoint of this tradition of German humanism can be found in Ernst Cassirer's philosophy of symbolic forms. His philosophy of symbolic forms—a metamorphism of the various aspects of this "humanistic" philosophical tradition into a total philosophy of culture—is a passionate defense of philosophy as a humanist enterprise. Cassirer interprets the various cultural systems (i.e., language, myth, art, science) as a function that relates phenomena in their own respective ways. An artist and a mathematician will, for example, relate the same phenomena according to their own respective paradigms, and produce different world pictures. It is, furthermore, these functional systems—culture—through which ones achieves humanity. For Cassirer, this humanist tradition was very much concerned with overcoming the metaphysical dualism between the noumenal and the phenomenal, between the freedom and determinism of Kantianism. Crucially, it was in language, and for Cassirer the symbol, that they found the resolution. In the next section we will see how Cassirer understood this to be the case, and it will be suggested that the *Xici* understands the relationship between symbol and reality in the same way as Cassirer's "symbolic idealism."[18]

Naive Realism versus Symbolic Idealism

Under the paradigm of "a copy theory of meaning" (which, as we will see, is the most common interpretation of how the sages created the hexagrams of the *Xici*), there are certain a priori truths or determinations that are objectively present about this world, which language merely imitates or repeats. It is a model of language that operates under a "correspondence theory of truth," in which truth consists of a relation to reality. A famous pronouncement of such a correspondence theory of truth was given by Thomas Aquinas when he wrote, "*Veritas est adaequatio rei et intellectus*" (truth is the conformity/equality of thing and intellect). Truth is when the form of the thing (be this object or fact) and the form in the intellect are equal. This epistemological model was famously described by Richard Rorty in *Philosophy and the Mirror of Nature* as the metaphor of the mind being a great mirror, merely reflecting the world (1979, 12). This model of language is a companion to "naive realism," which holds that objects, properties, and relations of the world are independent of our thinking or perception of them—what Wilfrid Sellars called the Myth of the Given. By naive realism, I refer to a view that considers things (or phenomena) as they appear to us to be these things as they exist independently of knowers. This realism would assume that all knowledge conforms to objects, and that our perceptual or cognitive processes do not conceal or distort the real properties of the things that our perceptual or cognitive processes discover. Nor would this view hold that our perceptual or cognitive processes contribute new features to the appearances of things. A naive realist would hold, for example, that physical objects have exactly the same color and shape as we sense in them. The copy theory of meaning commits to a naive realism and thus an ontological dualism between the mental and the physical. In *The Ambivalence of Creation*, for example, Michael Puett writes that the sages' creation of the hexagrams is described "in purely passive terms: they did nothing but imitate and pattern themselves on what the natural processes had generated"[19] (2001, 87). A "copy theory of meaning" is similarly espoused by two other contemporary Western commentators on the *Xici*: Mark Edward Lewis[20] and Willard Peterson.[21]

For Cassirer, a necessary logical result of this naive realism, which regards the objects of reality as something directly and unequivocally given, is an attitude of skepticism toward language (and all mediating signs). If language is not understood as an *organ* of reality, as possessing its own spontaneous law of generation, but as a mere imitator of an already complete reality, then skepticism toward language is inevitable.[22] It leads to a dualism whereby imitation, as mediacy, is merely subjectivization, against the immediate "objectivity" of the "truth" of the object depicted. It leads to a dualism between subject and object. Representation in signs is merely a phantasmagoria created by the subject that obscures reality. What we find in the *Xici*, however, is an ebullient celebration of the creation of the hexagrams: the *Xici* is evidently not skeptical about language. On this count, we can rule out Puett, Lewis, and Peterson's attribution of a naive realist position to the *Xici*. If a naive realist position necessarily entails skepticism about language,[23] then the *Xici*'s lack of skepticism toward language indicates that it does not hold a naive realist position. Two possible explanations remain for explaining the *Xici*'s positive attitude toward language. First, it is operating under a mythic consciousness that assumes that the sign *is* the essence of its object, and that the potency of the real thing is contained in the sign. Second, and it is this latter view that I shall defend, the *Xici*'s position toward language is what Cassirer calls a "symbolic idealism." Under this position, it is the symbols of our creation that allow us epistemic access to a world that would otherwise be closed to us. Symbolic idealism differs from "idealism" in that it is not anti-realist about a mind-independent world. Symbolic idealism can be characterized as affirming an epistemological as opposed to metaphysical idealism (the view that all reality consists of minds and their mental states): the world exists, but it can only be known through humanly created symbols.

As a neo-Kantian, Cassirer's symbolic idealism can also be understood as related to Kant's "transcendental idealism." Kant's "Copernican Revolution" leads Kant (and Cassirer) to endorse empirical realism and transcendental idealism as two sides of the same coin. Where Cassirer differs from the Kantian position is that for Cassirer's symbolic idealism, our experience of the world is bound not merely by the a priori conditions of human experience (space, time, the categories, the schemata, transcendental subjectivity) but also by a symbolic system. In order for human beings to experience reality, they need to form, understand, and partake of "symbolic forms." Cassirer's symbolic idealism is thus an expansion of the principles of philosophy's linguistic turn, and by "philosophy's linguistic turn," I mean that "thought is essentially dependent on and bounded by language" and that "meaning consists in the use of words" (Forster 2010, 1).[24] In the Cassirerian variation on the linguistic turn—which we could call "symbolic turn"—however, thought (and much of experience) would be essentially dependent on and bounded by symbolic forms, and meaning would consist in the use of symbolic forms. Under this paradigm, the sages' creation of the hexagrams was not merely the creation of a writing system for recording what they understood about the world; instead, the hexagrams *enabled* the sages to *understand* the world. Under this framework, then, there would be no ontological dualism between the mental (subject) and the physical (object)—there would be no alienation of the human being from nature—for, it was the symbolic forms that *enabled* our relationship with nature in the first place; and this is the *tian ren he yi* to which I refer. The symbolic forms are epistemo-logically prior to the distinction between nature and culture. Cassirer's "symbolic idealism" as related to Kant's transcendental idealism must thus be understood apart from "metaphysical" or "ontological" idealism. Idealism in this sense holds that something mental—that is, the mind, spirit, reason or will—is the ultimate foundation of all reality. An example of this view would be George Berkeley's "immaterialism," according to which all that exists are ideas and the minds that have them. Cassirer's symbolic idealism can be understood as a "constructivism" in that the subject constructs the cognitive object through the use of symbols.

There are six interrelated characteristics of "symbolic" idealism, and because my thesis is that the *Xici* is operating under a symbolic idealism, it will be shown (in the next chapter) that these six characteristics also describe the *Xici*. First however, to highlight the implausibility of reading the *Xici* under a naive realism, let's first see what the implications of the *Xici* as operating under a naive realism would be.

Six Characteristic Corollaries of Naive Realism

For Cassirer, a copy theory of meaning describes the view of language under naive realism—which Cassirer associates with the philosophy of substance. This philosophy of substance necessitates, or is simultaneous with, certain views about language and its relationship to mind and the world. The philosophy of substance views (1) relationality as accidental to the ultimate substances lying behind our representations and is thus (2) the antithesis of a "structuralism" that sees the part and whole as *essentially* related. This philosophy of substance is thus simultaneous with (3) the prioritization of Being, which is antithetical to particularity, becoming, and pluralism. (4) The philosophy of substance commits itself to metaphysical dualisms that result in antitheses between realism-idealism, particular-universal, being-becoming, freedom-necessity. The philosophy of substance is committed furthermore to a view (5) of the human agent as a passive mirror reflecting objective things or facts in the world, (6) of symbols as merely simulacra that reflect a priori truths or determinations that are objectively present about this world. I think it is fairly uncontroversial that points 1, 2, 3, and 4 do not describe the philosophical characteristics of the *Yijing*. I will defend the thesis, following Cassirer's synopsis of the characteristics of a philosophy of the function, that the *Yijing* is further consistent with a functionalist philosophy in that points 5 and 6 also do not describe it.

The following sections of this chapter will suggest that the *Xici* is operating under the logic of a linguistic turn (and symbolic idealism) before detailing how Cassirer understood the European linguistic turn to have been actuated. The characteristics of the *Xici* and the *Yijing*, it will be argued, closely follow the six philosophical characteristics associated with the paradigm shift simultaneous with the European linguistic turn. These six philosophical characteristics will be addressed from a comparative perspective. Points 1, 2, 3, and 4 will be addressed under "Holism and Structuralism," and points 5 and 6 under "Language and Freedom."

From Substance to Function

The ordering of the world through functional laws as the precondition for the liberation of the human mind and the human subject is a recurring point of emphasis through Cassirer's entire oeuvre. For Cassirer, the European Renaissance liberated the human mind and human subject from the "reactionary and restrictive element" (2001, 42) of the Aristotelian concept of substance (*ousia*). In the medieval "harmony of the spheres"—which gained its theoretical foundation from Aristotelian and Neo-Platonic ontology—there was a hierarchical, fixed order of being that steadily led from the most imperfect to the most perfect (Being), and through which all limited and dependent being was fixed in an eternal order. With the Copernican-Kepler Revolution, the harmony of the world is no longer a substantial, fixed, spatial order that exists independently of mind. Instead of partaking of the whole through the fixed order of being, the harmony of the whole is to be gained through the mind's ability to grasp/form the internal principles of the natural order. For Cassirer, what the Copernican-Kepler Revolution achieved against the medieval harmony of the spheres is paralleled by what formal logic achieved against traditional logic, and what the linguistic turn achieved against a copy theory of truth.

In *Substance and Function*, inspired by the modern mathematical logic implicit in the work of Dedekind and Hilbert and explicit in the work of Frege and the early Russell, Cassirer criticizes the Aristotelian "abstractionist" theory of concept formation in which general concepts are arrived at by ascending inductively from sensory particulars. For Cassirer, this theory is premised on a substance ontology of a fixed order and so understands logical relations in terms of superordination and sub-ordination, genus and species. An inevitable outcome of this substance ontology is a metaphysical "copy" theory of knowledge, according to which our sensory representations are a copy of the ultimate substances lying behind our representations.[25] In *Substance and Function* and in his entire oeuvre, Cassirer sought to overcome this substance ontology. He does so through a turn to the logic of relations whereby our sensory representations are related to the (metaphysical) object not through a copy theory of knowledge, but by embedding the empirical phenomena themselves in a formal structure of symbolic relations. The truth and stability of our representations that used to be secured through appeal to an enduring substrate behind empirical phenomena is now secured by the stability of the laws (of our own creation) of relations governing the symbols, be this mathematical symbols, language, myth, law, or art (i.e., symbolic forms).[26] In *The Logic of the Cultural Sciences*, which was published in 1942, Cassirer explained the function-concept of the phi-losophy of symbolic forms thus:

> In *this* respect a "philosophy of symbolic forms" can maintain the claim of unity and universality that metaphysics had to abandon in its dogmatic form. Not only can it unite these various ways and directions of our knowledge of the world in itself, but in addition it is capable of recognizing the legitimacy of every attempt to understand the world, every interpretation of the world that the human spirit is capable of, and of understanding them in their specificity. It is in this way that the problem of objectivity first becomes visible in its full scope, and taken in this sense it encompasses not only the cosmos of nature but also that of culture. (LCS 19–20)

An object possesses "reality" when it has a functional place within a conceptual system (i.e., the symbolic forms). The function concept becomes the basis of Cassirer's conception of the symbolic form.

Cassirer's Account of Functionalism

Both the Copernican-Kepler Revolution and revolution in symbolic logic of modern mathematical logic replaced substance with function as the foundations of their theoretical knowledge. While in traditional logic the category of relation is forced into a dependent and subordinate position as the nonessential properties of a concept that could be left out of its definition without fallacy, in formal logic, it is relationality that is taken as prior. In Cassirer's view, therefore, a shift in ontology necessitated a paradigm shift in epistemology. There are six mutually conditioning outcomes of the Copernican-Kepler revolution against Aristotelian and Neo-Platonic metaphysics. These mutually conditioning outcomes can be seen in both Cassirer's account of European intellectual history since the Renaissance[27] and in his own system of the philosophy of the symbolic forms. I think we can understand Cassirer's own project as expanding the "universal characteristic" that Leibniz sought for cognition (*PSF* 1:86) married with his own interpretation of Kant's third critique by way of Humboldt's philosophy of language.

I will lay out these six mutually conditioning outcomes before describing Cassirer's account of them historically. (1) Relations are not already existing *objects* in the world that one makes a copy of in a symbolic medium. Relations were only ever a creation of the human mind. Against dogmatic sensationalism, Cassirer would say that the immediate content of particular impressions is meaningless. Hume's "'five tones on a flute'" does not "add up to" the idea of time, but rather temporal relationality is already tacitly drawn into perception (*PSF* 1:94). (2) Functionality presupposes and allows for a deeper relationship between the part and the whole, in the sense that a particular no longer has *essential* meaning; it gains its meaning in connection with laws which only result from the whole. (3) Functionality gives philosophical place to particularity, becoming, and pluralism. As we see from the philosophy of Parmenides,[28] to take Being or a substance ontology as a metaphysical a priori necessarily entails homogeneity (wholeness and indivisibility) as well as timelessness. Being must be whole and indivisible, as divisibility would entail change and so time. The things of the phenomenal world undergo change and so are non-Being, and thus illusory, and cannot be thought about. A metaphysics of Being thus logically entails monism and timelessness. It is the intellectual revolution against a metaphysics of substance that results in an elevated status for the power of the human mind in constituting reality; for this reality is now *a system of relations* that is constituted and organized by the human mind and the symbols of its creation. Put another way, once we substitute a functional description of the world with a substantial one, it is more conceivable that there is a plurality of ways to describe the same phenomena. In a functional description, the relations of things are constructions of pure thought; unlike a description under substance ontology, there is no claim that we are ontologically describing the nature of the thing in itself. In a functional description, an atom, for example, can be understood as both waves and electrons; and these two descriptions can be complementary. This point about pluralism will be explored in greater detail in the final chapter. (4) A philosophy operating under metaphysical dualisms always faces the problem of how the universal in the form of the concept can combine with the sense impression of the particular. In the Platonic framework, it is the *chora* that fulfils this function. When this paradigm began to lose its grip in the Renaissance, it was no longer necessary to think of the sensuous, particular content as separate from the universal form.[29] One can begin to think of language (as a sensuous particularity) as constructing meaning. "If with dogmatic metaphysics we take the concept of absolute *being* as our starting point, this question must seem ultimately insoluble. For an absolute being implies ultimate absolute elements, each of which is a static substance in itself, and must be conceived for itself. But this concept of substance discloses no necessary or even intelligible transition to the multiplicity of the world, to the diversity of its particular phenomena" (*PSF* 1:97). (5) As a result of a functional or relational description, the human factor becomes important: the formative powers of the mind are needed to establish these very relations. (6) The establishment of these functional laws requires *symbols* through which we can represent these functional relations. In the next sections, we will see how Cassirer interpreted the actualization of these paradigm shifts in European intellectual history.

The Six Characteristics in History

For Cassirer, the birth pangs of the linguistic turn began with Galileo. Instead of an appeal to a substantial core, Galileo's metaphor of the "'book of nature'" showed that knowledge of nature was only available through mathematical ciphers (*PSF* 1:85). The development of the natural sciences is thus indebted to "the increasing refinement of its *system of signs*" (PSF 1:85). A clear understanding of the fundamental concepts of Galileo's mechanics, for example, became possible only with the creation of the algorism of differential calculus. It was only with Leibniz, however, that the universal problem inherent in the function of symbolism was raised to a philosophical plane. In Leibniz's *characteristica generalis*, therefore,[30] Cassirer sees the roots of the linguistic turn.[31] The algorism of differential calculus proved for Leibniz that the sign not only *represents* what had already been discovered but is an *organ* of inquiry (PSF 1:130).[32] Without the universal sign provided by arithmetic and algebra, the laws of nature could not be expressed. The concepts of mechanics such as mass and force, material point and energy, atom or ether are "free 'fictions'" created by the logic of natural science for understanding reality as lawful (PSF 1:85).

With this revolution in science, the "object" of science is no longer a set of given facts, and with it the naive copy theory of meaning becomes discredited. It is the fundamental concepts of science, its *symbols*, that become an *organ* of inquiry (PSF 1:75).[33] With this "critical" insight, science renounces its claim for grasping immediate reality. The unity of knowledge can no longer be secured by appealing to a transcendent prototype to the empirical copies. With this "linguistic turn" we overcome the dualism between the *mundus sensibilis* and the *mundus intelligibilis*. Language is no mere passive instrument for re-presenting given *facta*; language is an active, spontaneous organ for discovering meaning, and conversely the conceptual definition of a content requires its stabilization in a sign (PSF 1:86). All "truly strict and exact thought is sustained by the *symbolics* and *semiotics* on which it is based" (PSF 1:86). In language, we find that the universal requires the particular in order to be perceived, but the particular requires the universal (the whole of language) in order to be thought. In other words, the contents of spirit are only disclosed in particular, sensuously tangible forms; but these particular forms would have no meaning without reference to a larger whole.[34] The Chinese equivalent of the idea that the human sign is that which enables the furtherance of "ideas," as we will see, is expressed by the idea that *wen* is a vehicle for the Dao (文以載道) and when Confucius says in *Analects* 15.29 that it is humans who enlarge the Dao, not the Dao that enlarges humans.[35]

As commentators have pointed out, Kant's Copernican Revolution—the turn from a naive realism towards a transcendental critique that is thus a turn towards the subject—lends itself to a turn toward language, that is, the linguistic turn. As soon as we turn from the idea that there is a given reality to the idea that we *represent* reality, then it is a short step from noticing that reality and thought are essentially tied to (representation in) language (Glock 2015, 373). It was for these reasons that all " 'metacritique'[36] that attempted to surpass the *Critique of Pure Reason* was always bound to this point," that is, how could "reason" be developed and laid out for us without the *logos* of language? (*KEH* 104). For Cassirer, once we have made the turn toward the subject and her language as that on which reality is essentially dependent, holism and structuralism are *also* necessary corollaries. As we will see in the next section, a part-whole structuralist relationship is antithetical to a substance ontology.

Holism and Structuralism: Points 1, 2, 3, and 4

For Cassirer, a nonsubstance ontology leads to both a linguistic turn view of language, whereby language creates meaning, and a structuralist understanding of language. For Cassirer, the "holism or organicism" of "idealistic morphology" found in Goethe's *Metamorphosis of Plants*, "bears a close relationship to linguistic structuralism" (1945, 109) in that neither "consist[s] of detached, isolated, segregated facts"—as in a physicalist/ mechanical view—but rather, they form "a coherent whole in which all parts are interdependent upon each other" (110). In both Goethe's "idealistic morphology" and linguistic structuralism,[37] the individual parts are mutually interrelated, no part can change without the whole changing, leading to a relationship whereby the whole is manifested in the part. Structuralism is thus for Cassirer "no isolated phenomenon"; it is, rather, "the expression of a general tendency of thought" (120)—a tendency of thought that was enabled by Leibniz and came to fruition in Goethe. In "Structuralism in Modern Linguistics," Cassirer quotes Viggo Brøndal (1887–1942)—one of the pioneers of linguistic structuralism: " 'I am in agreement with the universalism demonstrated and practiced a hundred years ago by the great master of general linguistics who was Wilhelm von Humboldt.' " The "program of structuralism developed by Brøndal" Cassirer goes on to say, "is, indeed, very near to Humboldt's ideas" (quoted in Cassirer 1945, 117; my translation). Similarly, toward the end of his life he wrote, "Knowledge is 'organic' insofar as every part is conditioned by the whole and can be made 'understandable' only by reference to the whole. It cannot be composed of pieces, of elements, except to the extent that each part already carries in itself the 'form' of the whole" (*PSF* 4:193).

Zhang Dongsun (also Chang Tung-sun)[38] (张东荪; 1886–1973)—one of the first scholars to describe Chinese thought as "correlative" (Chang 1952)[39]—agrees with Cassirer's analysis. He writes that traditional "Western thought is in the last analysis confined to Aristotelian logic" before the revolution of symbolic logic (Chang 1952, 211), and that Aristotelian logic presupposes a substance ontology that understands the world through a logic of identity.[40] "The Chinese are merely interested in the inter-relations between the different signs, without being bothered by the substance underlying them. Hence the relational or correlational consideration" (215). For Zhang, without a substance ontology, Chinese epistemology is based on a correlation logic of signs.[41] This correlation logic, I argue (following Zhang and Cassirer), is symptomatic of a non-substance-based ontology; instead of understanding the part in relation to a substance, it is understood in relation to the whole. Cassirer's own view of science as a gradual progress from the substance concept (i.e., an atomistic theory of concept formation) to the function concept (which is premised on a part-whole structuralism of measurements)[42] is in line with this view.

As an example of this correlation logic, Zhang gives the following example: whereas Western definitions define the subject in terms of its attributes, the Chinese language tends to define the subject in relation to other subjects. This "indicative" method of definition is, for Zhang, everywhere in the Chinese classics. The *Shuowen*, for example, defines *tian* as "that which is above the human head"; but in "Western logic," this would be "condemned as a fallacy" or "begging the question," for there are many things, such as birds and clouds, that are above our heads and don't refer exclusively to heaven. For Zhang, the "correlation-logic" that characterizes Chinese logic is one by which one term "awaits its opposite for a complete illustration of the connotation" (Chang 1952, 215). Zhang takes the example of " 'wife' " which in Chinese would be defined as " 'a woman who has a husband' " (213); whereas a definition that corresponds with the law of identity might be "a wife is a married woman." The difference between the classical Chinese definition of "a woman who has a husband" and the Western definition of "a married woman" is that in the Chinese example the definition of wife rests on a relationship with a husband. There is no exclusiveness in the Chinese definition of wife; she is never self-identical with herself. In the Western case, however, a wife is defined by the attribute of married-ness. In the Western case, one should not seek beyond the properties of the wife herself to define her status as that of a wife (law of identity, analytic truth). In the case of *tian*, the *shuowen* definition seems fallacious by the standards of Western logic because it does not define *tian* (sky/heaven) through attributes of *tian* itself. For Zhang, Chinese thought differs from this stark dichotomizing in that it "puts no emphasis on exclusiveness, rather it emphasizes the relational quality. . . . All these relatives are supposed to be interdependent" (Chang 1952, 213). At no point can any one of the subjects be defined per se, without reference to another subject. For Zhang, this kind of "correlation-logic" or "logic of correlative duality" is expressed in the *Yijing* whereby the definition of *yang* is dependent on its negative, *yin*, and vice versa. Each principle is dependent upon the other for its completion (214). The correlation logic that Zhang speaks about is, I argue, comparable to linguistic structuralism (and thus Humboldt's account of language) and Goethe's idealistic morphology.

In his article "The Mosaic and the Jigsaw Puzzle: How it all Fits Together," Thomas Kasulis (2015) characterizes two models of knowing how the part relates to the whole, what he calls the paradigms of "external" and "internal" relations. In his own analogy, the paradigm of external relations is that of a "mosaic" (atomistic model), whereas the paradigm of internal relations is that of a "jigsaw."[43] The distinction that Kasulis makes between these two models of part-whole relationships is useful for understanding the part-whole logic under the structuralist-correlative logic. In the external-mosaic paradigm, each part of the overall mosaic is identical, and differing only in certain respects, let's say color. How all the different mosaic parts fit together cannot be deduced by looking at each piece of the mosaic itself; the structure of the whole is not contained in the individual part. How the different mosaic parts go together is *external* to the pieces themselves; we require external information—perhaps a design or photograph—to tell us how all the different parts should relate. In the internal-jigsaw paradigm on the other hand, each jigsaw part is unique. The combination of colors and shapes of each piece will be unique. How the jigsaw pieces fit together, the overall configuration of the jigsaw puzzle is thus contained in each piece itself. How the different jigsaw parts go together is *internal* to the pieces themselves, and we require no information external to the pieces themselves to project the nature of the whole. The external-mosaic model, furthermore, has an "aversion to variety and uniqueness," because the less content each mosaic piece has, the easier it is to reconfigure them to different patterns.

The Chinese example thus corroborates Cassirer's thesis that substance ontology is antithetical to a correlative-structuralist logic. Similarly, I would argue that "correlative thinking" has been seen as a uniquely Chinese mode of thought because the Chinese tradition, unlike the Western tradition, did not operate under a substance ontology. Chinese correlative thinking is anti-essentialist in the sense that there is no distinction between the intrinsic and extrinsic features of things: the intrinsic features of things are its ("extrinsic") relations. This anti-essentialist way of thinking is inherently more pluralistic and is, I think, related to the problem of freedom. In the Western, dualistic paradigm, freedom belongs to the transcendent realm of forms (because it is being). On the other hand, the empirical particular (i.e., nature) is unfree because it is formless (because it is particular and becoming). Under the Chinese, jigsaw paradigm, each particular already has form in the sense that it has relations holographically within it. Under the Western, mosaic paradigm, form is extrinsic to the particular. The fact that the Confucians were able to see nature as both particular and *formed* (in the sense that it contains relations within) is, I think, why "Confucians hold as a fundamental point of faith that the universe is ultimately harmonious" (C. Li 2014, 43)—freedom and form is already possible in the empirical particular. This point will be picked up in chapter 2 and chapter 6.

A Cassirerian take on this structural-holist logic is, as we have already seen, to see it as inseparable from the linguistic turn. For Cassirer, these structuralist-correlative relationships can only be expressed via symbols that are mediated representations of observed phenomena. We can make no claims of objectivity beyond the correspondence between the logic of our laws and the observable data. Objectivity lies in embedding our mediated observations within the whole of a symbolic system, and this can be shown through Cassirer's interpretation of modern physics. In the first formulation of Bohr's theory, electrons move continuously in stationary orbits without radiating. However, this is impossible to observe because electrons are immunized against radiation: radiation being the only means by which the movement of electrons could be observed. This paradox is archetypical for Cassirer. The history of physics repeatedly displays this idea of a substantial core that again and again takes precedence over what can be empirically observed. This, is the substance-based ideology of classical science; and it is only the development of quantum mechanics that has managed to overcome it.[44] Unlike classical physics, quantum mechanics is not founded upon the substantial interior of atoms, but rather on "functional relations between observable magnitudes" (*DI* 135). These functional relations, furthermore, can only be expressed via symbols that are mediated representations of observed phenomena.[45] As in his mature philosophy of the symbolic forms, there is no form of knowledge that offers direct access to reality. The most that knowledge can achieve is an ordering of observed phenomena through certain laws of relationality.[46] Scientific knowledge, as any other type of knowledge, is a creative collaboration between the representational system and phenomena as observed. Knowledge is created, not found, and the only way it is created is through a system of "pure signs." We can make no claims of objectivity beyond the correspondence between the logic of our scientific laws and the observable data. We see the same relationship in the 64 hexagrams of the *Yijing*; the truth about the world as it is for the modern physicist is a totality not of existing things or properties, but a totality of abstract symbols of thought that express determinate relations and functional coordinates. With the understanding that knowledge is the symbolic articulation of external, observable phenomena, we put aside the dogma of a posited essence (which we cannot observe). The truth about the world, and about human beings lies in their external, observable manifestations, in their work. It is for this reason that Cassirer's philosophy of symbolic forms is so pluralistic. An illuminating example of this pluralism is Cassirer's attitude to technology. This point about pluralism will be the focus for the final chapter of this book.

In "Form and Technology" (Cassirer 2012; original German article published in 1930), Cassirer argues that technology is a means by which the human *Geist* manifests itself and through which greater freedom is won for human *Geist* (culture). As a symbolic form, technology can never be understood as alienated from man, cancerously engendering its own laws of growth to the detriment of the human being that spawned it.[47] The historical background to this essay is the rise of the new technologies, the mechanization of war in World War I, and with it, the thrown-ness of man's fate to the irrepressible march of the machine. *Technik* became the name for both the enemy and the savior of mankind; and Fritz Lang's *Metropolis* (1927) typifies the fascination and fear surrounding the "machine age." Like Hegel's *Weltgeist*, technological progress was understood as driven by deep forces and motives that were beyond human control and human understanding; it was a whirlwind to which humans can only passively submit, taking us where it will.

The key to Cassirer's ability to embrace technology is his stress on the fact that spontaneity *always* lies with the human subject, and that human spontaneity realizes itself in its work. Geist always manifests itself in a material form—in the *work* of humans—and so is empirically observable; conversely, what is empirically observable as work is always a sign of the spontaneity of *Geist*. In this regard, it is useful to contrast Cassirer's attitude to technology with the Confucians. Whereas *Xici* 2.2 celebrates the creation of technology as that which *enabled* civilization, "cultural pessimists" such as the Daoists of the "Outer Chapters"[48]—similar to the cultural pessimists of the twentieth century—see technology as a manifestation of the utilitarian spirit that alienates us from the oneness of life (Dao). For the cultural pessimists and the Daoists of the outer chapter, Mind, "whose goal and power emerges in technology" (Cassirer 2012, 35), is the irreconcilable opponent of life. This mind seeks to rapaciously dominate everything at the expense of life. The Cassirerian and Confucian attitude against such primitivistic renunciation of technology through the foil of a pretechnological "state of nature" is to stress that freedom is always to be *made* by human beings through their work. Freedom is not an existing fact of the world that culture takes us away from; freedom is to be made through culture itself. No aspect of culture can therefore be alienated from the human being. For Anthony Appiah, the Roman playwright Publius Terentius Afer's similar dictum in *The Self Tormentor*, "Homo sum: humani nil a me alienum puto" (I am human: nothing human is alien to me), is the golden rule of cosmopolitanism (Appiah 2007, 111). Likewise, we can say the same about the Cassirerian and Confucian view of culture. Nothing that is the work of humans can be alienated from humans, hence their embrace of pluralism and holism.

Language and Freedom: Points 5 and 6

Cassirer's understanding of human freedom is best explained via his understanding and advance upon Kantian freedom. Famously, for Kant, as phenomenal creatures we are determined by the laws of nature, but the possibility of ethics demands that we assume the unconditioned, that is, freedom and autonomy. There is thus a dualism in the Kantian system between the conditioned and the unconditioned. In theoretical judgment, there are forms of judgment (quantity, quality, relation, and modality) by which a representation obtains generality and necessity and thus becomes an object of possible experience. In practical judgment, it is only when the subject acts according to the categorical imperative that the subject is "free."

For Cassirer, the kind of "judgment" needed to see nature as "purposive" indicated to Kant that there was a form of judgment that could not be encompassed by the theoretical and practical judgment outlined in the first two critiques. Kant's understanding of "purposive," as Cassirer interprets it, is in line with its general linguistic usage in the eighteenth century—derived from Leibniz's concept of "harmony"—wherein

> a totality is called "purposive" when in it there exists a structure such that every part not only stands adjacent to the next but its special import is dependent on the other. Only in a relationship of this kind is the totality converted from a mere aggregate into a closed system, in which each member possesses its characteristic function; but all these functions accord with one another so that altogether they have a unified, concerted action and a single overall significance. (KLT 287)

For Cassirer, the scientific understanding of nature cannot be explained solely by the forms of judgment of the pure understanding. The three general laws of the understanding ("three analogies of experience": substantiality, causality, and reciprocity), for example, correspond to the three basic laws laid down by Newton: the law of inertia, the law of the proportionality of cause and effect, and the law of equality of action and reaction. The structure and historical development of mechanics is not, however, sufficiently described through these. What the empirical sciences describe is an integrated order of empirical laws; and the comprehensibility of this order cannot be reduced to the pure laws of the understanding alone. Science is an interconnected, "harmonious" system of concepts that does not prescribe a priori any content (legislate the conditions of possibility of the object) but makes science as a mode of knowledge possible. If we were not able to systematically comprehend the totality of empirical laws as a unitary series, then our experience of nature would be merely a crude chaotic aggregate.[49]

The necessity of seeing nature as "purposive" and the need for higher order concepts in our description of nature emerges most clearly in the biological sciences. Different organisms, for example, seem dividable into a systematic hierarchy of genera and species, but this "law-likeness" of nature cannot be demonstrated as a priori necessary through the pure laws of the understanding. Whereas the pure understanding contains the conditions of possibility of its object and is thus a "legislator for nature," the kind of judgment necessary for scientific laws is not constitutive and determinative but regulative and reflective. Whereas the determinative judgment of the pure understanding subsumes the particular under a given universal in order to specify its nature, in reflective judgment, one starts with the particular and attempts to find concepts and rules that describe the *connections* that the different parts show with respect to one another. The lawfulness or order that we perceive in nature is called "purposive" in the sense that there is an appropriateness of appearances to the conditions of our judgment. Regarded as an object of experience, nature is nothing but the totality of appearances governed by universal (mathematico-physical) laws. The fact that there does appear to be a regularity to nature indicates that there is a "second-stage creative process" (*KLT* 296). The *experience* of nature is thus fundamentally informed by the scientific principles and laws that the human subject constructs.[50] We "discover" nature inasmuch as we "create" it with scientific means: the purposiveness of nature is thus a heuristic principle for judging nature (*KLT* 298). Despite being a mere heuristic principle, it is, however, *necessary* for understanding nature, as knowledge of phenomena would be incomplete and defective without the concept of purpose.[51] The "purposiveness" or harmony of content that our scientific laws "discover" in nature is thus *regulative*, as it does not relate to things and their inner natures, but instead to concepts and their connections in the mind of the subject. What the mind discovers are harmonious relations that, although merely "formal," are nevertheless "objective" in the sense that they are the conditions of possibility ("transcendental" conditions) of the empirical sciences, and a scientific understanding of nature.

This recognition that it is relationality (i.e., an interconnected, "harmonious" system of concepts) that characterizes our understanding and description of nature, and especially biological nature, along with the stress on the fact that these relations are constructed by the subject (merely a heuristic), leads Cassirer to the idea that there are more "heuristics" for our understanding of the world. Cassirer, following the Marburg neo-Kantians, rejects Kant's two-stem doctrine. Nature is no longer something we experience, but something we understand through the creation of our scientific theories. In organic life, we see the inextricable mutuality between our own (evolving) heuristic laws and the orderliness we perceive in the natural world: the spontaneity of spirit is present in how we understand the orderliness of nature. Cassirer's "Kantianism" thus leaves aside the enterprise of finding a universal and necessary description of cognition and sees the a priori as dynamic and evolving[52] with the progress of the sciences.[53] The "creation" of scientific laws under reflective judgment, however, is a sign of the "freedom" of spirit. Scientific laws are a sign of freedom because (1) they are a free creation of spirit, and (2) it is through their creation that we can better understand our world. It is the creations of spirit that allow us to discover *meaning* in the world, and thus achieve freedom.

The fact that there is a domain of knowledge that does change and evolve—the organic—showed Cassirer that our heuristic tools must be commensurably dynamic. It is for this reason that he associates language—the paradigmatic "heuristic"—with the organic. Like the heuristic laws that we use to understand the organic, "language as an organism, which situated the organic process *between* nature and freedom, hence subjected it to no absolute necessity but left a certain amount of free play between the different possibilities" (*PSF* 1:169). Language, as a *free* creation of the subject like the heuristic laws used for understanding nature, overcomes the determinism of the phenomenal and the freedom of the noumenal:

> There is a domain of spirit, even in the case of the practical and teleological sciences, that is fulfilled neither by the analogy of the mathematical concept of necessity nor by the model of ethical values or the concept of norms. . . . We find ourselves, here, face to face with a pure and true spiritual *creation* to which all mere arbitrariness of reflection is related and according to which it itself appears as a *product* of nature. Here, the basic opposition that rules over the whole Kantian system does not appear sufficient to determine and delimit this new sphere—the domain of *language*, which is distinctly spiritual. (*KEH* 103–4)

For Cassirer, the only objectivity that transcendental analytics analyses is the synthetic unity of the understanding, which is determined by purely logical attributes, but this does not exhaust all the workings of the creative spontaneity of the human spirit (*PSF* 1:78–80). It is for this reason that the analysis of consciousness must be supplemented by a philosophy of culture, for, otherwise, "the true concept of freedom" could not be demonstrated (*SMC* 89). There are thus times when Cassirer criticizes the dualism between freedom and determinism in the Kantian system. In his lecture to the Warburg Institute in 1936, "Critical Idealism as a Philosophy of Culture," for example, he says:

> We cannot restrict freedom to morality; for in doing so we should include it within the limits of mere subjectivity, of subjective reflection. But freedom means much more; it means the ultimate end of the absolute mind and at the same time the path it had to traverse in order to come to this end. Freedom is no mere fact of consciousness that must be believed on the testimony of this consciousness, it is to be made and acquired and it cannot be acquired but by the work of the mind's self-realization." (*SMC* 88)

Freedom cannot be merely abstractly proved via transcendental analysis—and thus remain merely subjective—but rather it must be seen in the communal, concrete work of spirit, in the *facta* of culture. As long as we limit freedom to the analysis of pure cognition, we cannot wholly discredit the naive-realistic view of the world (*PSF* 1:80). But, in culture, "being" can only be apprehended in "action." The "being" of culture, the *forma formata*, as it were, is a proof of the "action" of culture, the *forma formans*. We need not prove the fact of the freedom of spirit through transcendental analysis, as the mere physical reality of the works of culture is proof of its existence.[54] Only insofar as the aesthetic, religious, or mythic imagination exists *can* there be the sphere of aesthetic, religious, and mythic objects. "For the content of the concept of culture cannot be detached from the fundamental forms and directions of human activity" (*PSF* 1:80). The work of culture, in the nominal sense, is the physical proof of the work of culture and the cultural imagination, in the verbal sense. Thus, "beside and above the world of perception, all these spheres produce freely their own *world of symbols* which is the true vehicle of their immanent development" (*PSF* 1:87). Spirit *needs* physical embodiment in the physical work (in the nominal sense) of culture, in order for its work (in the verbal sense) to actuate. Spirit creates the concrete symbols in which and only in which it can exist and develop. And so, "the critique of reason becomes the critique of culture" (*PSF* 1:80). To understand culture is to understand spirit (*Geist*).

Cassirer's Linguistic Turn

The six characteristics that were outlined at the beginning of this chapter are all linked to a "linguistic turn" view of language. Relationality, part-whole structuralism, pluralism, and concrete universality are all related to the concession that it is the human mind that freely creates these relations through the linguistic sign. Cassirer's interpretation of the history of language thus follows the same logic of a gradual liberation from a substance-ontology: the copy theory of meaning is a manifestation of traditional (Aristotelian) logic that was replaced by a functional understanding of language. According to traditional logic, the mind forms concepts by abstracting common properties from a certain number of objects: the *concept* is that which presents the shared *essential* properties. The formulation of concepts under traditional logic thus presupposes the existence of definite, fixed properties, which *objectively* obtain. This traditional logic is thus a counterpart to the copy theory of language whereby language merely reproduces the essential nature of things. According to the substance or copy-theory of knowledge, or "pictorialism" (*DI* 151), *truth* is explained in terms of the object; a representation is true if it manages to mirror the properties of the object. The mind under this framework would literally be passive. With the Copernican-Kepler Revolution, the removal of the fixed hierarchy of being, and the attendant elevated status afforded to mind of the subject, the copy theory of meaning runs into problems. If properties are not always already in the world, which the mind passively mirrors, then we cannot explain how the finished world of concepts and ideas were originally determined before their reproduction in language. For Cassirer, the philosophy of language before Herder (1744–1803) was limited to a copy theory of meaning, merely reproducing the "finished world of concepts and ideas [*Vorstellungen*]" of either externally received cognitive data or internally derived ideas (*KEH* 110). Under the Herderian and Cassirerian view of language, however, language does not merely mechanically reproduce given determinations; rather, there is an autonomy and spontaneity in language that *creates* those very determinations.

Cassirer's concept of the symbol can be seen as the Kantian schema in observable, phenomenal form. The symbol is *functional* and so able to relate to both the phenomena and the "category." The symbol, because it is created by the subject and *constitutes* reality, overcomes the Kantian dualism of objectivity of being and objectivity of freedom. The symbol is *objective* because it has intersubjective validity among the members of the symbolic community who employ it and because each symbol is internally coherent with the overall symbolic system. The symbols are the forms of *culture*. Cassirer's philosophy of the symbol thus extends the productive spontaneity of Kantian reason to the entirety of human life. As symbolic animals, our "empirical" and "rational" natures are reconciled through cultural forms; these forms being, in turn, the enabling conditions of our freedom as well our relationship to the "empirical" world.

As we will see in chapter 4, the reason *wen* can be a vehicle for the Dao (文以載道)—as Cassirer asks, "How can a finite and particular sensory content be made into the vehicle of a general spiritual 'meaning'?" (*PSF* 1:93)—is because language is both universal, a creation of spirit, and takes form in the particular and the concrete. Language, further-more, extends the "principles" of Dao itself, which is why, in *Analects* 15.29, Confucius said it is humans who enlarge the Dao, not the Dao that enlarges humans. Like the Confucian relationship between *ren* and *li*, *ren* is only ever *manifested* in specific instances of *li*. Like the Daoist relationship between *Dao* and *De* (德), the Dao is only ever manifested in specific instances of *De*. "The content of the spirit is disclosed only in its manifestations; the ideal form is known only by and in the aggregate of the sensible signs which it uses for its expression" (*PSF* 1:86). It is for this reason that Cassirer writes of Humboldt's philosophy of language, "The true synthesis and the genuine reconciliation of the great funda-mental antagonisms of metaphysics were achieved in it. Spirit, in its pure particularity and full generality, exhibits itself in language as both limited and unlimited, as free and necessary. Here, it first shows itself, according to Humboldt, to be that ideal of a concrete generality with which the whole of post-Kantian speculation wrestles" (*KEH* 115). Language, as this concrete generality, overcomes the dualisms of subject-object, free-dom-determinism, and universal and particular.

The Confucian tradition, I argue, *assumed* from its formative beginnings such a relation between humanism, language, and freedom. The Confucian tradition, that is, assumed the six characteristics associ-ated with a "linguistic turn" view of language. Language is a concrete universal that is both a demonstration of the spontaneity and freedom of spirit *and* that in which it can further itself. This concrete universal operates through a part-whole structuralism, in that the meaning of any one symbol rests on reference to the whole system of such symbols. It is for this reason that *xiang* (象) and relatedly *wen* (文) became such loaded and exalted terms in the Chinese tradition, comparable in their aggrandizement to the "truth, goodness, beauty" of the Western tradition: language and symbols are a demonstration of our freedom.

Nature, Organism, and *Ziran* (自然)

In "The Expressivist Turn" chapter of Charles Taylor's *Sources of the Self*, there is a discussion about Romanticism that also relates the several points that I have been making, and it is worth quoting in full:

> The creative imagination is the power which we have to attri-
> bute to ourselves, once we see art as expression and no longer
> simply as mimesis. Manifesting reality involves the creation
> of new forms which give articulation to an inchoate vision,
> not simply the reproduction of forms already there. This is
> why the Romantic period developed its particular concept of
> the symbol. The symbol, unlike allegory, provides the form of
> language in which something, otherwise beyond our reach,
> can become visible. Where the allegorical term points to a
> reality which we can also refer to directly, the symbol allows
> what is expressed in it to enter our world. It is the locus of
> a manifestation of what otherwise would remain invisible.
> As A. W. Schlegel put it: "Wie kann nun das Unendliche
> auf die Oberfläche zur Erscheinung gebracht werden? Nur
> symbolisch, in Bildern und Zeichen" ("How then can the
> infinite be brought into manifestation on the surface? Only
> symbolically, in pictures and signs"). And Coleridge takes up
> the same idea. He defines the symbol as "characterized by a
> translucence of the eternal through and in the temporal." It
> can't be separated from what it reveals, as an external sign
> can be separated from its referent. It "always partakes of the
> Reality which it renders intelligible; and while it enunciates
> the whole, abides itself as a living part of the Unity, of which

it is the representative." Or again, the perfect symbol "lives within that which it symbolizes and resembles, as the crystal lives within the light it transmits, and is transparent like the light itself."

This concept of the symbol is what underlies the ideal of a complete interpenetration of matter and form in the work of art. Coleridge's image of translucence makes this connection understandable. In a perfect work of art, the "matter"—the language of a poem or the material of a sculpture—should be entirely taken up in the manifestation; and reciprocally, what is manifested ought to be available only in the symbol, and not merely pointed to as an independent object whose nature could be defined in some other medium. (1989, 379)

As Taylor writes here, historically, once we give up the idea that our work—in this instance art—is merely a copy of a preexisting reality (mimesis), this *requires* the concept of a creative imagination. It requires that we dignify the productive capacities of the human mind. It is precisely this ontological-epistemological shift that necessitated the idea of the *symbol*. The symbol, as distinguished from allegory, is not premised on a dualistic worldview. (This point will be picked up in chapter 3 in relation to poetry.) The symbol, like Leibniz's *characteristica generalis* realizes the "matter" or potential of the thing. The symbol manifests a potential that is shaped by this very manifesting. For Taylor this expressivist turn, whereby the very manifesting of something in a concrete medium is not merely a mimesis of what was already formulated, but a means of realizing something inchoate or only partly formed, is rooted in biological ideas of growth and so a naturalistic paradigm (1989, 374). "The philosophy of nature as source was central to the great upheaval in thought and sensibility that we refer to as 'Romanticism'" (368).[55] What Taylor defines here in terms of expressivism and a biological notion of growth Cassirer takes to be the nature of *Geist*. *Geist* requires a concrete corporealization; and this corporealization also furthers *Geist* itself. For Cassirer, language is one of the symbolic forms that exemplifies this principle, and so I have used the "linguistic turn" to talk about what Taylor here refers to as "expressivism."

It is worth bearing in mind that, for Taylor, there are two important sources for this "expressivism": Leibniz and Herder. These two figures, as we will see throughout the rest of this project, and especially in chapter

6, are important influences on Cassirer. As we will see in chapter 5, for Charles Taylor, this "expressivism" is also relevant as a paradigm in the developing of oneself (*Bildung*) that resonates with Confucian ideas about self-development. Taylor's definition of expressivism will also be very useful for chapters 3 and 4.

In a discussion of *xiang* in *Xici* 1.12 (which will be discussed in the next chapter), Roger Ames defines *xiang* in a very similar way to Charles Taylor's summary of the symbol:

> The meaning resident in the image as established is the act of establishing the image itself. Contrary to one's own naive expectations—and the advice of many subtle aesthetic theories—what one finally "sees" in a work of art is the creative act that produced it. The creative process, not the object, is the repository of meaning. What is imaged is the process. (Ames 1991, 229)

Many of the points Ames alludes to here will be picked up in greater detail in the next chapter. Suffice it to say that Ames's summary of the nature of *xiang* echoes Taylor's discussion of the Romantic conception of the symbol. (1) The material presentation of the idea through the creative imagination *is* to establish meaning. This is what I have called a "symbolic idealism." (2) This is opposed to a naive realism/copy theory of meaning. Ames's point that (dualistic) aesthetic theories that understand art as mere mimesis miss these two points will be picked up in chapter 3.

That the Romantic paradigm of the organic or nature can be interpreted as the source of the six characteristics that I have described and is shared with Chinese/Confucian philosophy is no accident. The Romantic paradigm of "nature" that replaced the substance ontology of Aristotelianism is much more comparable to Chinese cosmology. In the classical Chinese tradition, one did not have a term "nature" to refer to the immanent, changing world. The modern translation for nature, *ziran* (自然), is taken from the *Daodejing* and means that which is so on its own: each thing is its own spontaneous source of action. In chapter 25 of the *Daodejing*, for example, we read that the Dao models itself on *ziran* (道法自然).

Once one replaces the mechanistic Aristotelian paradigm of linear causality with a "nature," self-so, paradigm where there are a myriad self-soing entities, then order is understood as emergent, as opposed to predefined. If there is not one stable ontological order, then it is harder to abide by the Aristotelian concept that each thing in nature has just one telos, and is thus defined *in se est et per se concipitur*. A thing is instead only defined momentarily and relationally (both in time and in space, i.e., in relation to past and present, and with other things). This naturalistic cosmology, in its rejection of an extratemporal *arche*, is an-archic: no order can be defined for all time, or even momentarily, before it becomes superseded in the face of a new order. Once one gives up this idea of a single ordered universe, then one is pushed toward a more relational view of things. This relationality furthermore *requires* the human creative imagination to be seen, because there are so many relations that a single, creative perspective is needed to describe a particular relational nexus. Once one realizes the importance of the human creative imagination, then it is a short step to the realization that our thinking is dependent upon the linguistic sign.

This, then, is the metaphysical background for taking "culture" seriously, and I will pick up this discussion in the final chapter. This chapter has provided a metaphilosophical background, through the foil of Cassirer's own interpretation of the linguistic turn, of why the Confucian tradition took *xiang* and *wen* so seriously. The six characteristics of Cassirer's interpretation of the linguistic turn are seen to match the characteristics of the *Xici* and *Yijing*. In the next chapter, we will read the *Xici* closely, and see that in many crucial aspects, it does indeed follow Cassirer's "Symbolic Idealism."

2

Li Xiang Yi Jin Yi (立象以尽意)

Giving (Symbolic) Form to Phenomena

In this chapter, I argue that *xiang* (象) is a "concrete universal"[1] created by the sages through dialogue with the "symbolic pregnancy," that is, the inherent expressiveness, of the world. The "symbolic pregnancy" of the world is comparable, it is suggested, to the concept of *qing* (情) found in the *Xici*. It is the "invention" of this concrete universal that allowed the sages to better understand the world, which is why *xiang* becomes a metonym for culture and civilization itself. The meaning of *xiang* is derived from a part-whole structuralism. It overcomes the subject-object dualism and is therefore the Confucian paradigm of *tian ren he yi*. Importantly, for Cassirer, the Western counterpart to this "concrete universal" that overcomes the subject-object dualism is language. It is therefore unsurprising that, as we have already seen, the philosophical rationalization of *xiang* of the *Xici* ("Commentary on the Appended Phrases"; 系辞) is also the philosophical rationalization of *wen* (language).

Xiang (象) in the *Xici*

Xiang is used in three main ways in the *Xici*. In its first meaning, it signifies a naturally occurring phenomenon, or the image of a naturally occurring phenomena.[2] In its second usage, it is used like the homophone of *xiang* (象)—*xiang* (像), that is, with a person radical added—meaning

51

resemblance, semblance, or to make semblances.[3] In its third meaning, it refers to the graphic representations of the trigrams ☲ and, compounding them, the hexagrams ䷜.[4] Most of the commentators agree with this categorization.[5] In the *Yijing* as a whole each trigram/hexagram is associated with a particular "image" (*xiang* 象), that is, principle of a natural process.[6] The eight trigrams are associated, for example, with the images of heaven, earth, thunder, water, mountain, wind, flame, and lake respectively. The Russian sinologist, Iulian Shchutskii, expresses the nature of "images" (*xiang*) most incisively:

> Each hexagram is a symbol of some life situation which develops in time. Each text to a hexagram is a short characterization of this situation, basically or completely. Each text to a line is a concrete characterization of some stage in the development of the given situation. With this, one must take into account that, in view of the authors' level of thinking and language techniques, such characterizations almost never are expressed in the form of precise ideas. The elements of the *Book of Changes* are elements of imagery. (1979, 226)

The lexical ambiguity of *xiang*, its semantic multivalence or its polysemy, has traditionally beleaguered attempts at defining and understanding it: How can *xiang* refer to physical objects, and abstract, conceptual ideas, as well as hermeneutic symbols? How can it, furthermore, combine the idea of a phenomenon with the idea of its representation? As Pauline Yu writes, "It is difficult, if not impossible, to distinguish among an object, one's perception of it, its image or representation, and its significance. Indeed, the first three are all rendered by the same word" (1987, 38).

We can see the difficulty in getting to grips with the concept of *xiang*—especially for a dualistic framework (i.e., naive realism or idealism)[7] when Dai Lianzhang (戴璉璋; 1932–) writes in *The Formation of the Ten Wings and Its Four Xiang* (易传之形成及其四象) that

> *xiang* is the product of the powers of human imagination. When people are focused on an object, a lively imagination, or through a sudden flash of inspiration, or through the power of association, a "meaningful image" [*yixiang* 意象] or images [*tuxiang* 图象] will be produced. Art, sculpture, music, dance, drama, literature are all the art [*yishu* 艺术] of *xiang*, whereas language, the written graph, and various symbols and signs

are the information [zixun 资讯] of *xiang*. *Xiang* is essentially the imitation of an object. But with regard to the imitation of the object, to the intention behind, and method of, imitation [*moni* 模拟], there is an authorial action and implicit authorial intent. . . . This is to say, *xiang* is not a re-presentation [*zai xian* 再现]; what it in fact demonstrates or evokes is an idea [*yinian*, 意念]. (Dai 1988, 158; my translation)

The picture that emerges from Dai's description of *xiang* is of a kind of idealism, and yet the *Xici* claims to be rooted in cosmic processes itself, because *xiang* refers (in its first usage) to natural phenomena themselves. Even Dai himself seems to complicate the picture by saying that "*xiang* is essentially the imitation of an object." At first glance, Dai seems to be merely confused about what *xiang* is, because it can't be both operating under a realism and an idealism. In a similarly "idealistic" description, Richard J. Smith describes the physical objects in the first definition of *xiang* as "representation" and "symbols" (see Smith 2008, 39). Likewise, Mark Edward Lewis refers to this first definition of *xiang* as "schematized forms of real entities" (1999, 266; my emphasis), thereby suggesting an idealism as it points to a human subject who did the schematizing. In reference to *Xici* 2.3 and 2.2, Hu Shi writes that, for Confucius (the reputed author of the Ten Wings), "first there is *xiang*, then there are things [*wu* 物; *xiang sheng er hou you wu* 象生而后有物]. The *xiang* are the primeval archetype after which things are modelled" (Hu 1997, 59; my translation). Again, this seems to point to an idealism whereby *xiang* creates reality. Using this citation from Hu Shi, Zhang Dongsun (张东荪) emphasizes that *xiang*, despite superficial similarities, should not be confused with self-subsisting Platonic forms. The signification of *xiang* is "only concerned with human affairs" (Chang 1952, 216). An antinomy seems to result from the descriptions of these scholars. If *xiang* has an exclusively subjective orientation, then why does the *Xici* claim that *xiang* is a manifestation of things themselves, as a naturally occurring phenomenon?

Symbols and Reality

In "The Roots of Chinese Philosophy and Culture: An Introduction to 'Xiang' and 'Xiang Thinking,'" Wang Shuren argues that "to grasp the truth in traditional Chinese classics, we need to uncover the long obscured '*xiang*' 象 (image) thinking, which has long been overshadowed by Occidentalism" (Wang 2009, 1). For Wang, whereas Western thought is centerd in substance, objectivity, and the "ready-made," the key ideas of the Chinese tradition, such as *Dao*, *Qi*, *Taiji*, "manifest themselves in the framework of 'the syncretism of man and nature,' or that of 'subject-object integration' which, nevertheless, is dynamic"[8] (4). I very much agree with Wang's assessment of *xiang* and its syncretic nature. I will build on Wang's argument and contend that the "truth" about "*xiang*" thinking and thus the key to the traditional Chinese classics, lies in the fact the *Xici* operates under a "symbolic idealism" that integrates the subjective and objective poles.[9] Symbolic idealism operates, as Wang writes of *xiang*, as a human observation "which is dynamically integrated with intuition or comprehension" (4). When we read the *Xici* under "symbolic idealism," there will be no antinomies in seeing *xiang* as referring to both phenomena and conceptual ideas (and its representation in symbolism) that we might have found to be so problematic in the previous section. Consider what happens when we read the *Xici* according to the symbolic idealism that takes symbols to be necessary in understanding reality.[10]

In *Xici* 1.8 we read that

> the sages had the means to perceive the confusion [*ze* 赜] of the world and, drawing comparisons [*ni* 拟] to them with analogous things, made images [*xiang* 象] out of those things that seemed appropriate.[11] (Lynn 1994, 56–57; modified)

I have translated *ze* (赜) here as "confusion," following Zhu Xi[12] (1130–1200) (Zhu 1992, 143), and Gao Heng's (高亨) (1900–86) commentaries.[13] Gao Heng comments on this passage that

> *ze* (赜) means confusion. *Ni* (拟) means "compare; draw a parallel; match or analogy; metaphor." *Zhu* [诸] means "in relation to" [*hu* 乎]. The nature [*xing* 性] of each of the myriad things has what is suitable [*yi* 宜] to it, thus it is called "things that are suitable" [*wu yi* 物宜]. This means that the sages had the means to see the complexity of the world; from this they used the hexagrams to analogize [*ni* 拟] its form/shape/patterns [*xingtai* 形态], symbolize [*xiangzheng* 象征] what are suitable to them; thus the hexagrams are called *xiang*.[14] (Gao 1979, 518; my translation)

From this passage, we can see that there was an aspect of human creativity involved in the creation of the hexagrams. Prior to the ordering of the world by the sages, the world was/appeared as a confused, amorphous mass. The sages then distinguished the natures of things, and then *analogized* what they distinguished or judged the natures of things to be, in terms of suitable symbolisms. There is thus a double human act of creativity or judgment present: the natures of things needed to be distinguished out of chaos—by a human agent—and then the human agent *chose* an appropriate analogy for them. The human agent is thus not a passive mirror reflecting given properties of the world; the human agent was necessary for discerning those very properties. We can go further in our interpretation and say that the act of discerning the properties of things from chaos, and the act of analogizing them in terms of an appropriate symbol, are not successive stages, but rather simultaneous with each other. It is only when the sages symbolized the natures of things—what Gao Heng called *xing tai* (形态)—in terms of what was suitable for them that their natures were *known*: their natures were known through analogy.[15] This interpretation stressing the essential role of human creativity and judgment in the formation of the hexagrams is coherent with *Xici* 1.10, 1.12, and 2.2.

In *Xici* 1.10, we read,

> It is by means of the *Changes* that the sages plumb [*ji* 极] the utmost profundity and dig [*yan* 研] into the very incipience "*ji*" [几] of things.[16] (Lynn 1994, 63)

Han Kangbo comments on this passage that " 'to plumb the principles that underlie the prephenomenal world' is what is meant by the term *profundity*, and 'to be ready just at the moment when the imperceptible beginnings of action occurs' is what is meant by the term *incipience*"[17] (Lynn 1994, 63). It is significant that the *Changes* were necessary to understanding the "prephenomenal" principles of the world, for it seems to imply that if the *Changes* did not exist, then the sages could *not* have understood these principles. It can thus be inferred that the *Changes* *precedes* understanding phenomenal laws, for if the *Changes* was merely an exact replica of the phenomenal laws that the sages had the means to access, then why would they need the *Changes* before they could understand phenomena?

In *Xici* 1.12, we read,

> They [the sages] appended phrases to the hexagram lines
> in order to judge [*duan* 斷] the good and bad fortune
> involved. . . . To plumb the confusion [*ze* 賾] of the world
> to the utmost is dependent on the hexagrams. (Lynn 1994,
> 68; modified)

In saying that the sages needed to append phrases to the hexagrams
before they could judge the nature of a situation, the *Xici* is implying
that the sages could not have judged the nature of a situation *without*
the phrases and the hexagrams. It is for this reason that understanding
and ordering the world is *dependent* on the hexagrams.

A series of examples demonstrating that ordering the world is *dependent* on the hexagrams is to be found in *Xici* 2.2, which will be explored
in more detail. For the moment, let us take hexagram 17, "Following"
(*sui* 随), which, *Xici* 2.2 tells us, inspired the sages to domesticate the
ox and to harness the horse to conveyances. The hexagram "Following"
☰ is composed of two trigrams, "Quake" (*zhen* 震) ☳ below and "Joy"
(*dui* 兑) ☱ above. "Quake" is the initiator of moment; it is a "yang"
trigram, while the "Joy" trigram is a "yin" trigram. In total, this hexagram
is supposed to convey the idea that the hard are happily submitting to
the soft. It is thus the (relational) principle embodied in this hexagram
that, according to the *Xici*, the sages used and applied to the world and
so invented the idea of domesticating animals.

Xici 2.2

In the introduction, we have already seen that the *Yijng* trigrams were
understood as the most important account of the origins of writing in
Warring States and early imperial China, and that *Xici* 2.2 gives the most
complete account of the genesis of the trigrams. In *Xici* 2.2 we read that,

> when in ancient times Lord Baoxi ruled the world as sovereign,
> he looked upward and observed [*guan* 观] the images [*xiang*
> 象] in heaven and looked downward and observed [*guan* 观]
> the models [*fa* 法] that the earth provided. He observed [*guan*
> 观] the patterns [*wen* 文] on birds and beasts and what things
> were suitable for the land. Nearby, adopting them from his

own person, and afar, adopting them from other things, he thereupon made the eight trigrams in order to become thoroughly conversant [*tong* 通] with the virtues [*de* 德] inherent in the numinous [*shen* 神] and the bright [*ming* 明] and to classify the myriad things in terms of their true dispositions [*qing* 情].[18] (Lynn 1994, 77; modified)

This is perhaps the most explicit statement in the *Xici* that the invention of the trigrams *preceded* understanding; there is, however, a paradox. The text says that Baoxi could not have completely understood the highest things—the numinous and the bright—without the trigrams; but Baoxi was evidently able to understand (*guan* 观) the phenomenal patterns in the sky and on earth *prior* to the invention of the trigrams, for it was his perception of these patterns that inspired the very creation of the trigrams. For Hu Shi, there are two types of *xiang* in the *Xici*; one is the natural phenomena (*xian xiang* 现象) found in nature; the second type is that of a "meaningful image" (*yixiang* 意象) (Hu 1997, 60). With regard to this passage, Hu Shi notes that the first type of *xiang*, the *xiang* that Baoxi observed in heaven, are the *xiang* of natural phenomena. These observations gave rise to *yixiang* that are then captured in the hexagrams (60). I will propose that these two successive stages of *xiang* that Hu Shi notes are comparable to the relationship between the two stages of Cassirer's own phenomenology of perception: "symbolic pregnancy" and the symbolic form. To make clearer the relationship between phenomena, symbolic creation, meaning, and the subject in the *Xici*, we should thus make a detour through Cassirer's conception of symbolic pregnancy.

Symbolic Pregnancy

For Cassirer, the symbolic forms of human culture—language, art, science, and so on—are "artificial" symbolism, as they involve the "giving of signs"[19] (*Zeichengebung*; *PSF* 1:105–7; Cassirer 2010, 41). For Cassirer, however, neither culture nor the artificial symbols create the phenomenon of meaning itself; our sensory perception itself is already inherently meaningful.[20] The ultimate ground of meaning is instead a nonreducible "symbolic pregnancy"[21]—the inherent meaningfulness of perception. Anything sensory always bears meaning of some kind:

By symbolic pregnance we mean *the way* [*die Art*] in which a perception as a sensory experience contains at the same time a certain nonintuitive meaning [*Sinn*] which it immediately and concretely represents. Here we are not dealing with bare perceptive data, on which some sort of apperceptive acts are later grafted, through which they are interpreted, judged, transformed. Rather, it is the perception itself which by virtue of its own *immanent* organization, takes on a kind of spiritual [*geistiger*] articulation—which, being ordered in itself, also belongs to a determinate order of meaning. In its full actuality, its living totality, it is at the same time *a life "in" meaning.* It is not only subsequently received into this sphere but is, one might say, born into it. It is this ideal interwovenness, this relatedness of the single perceptive phenomenon, given here and now, to a characteristic total meaning that the term "pregnance" is meant to designate. (*PSF* 3:202: my emphasis)

The best way to think of perception as symbolically pregnant is to contrast it with the kind of artificially attributed meaning found in medieval allegory. The allegory is a conventional sign for something not present in them; it is a cloak for a secret meaning hidden behind it. The dove in Christian allegory, for example, *symbolizes* the Holy Spirit, but this meaning is not *immanent* to the dove itself.

There is no raw data of perception; perception is always saturated with meaning. Symbolic pregnancy is thus the condition of possibility of the giving of signs and the giving of meaning (*Sinngebung*). Cassirer formulated his metaphysics in opposition to other forms of metaphysical foundationalism: logic, physics, immediacy, belief, and skepticism (*PSF* 4:115–26). Neither mere association, as it was for the empiricists, nor syllogism proves for Cassirer the origin of objective consciousness (*PSF* 3:235).[22] For Cassirer, all these methods commit a philosophical fallacy in thinking that meaning either lies within the subject or within the object: they are dualistic. For Cassirer, meaning is what is anterior to the *separation* between mind, object, and meaning. In symbolic pregnancy, sensory experience contains meaning; conversely, symbolic pregnancy pervades sensory awareness itself. Symbolic pregnancy is independent and originary, without which neither an object nor a subject, nor the unity of the self or objects could be possible for us (*PSF* 3:235).

The first use of Cassirer's idea of pregnancy as it is later developed in "symbolic pregnancy" is arguably in *Substance and Function*, which was published in 1910. Here he writes, in relation to the serial form and the members of the series, that, "by the side of what the content *is* in its material, sensuous structure, there appears what it *means* in the system of knowledge; and thus, its meaning develops out of the various logical 'acts,' which can be attached to the content. These 'acts,' which differentiate the sensuously unitary content by imprinting upon it different objectively directed 'intentions'" (*SF* 25). For Cassirer, the psychological act of perception is "intentional" in the same way that the serial form is intentional in a series.[23] While empiricism would regard the "similarity" of the contents of presentation as a fact of psychology, Cassirer argues that this is an untenable illusion. There is always a tacit frame of reference, a "point of view" that changes the nature of the perceptual data. Just as the (intensional) serial form cannot be reduced to the members of a series (extension), likewise the data of experience is organized by a peculiar form of consciousness that cannot be reduced to the individual data of sensation or perception.

To do so would be a category mistake. The "form" of the series is immanent in its extension but not reducible to it. This tacit frame of reference, or the "form" of the series is Cassirer's concept of symbolic pregnancy. Meaning does not inhere in the object itself, but nor is it separable from the object. Just as we cannot separate the serial form from the members of the series, we cannot separate meaning from objects; but nor can we simply reduce meaning to the discrete objects, for objects and meaning belong to different categories. Meaning and objects are inseparable from each other, but are not reducible to each other. From the mere juxtaposition of a, b, c . . . , for example, it is impossible to work out the special character of the organizing relation. This organizing relation, however, does not exist independently of extension; it cannot be abstracted as another individual, substantial element. The tacit frame of reference—the (law of the) whole—is holographically implicit in each member of the series.

For Cassirer, every content of consciousness, as in the serial form, exists in a structuralist part-whole relationship with the whole of consciousness. Each partial content of consciousness contains reference to the whole of consciousness: a present content has the power to evoke another content, because the whole is apprehended in the particular.

The part exists in a *structuralist* relationship with the whole (see point 2 in previous chapter). When a part of consciousness becomes bonded with the sensuous, however, when it becomes a sign, this part-whole structure becomes more stable and intelligible. The basic function of signification is thus present and active before the formation of the individual sign; but the creation of the sign *stabilizes* this signification, and, furthermore, makes the character of consciousness more definite and intelligible. In this process, a wholly new sphere of consciousness thus appears.[24] Furthermore, because we have now sensuously embodied certain formations of consciousness (with their inherent reference to the whole of consciousness), we are no longer bound to waves of passing impressions. We are *free* to evoke the sign at any moment. The creation of the sign thus both stabilizes consciousness and gives us a freedom from the passivity of conscious impressions. The symbol makes explicit the representative values and meanings that are embedded in perception itself. For Cassirer, this process of placing the individual content of consciousness within the whole of a symbolic system is not only a description of an intellectual process; it is also an ethical task. In *Language and Myth*, he talks of how this "synthesis cannot be achieved immediately and at a single stroke"; it is rather a progressive activity that requires a "will" (*LM* 26). We can say that, for Cassirer, "Form"—in the Kantian sense of forms of experience—that enables objectivity is never given; it must be striven for. This point about the freedom offered to the subject through symbolization will be picked up on in chapter 5.

    In his chapter "Pathology of the Symbolic Consciousness" (*PSF* 3), Cassirer provides a negative proof of why symbolic forms are integral for normal human perception. Cassirer surveys the impairment to speech in aphasia, the (mis)apprehension of objects and spatial, temporal, and numerical relations in "agnosia," and the disturbances in action in "apraxia." He concludes that, despite the variety of faculties affected, these pathologies can all be reduced to a common denominator, a failure of the "symbolic consciousness." This symbolic consciousness is *enabled*, furthermore, by our command of language (*PSF* 3:276–77). When our linguistic abilities break down, the various pathologies of aphasia, agnosia, and apraxia result. When we lose our linguistic abilities, our very intuition and perception of the world is affected (*PSF* 3:208). The inability to spontaneously use terms in relation to a given object, to understand spatial relations and number sequences and perform actions freely is understood by Cassirer to result from an inability to place the particular within a larger schematic/representational field (*PSF* 3:257).

A patient might be able use coins correctly in daily life but have lost all understanding of their abstract value (*PSF* 3:252). A patient might no longer recognize the actions of his hand and refer to it in the third person (*PSF* 3:264) A patient might not be able to recognize lampposts but see them merely in terms of their shapes—that is, long things (*PSF* 3:241n55). In perception, the sensory attains different degrees of symbolic significance, which becomes impaired in neurological disorders. What results in aphasia, agnosia, and apraxia is an inability to see the object or the self as anything else other than the concrete particular and thus to represent it in schematic terms within an abstract system of reference. In Cassirer's analysis of the importance of language for even intuitions and perceptions, he goes back to the Humboldtian principle that language *conditions* our intuition of objective reality (*PSF* 3:207)

For Cassirer, these neurological disorders blur the boundary between the biological sphere and the sphere of meaning, and the behavior of animals provide striking analogies with the behaviors of an apractic. A lower-order animal only knows rigid, stereotyped action sequences, and cannot recognize the individual characteristics of an object nor the separate phases of action removed from this usual fixed channel. A spider immediately attacks the prey in its net but runs away from it when the encounter occurs in situations unfamiliar to the spider. That is, the spider is unable to understand the object and the situation in a "symbolic," reflective way. Likewise, an apractic uses his spoon properly during a meal, but cannot recognize it under other circumstances (*PSF* 3:276). If we lost our symbolic capacity, then "man's life would be confined within the limits of his biological needs and his practical interests; it could find no access to the 'ideal world' which is opened to him from different sides by religion, art, philosophy, science" (*EM* 41). By "ideal," Cassirer is contrasting the horizons opened up to human beings through their symbolizing capacities that are unavailable to the animal, who is confined to the present and actual. In symbolic perception, however, we can escape the immediately perceived and desired, and make projections about an ideal (in the sense of ideas) world (*PSF* 3:276–77).

Symbolic Pregnancy and *Xici* 2.2

We can now offer an interpretation of *Xici* 2.2. The world was "symbolically pregnant" to Baoxi—the phenomena of the world were imbued with expressive meaning for him, it had *qing* (情)—a key term that I will explain—which is why he was able to observe the images (*xiang* 象) in heaven and the models (*fa* 法) that the earth provided. The world was evidently "symbolically pregnant" to Baoxi, but the creation of the trigrams allowed him to make clearer the structures that were nebulously present to him. The Cassirerian insight into the power of symbols for fixing impressions and thus creating a higher level of consciousness is thus paralleled by the narrative fiction that *Xici* 2.2 provides for the genesis of the hexagrams. What needs to be stressed is that, for Cassirer, the relationship between symbolic pregnancy and the symbolic form is not strictly genetic, the perceptual world and the symbolic world are inextricable, and not temporally successive (*PSF* 3:228, 230–31). His ideas on the "pathology of the symbolic consciousness" proves this. Once patients lose their linguistic capacities, their very ability to *see* the concrete particular in terms of an abstract, *symbolic*, or representational meaning becomes impaired. It is for this reason that I have called *Xici* 2.2 a "narrative fiction." For I think the point that the writers of this passage are making is that symbols were necessary for higher levels of human consciousness and thus civilized human behavior.[25] To do this, they posited a "state of nature" narrative fiction,[26] in which there was a time *before* the existence of symbols:

> When in ancient times Lord Baoxi ruled the world as sovereign, he looked upward and observed the images [*xiang* 象] in heaven and looked downward and observed the models [*fa* 法] that the earth provided. He observed the patterns [*wen* 文] on birds and beasts and what things were suitable for the land. Nearby, adopting them from his own person, and afar, adopting them from other things, he thereupon made the eight trigrams in order to become thoroughly conversant with the virtues inherent in the numinous and the bright and to classify the myriad things in terms of their true, innate natures [*qing* 情].
>
> He tied cords together and made various kinds of snare nets for catching animals and fish. He probably got the idea for this from the hexagram *Li* "Cohesion."
>
> After Lord Baoxi perished, Lord Shen Nong applied himself to things. He hewed wood and made a plowshare and bent wood and made a plow handle. The benefit of plowing and hoeing he taught to the world. He probably got the idea for this from the hexagram *Yi* "Increase."

He had midday become market time, had the people of the world gather, had the goods of the world brought together, had these exchanged, had them then retire to their homes, and enabled each one to get what he should. He probably got the idea for this from the hexagram *Shihe* "Bite Together."

After Lord Shen Nong perished, the Lord Yellow Emperor, Lord Yao, and Lord Shun applied themselves to things. They allowed things to undergo the free flow of change and so spared the common folk from weariness and sloth. With their numinous powers they transformed things and had the common folk adapt to them. As for "the Dao of" change, when one process of it reaches its limit, a change from one state to another occurs. As such, change achieves free flow, and with this free flow, it lasts forever. This is why "heaven will help him as a matter of course; this is good fortune, and nothing will be to his disadvantage." The Yellow Emperor, Yao, and Shun let their robes hang loosely down, and the world was well governed. They probably got the idea for this from the hexagrams *Qian* and *Kun*.

They hollowed out some tree trunks to make boats and whittled down others to make paddles. The benefit of boats and paddles was such that one could cross over to where it had been impossible to go. This allowed faraway places to be reached and so benefited the entire world. They probably got the idea for this from the hexagram *Huan* "Dispersion."

They domesticated the ox and harnessed the horse to conveyances. This allowed heavy loads to be pulled and faraway places to be reached and so benefited the entire world. They probably got the idea for this from the hexagram *Sui* "Following."

They had gates doubled and had watchmen's clappers struck and so made provision against robbers. They probably got the idea for this from the hexagram *Yu* "Contentment."

They cut tree trunks to make pestles and hollowed out the ground to make mortars. The benefit of pestles and mortars was such that the myriad folk used them to get relief from want. They probably got the idea for this from the hexagram *Xiaoguo* "Minor Superiority."

They strung pieces of wood to make bows and whittled others to make arrows. The benefit of bows and arrows was such that they dominated the world. They probably got the idea for this from the hexagram *Kui* "Contrariety."

In remote antiquity, caves were dwellings and the open country was a place to stay. The sages of later ages had these exchanged for proper houses, putting a ridgepole at the top and rafters below in order to protect against the wind and the rain. They probably got the idea for this from the hexagram *Dazhuang* "Great Strength."

In antiquity, for burying the dead, people wrapped them thickly with firewood and buried them out in the wilds, where they neither made grave mounds nor planted trees. For the period of mourning there was no definite amount of time. The sage of later ages had this exchanged for inner and outer coffins. They probably got the idea for this from the hexagram *Daguo* "Major Superiority."

In remote antiquity, people knotted cords to keep things in order. The sages of later ages had these exchanged for written tallies, and by means of these all the various officials were kept in order, and the myriad folk were supervised. They probably got the idea for this from the hexagram *Kuai* "Resolution." (Lynn 1994, 77–80; modified)

Prior to the invention of the trigrams, Baoxi was clearly able to see what was in heaven, on earth, and on the animals. The world was "symbolically pregnant" to Baoxi, but this is *not* what the writers of the *Xici* are celebrating.[27] What is being celebrated is the creation of the trigrams, which, derived from the symbolic pregnancy of the world, then allows Baoxi to go back to the original phenomena and better understand them. It is the creation of the symbols that the text goes on to panegyrize. From mere symbolic pregnancy itself, the various implements and institutions of culture could not have arisen: the higher order of meaning is not already present in the world; it has to be created. This creation, however, is a consummation of what was already implicit. As Cassirer writes:

The process of language formation shows for example how the chaos of immediate impressions take on order and clarity for us only when we "name" it and so permeate it with the function of linguistic thought and expression. In this new world of linguistic signs the world of impressions itself acquires an entirely new "permanence," because it acquires a new intellectual articulation. This differentiation and fixation of certain contents by words, not only designates a definite intellectual quality through them, but actually endows them with such a quality, by virtue of which they are now raised above the mere immediacy of so-called sensory qualities. Thus language becomes one of the human spirit's basic implements, by which we progress from the world of mere sensation to the world of intuition and ideas. (PSF 1:87–88)

It is from the principles embedded in the hexagrams that the sages were able to derive the cultural tools and institutions that constitute civilization. This is the reason Xici 1.12 says, "Therefore what is above physical form [xing 形] pertains to the Dao, and what is below physical form pertains to concrete objects [qi 器]."[28] If we take "physical form" (xing 形) here to refer to the hexagrams, then it is the hexagrams that allow us to have access to the Dao and thus create the "concrete objects" (qi 器)—the material tools of culture and civilization. The ultimate foundation of civilization is the symbolic imagination of human beings, who, by fixing the symbolic pregnancy of the world in a symbol, are able to stabilize that original (subjective) understanding into a concrete, material structure that allows us to order the world in a way that would have been inaccessible to a consciousness without symbols. This ability to create the hexagrams, because it is the roots of civilization, is thus an ethical endeavor. In both the Xici's and Cassirer's account of the origins of civilization, (1) there is already an inextricable relationality between the self and the world and (2) civilization is immanent in the world; but the catalyst is the human being whose symbolic imagination forms a triad with symbolic pregnancy, and the symbol—which, as I have interpreted it, is a form of tian ren he yi.

In the last line of Xici 2.2 that I cited above, we read that with the invention of the trigrams, the sage Baoxi was able to "classify the myriad things in terms of their true, innate natures [qing 情]" (Lynn 1994, 77). The term qing, which is here translated as "nature," also means disposition or emotions. As Brian Bruya explains, qing "has a side to it that draws on the shared, implicit early cosmology of spontaneous interrelations among things (humans included) in a way that imbues it with a sense that we can call 'emotional'" (2003, 163). It would otherwise be hard to explain, he argues against A. C. Graham, "how a term which originally meant something like our 'quintessence' came to mean emotions" (163). Only when the world is inherently expressive to people can a word that originally meant the disposition of something come to mean emotions. With regard to Graham's description of *qing* as bearing two seemingly disparate meanings—quintessence and emotions—Ames and Hall write, "It may indeed be said that *qing* is 'how things are in themselves' if we recognize that 'how things are' always involves a perspectival claim. Further, this perspective is not a narrowly perceptual or noetic one, but an *affective* one that shapes the emotional character of the situation and one's role in it" (Ames and Hall 2001, 36). *Qing*, as Ames and Hall go on to explain, is "'what something really is' in the sense that the unmediated experience itself resides in affective transactions that become selective and abstract when reduced to the cognitive structures of language" (73). *Qing* is, in Cassirerian terms, the symbolic pregnancy of the world. If we look at the composition of the word *qing* (情), we will see that it is composed of the heart-mind radical 忄 that signifies emotion, feeling, mind, or thought. The right-hand side is the phonetic component. From the composition of the word itself, we therefore see Bruya's and Ames and Hall's point that *qing* means what something *is* through an affective, personal, perspective.

One could say therefore that the symbolic pregnancy of the world that Baoxi observed is the *qing* (情) of things. This understanding of the sage as reading the symbolic pregnancy or *qing* of things will help elucidate another heavily loaded passage in the *Xici*, 1.4.

Tian Ren He Yi (天人合一) and Symbolic Idealism

We have already seen that *Xici* 1.10 and 1.12 follow the logic of *Xici* 2.2 in stating that it was the creation of the hexagrams that enabled a previously unavailable meaning. I have explained the rationale at work through *Xici* 2.2, whereby in stabilizing the symbolic pregnancy of the world, the sages were able to create a higher level of meaning. In *Xici* 1.4 we see a similar logic whereby it is the Yi (易; either meaning the sage or the technique of the *Changes*) that consummates the processes of heaven and earth. The text, interestingly, states that it is *because* the

Yi has complete knowledge of heaven and earth that it *doesn't* transgress
against heaven and earth:

> *Yi* is a paradigm of heaven and earth, and so it shows how
> one can fill in and pull together the Dao of heaven and earth.
> Looking up, we use it [*Yi*] to observe the configurations of
> heaven, and, looking down, we use it to examine the patterns
> of earth. . . . As *Yi* [i.e., the sage/*Changes*] resembles heaven
> and Earth, he/it does not go against them. As his/its knowl-
> edge is complete in respect to the myriad things and as his/
> its *Dao* brings help to all under heaven, he/it commits no
> transgression. Such a one extends himself/itself in all directions
> yet does not allow himself/itself to be swept away. . . . He/it
> perfectly emulates the transformations of heaven and earth
> and so does not transgress them. He/it follows every twist and
> turn of the myriad things and so deals with them without
> omission. . . . Thus the numinous is not restricted to place,
> and *Yi* [i.e., sage/*Changes*] is without substance.[29] (Lynn 1994,
> 51–53; modified)

There is very much the same logic at play here as in *Xici* 2.2. There are
two points of interest about this text in relation to Cassirer's symbolic
pregnancy. Firstly, as Richard John Lynn writes, this passage may be
deliberately amalgamating the sage, whose power is commensurate with
that of heaven and earth, with the "technique of the *Changes*" and the
power of heaven and earth per se (Lynn 1994, 70n11). I think this
amalgamation belies a significant philosophical assumption: the sage
(as a functional subject) is identified with the functional, hermeneutic
law of the *Changes*.[30] Secondly, the text states that *because* the sage/
the "technique of the *Changes*" has complete knowledge of the myriad
things, he/it does not transgress them, and because he/it commits no
transgressions his/its Dao is, in turn, able to bring help to all under
heaven. I would propose that we can understand these two points in
relation to Cassirer's concept of the symbol, in the sense that the symbol
(and the subject) is comparable to the sage providing a correlative point
in organizing disparate phenomena.

Cassirer's concept of the symbol, like his concept of symbolic
pregnancy, is also based on his understanding of symbolic logic.[31] For
Cassirer, as I have already mentioned (in relation to *Substance and*

Function), the rule of relation F that binds the elements of the series F (*a*, *b*, *c* . . .) together is present in each member of the series, but it is not itself a new element in the series, and so cannot itself be abstracted as a member or "substantial thing." The function is, "a representation, an objective description":

> We must recognize first of all that the order in a certain "bunch" [*Schar*] of elements never adheres to the individual elements themselves nor is given with them as a fixed, fin-ished characteristic, but rather that it is first defined through the generating relation [*erzeugende Relation*] out of which the individual members proceed. (Cassirer 2001b, 45)

The function and the series are inextricable: each derives its respective meaning and so existence by its dependence on the other; but they are not to be conflated with each other, for they belong "to different dimensions" (*SF* 26). The sage/*Changes* and these existing elements, as in Cassirer's concept of function, are integrally dependent upon each other for their mutual existence, so much so that, as in the mathematical function they exist simultaneously or not at all. The functional relation in the mathematical series, when applied to every field of knowledge acquisition, becomes the cultural-historical subject, represented by their hermeneutic tool—the symbolic form: the symbolic form is the name that Cassirer gave to any historically evolving *function* that orders the phenomenal manifold: "For each of these contexts, language as well as scientific cognition, art as well as myth, possesses its own constitutive principle which sets its stamp, as it were, on all the particular forms within it" (*PSF* 1:97).

In the Cassirerian framework, the subject is identified with the symbolic forms of his own creation: the subject could not feasibly *be* a subject without the symbolic forms.[32] Cassirer thus abnegates on an essentialist understanding of the subject: the self, like the sage in the *Xici*, is functional. No matter how much potential, innate tendency these existing elements had, without an external, generating relation provided by the human subject/the hermeneutic law of the human subject, these elements could not have gained meaningful coherence. Conversely, every deepening and extension of our understanding of the world (via the symbolic forms) is a deepening of our own subjectivity. The self, the hermeneutic law, and phenomena are mutually dependent.

In the example from *Xici* 1.4, the sage is comparable to the rule of relation F that binds the elements of the series F (*a*, *b*, *c* . . .) together. The sage, however, does not exist *apart from* the elements of the series, but nor do the elements exist in a meaningful sense apart from the correlative point provided by the sage. The sage (as function) and the series (the myriad things) are mutually dependent. The sage exists ("perfectly") inasmuch as he can "emulate the transformations of heaven and earth"—that is, respect the innate tendencies of things, but he does not completely disappear, does not get "swept away," because he is that which allowed for the *possibility* that meaning could be exhaustively obtained. That he can bring to fruition the work of heaven, is because he provides a correlative point that organizes an existing, but otherwise disparate bunch of elements. It is *because* of this mutual dependency that the sage is understood as "without substance" (*wuti* 无体), and it is why he doesn't transgress against them. The sage exists *through* the myriad things; the sage does not inhere in the myriad things themselves, but nor is he separable from them.

For Cassirer, the ideal of a unity prior to the "abstraction" and "distortion" of culture is a dogmatic fiction. It is only once we have created cultural forms that we can have a relationship to nature. As he writes in a later work:

> This becoming conscious is the beginning and end, the alpha and omega, of the freedom that is granted to man; to know and to acknowledge necessity is the genuine process of liberation that "spirit," in opposition to "nature," has to accomplish.
>
> The individual "symbolic forms"—myth, language, art, and knowledge—constitute the indispensable precondition for this process. They are the specific media that man has created in order to separate himself from the world through them, and in this very separation bind himself all the closer to it. (*LCS* 25)

It is only through the creation of symbolic forms that we can bring ourselves closer to the world. The world that existed before its "mediation" through culture would be the world of the "pathology of the symbolic consciousness." The world would appear more concrete and immediate to us, but it is not a world of meaning—it is the world of lower biological organisms; and a world of meaning is the appropriately *human* world in which we *should* reside. The necessity of humanly created forms that consummate the implicit symbolic pregnancy of the world in order for it to become significant for us, and so bind us closer to it, is, I argue, the Confucian understanding of *tian ren he yi*,[33] and is what is seen in *Xici* 1.4 and 2.2.

Symbolic Idealism and the *Zhongyong* (中庸)

The same mutually dependent relationship between the self and phenomena as *Xici* 1.4 can be found in the *Zhongyong*.[34] What is interesting about the *Zhongyong* is that, like the *Xici*, it uses an ethical vocabulary to describe the sage's act of bringing to consummation the innate tendencies of things. The *Zhongyong* speaks of fulfilling one's nature through the virtue of *cheng* (诚) in order to consummate the innate tendencies of things:

> *Zhongyong* 22. Only those of utmost *cheng* (*zhicheng* 至诚) in the world are able to make the most of their natural tendencies (*xing* 性). Only if one is able to make the most of one's own natural tendencies is one able to make the most of the natural tendencies of others; only if one is able to make the most of the natural tendencies of others is one able to make the most of the natural tendencies [*xing* 性] of processes and events (*wu* 物); only if one is able to make the most of the natural tendencies of processes and events can one assist in the transforming and nourishing activities of heaven and earth; and only if one can assist in the transforming and nourishing activities of heaven and earth can human beings take their place as members of this triad [天地参].[35] (Ames and Hall 2001, 105; modified)

The "natural tendencies" (*xing* 性) spoken of here are comparable to the use of "innate tendencies" (*qing* 情) found in *Xici* 1.12 and 2.2. In these two *Xici* passages, it is the trigrams that allowed the sages to fully understand the innate tendencies of things. Although the *Zhongyong* does not speak about the hermeneutic sign, there is the same logic of the human subject consummating natural processes:

> *Zhongyong* 25. *Cheng* [诚] is self-consummating (*zicheng* 自成), and its way (*dao* 道) is self-directing (*zidao* 自道). *Cheng* [诚]

is a process (*wu* 物) taken from its beginning to its end, and without this *cheng*, there are no events. It is thus that, for exemplary persons (*junzi* 君子), it is creativity that is prized. But *cheng* is not simply the self-consummating of one's own person; it is what consummates events. Consummating oneself is authoritative conduct (*ren* 仁); consummating other events is wisdom (*zhi* 知). This is the excellence (*de* 德) of one's natural tendencies (*xing* 性) and is the way of integrating what is more internal and what is more external. Thus, when whenever one applies this excellence, it is fitting.[36] (Ames and Hall 2001, 106; modified)

Against the traditional rendering of *cheng* as "sincerity" or "integrity," Ames and Hall have translated the virtue of *cheng* as "creativity." Their rationale for doing so complements the relationship between the human subject and the symbolic pregnancy of phenomena that we have discussed so far. They note that the graph for *cheng* (诚) is composed of the speech classifier *yan* (言) and the phonetic component *cheng* (成), which means "to consummate, complete, finish, bring to fruition" (62). The thought that it is the consummation of things (*cheng* 成) that is implicit in the virtue of *cheng* (诚) leads Ames and Hall to its rendering as "creativity." What is consummated, it must be noted, is already implicit in the nature of things themselves. The creativity at work here is not a dualistic *creation ex nihilo* whereby the form (freedom) and the material (determinism) of the thing and events (*wu* 物) are radically separate. The form of things is already implicit in things themselves. We could say, following our discussion of symbolic pregnancy in relation to *Xici* 1.4 that things and events (*wu* 物) are already symbolically pregnant. It is *cheng* (诚) as a virtue in the subject that (creatively) brings things to completion. This interpretation of *cheng* (诚) as a virtue that consummates the implicit natures of things and events thus makes the conventional translation of *cheng* (诚) as integrity and sincerity tractable. As in *Xici* 1.4, it is because the sage abides by the innate tendencies of things that he is able to bring help to all under heaven. The creativity at work here is a virtue that is "sincere" with respect to the existing "integrity" of things.

A key assumption in this conception of creativity is that the world is a heterogeneous manifold (*wan wu* 万物) of fully individualistic self-soing (*ziran* 自然) potencies. There is no stark dichotomy between nature and freedom (creativity), because there is already self-willed action in nature. There is no dualism between spontaneous, free action (creativity) and merely passive nature (see also chapter 6). It is for this reason that the creativity of the sage in *Xici* 1.4 and the *Zhongyong* is spoken of in such wuwei (无为) terms: they are effortless actions, or uncoerced actions, because they are in accord with the implicit natures of things. The consummation of things is not an imposition of an external form:

> *Zhongyong* 20. Creativity (*cheng* 诚) is the way of *tian* (天之道); creating is the proper way of becoming human (人之道). Creativity is achieving equilibrium and focus (*zhong* 中) without coercion; it is succeeding without reflection. Freely and easily traveling the center of the way—this is the sage (*shengren* 圣人). Creating is selecting what is efficacious (*shan* 善) and holding onto it firmly.[37] (Ames and Hall 2001, 104)

In the *Zhongyong*, as in the *Xici*, this sincere respect in creatively realizing the integrity of things becomes an ethical injunction. Utmost attentiveness to things leads to the creative realization of their potential. That we need to create a form that not only respects the uniqueness of the particular but also brings it to completion is likewise the ethical moment in Cassirer's symbolic idealism. In Cassirer's symbolic idealism, this becomes the problem of reconciling the particular with the universal. The harmonization of the particular and the universal is Cassirer's version of *tian ren he yi*. Without an adequate way of reconciling the particular with the universal, we either have mere heterogeneity and so meaninglessness, and thus an inability to integrate humans into the world. Or we have a homogenizing universal that does injustice to the uniqueness of the particular. Cassirer's symbolic idealism is, in part, a solution to this dualism. This connection between *xiang*, symbolic pregnancy, and *qing* (情) will be picked up again in the next chapter in relation to poetry/music.

The Universal and the Particular

As we have already seen, Cassirer first develops the idea of symbolic pregnancy in *Substance and Function* in terms of objectivity in mathematical representation:

The fact must be granted unconditionally, that the particular "presentation" reaches beyond itself, and that all that is given *means* something that is not directly found in itself; but it has already been shown that there is no element in this "representation," which leads beyond experience as a total system. Each particular member of experience possesses a symbolic character, in so far as the law of the whole, which includes the totality of members, is posited and intended in it. The particular appears as a differential, that is not fully determined and intelligible without reference to its integral. Metaphysical "realism" misunderstands this shift of logical meaning when it conceives it as a sort of transubstantiation. . . . But this "other" need not at all be something actually heterogeneous; rather we are here concerned with a relation between different empirical contents, which belong to a common order. This relation brings it about, that we can pass from a given starting-point through the whole of experience in a progress according to rule, but not that we can pass beyond experience. The constant reaching out beyond any given, particular content is itself a fundamental function of knowledge, which is satisfied in the field of the objects of knowledge. (*SF* 300–301)

Cassirer's model of knowledge is a coherence model of truth. The universal is the functional law of the whole that the "particular" presentation is always tacitly and holographically signalling toward (see discussion on holism and structuralism in the previous chapter). In *PSF* 1, the same point about the "symbolic" relationship between the part and the whole is made, but with regard to the symbolic form. The symbolic form "does not reflect this impression in its sensuous totality, but rather selects certain 'pregnant' factors, i.e., factors through which the given impression is amplified beyond itself and through which the . . . synthetic spatial imagination, is guided in a certain direction" (*PSF* 1:108). A relationship whereby the whole imbues the (empirical) particular with meaning, but the whole can only be seen through the (empirical) particular, is Cassirer's symbolic form: the symbol is *symbolic* of the whole. The "pregnant" factors are the moments when this symbolic relationship between the part and the whole are especially prominent. In *Language and Myth*, Cassirer talks of the discipline of history as striving, "like the morphological thought of

Goethe, to find those 'pregnant' moments in the course of events where, as in focal points, whole series of occurrences are epitomized" (*LM* 27).[38] The intellectual labor of the historian, as in any symbolic form, lies in embedding a particular content into "the unity of a 'system'" (*LM* 25). This intellectual labor, Cassirer calls—in the fashion of Kant's third Critique—"judgment." Judgment "aims at overcoming the illusion of singularity which adheres to every particular content of consciousness. The apparently singular fact becomes known, understood and conceptually grasped only in so far as it is . . . recognized as a 'case' of a law or as a member of a manifold or series. In this sense every genuine judgement is synthetic; for what it intends and strives for is just this synthesis of parts into a whole, this weaving of particulars into a system" (*LM* 26). The judgment that Cassirer talks of here redounds of a symbolically pregnant evoking the whole. Cassirer calls this kind of judgment "discursive" in that it "starts with a particular case, but instead of dwelling upon it, and resting content in sheer contemplation of the particular, it lets the mind merely start from this instance to run the whole gamut of Being in the special direction determined by the empirical concept" (*LM* 26). The kind of discursive judgment that Cassirer is talking is about is the reflective and regulative judgment of Kant's third Critique. The particular is symbolic of the whole system, but the system is not already determined and given, it has to be produced; and because we recognize that the system does not correspond with some ontological reality, it is regulative as opposed to constitutive.

Goethe's Archetypal Phenomena (*Urphänomene*)

For Cassirer, the thinker who best reconciles the particular and universal according to this discursive judgment, is Goethe; and Cassirer's own account of symbolic formation is indebted to insights he saw in Goethe's work.[39] Goethe's concept of the "archetypal phenomenon" is a sensuous particular that is particularly *pregnant* or representative, or *symbolic* of the phenomenal series from which it emerges, and it is *discovered* by the subject through a dialectic between the *theorizing* subject and the phenomenon. Goethe's concept of the "archetypal phenomena" thus reconciles the particular with the universal, as well as subject and object. In this regard, Goethe's archetypal phenomenon is representative of "that ideal of a concrete generality with which the whole of post-Kantian speculation wrestles" (*KEH* 115). Goethe's concept of the archetypal phenomenon thus elucidates the simultaneously conceptual as well as sensuous nature of *xiang* (象). *Xiang* is that very concrete universal—which derives its meaning from the law of the whole—after which post-Kantian speculation was striving. *Xiang* is comparable to the Goethean concept of *Urphänomen*—an especially pregnant moment that evokes (or is "symbolic" of) the whole (series).

Cassirer regarded post-Kantian philosophy from Fichte to Hegel as an attempt to develop an adequate account of the particular in the universal (*KEH* 115),[40] and he saw Goethe's view of nature (*Naturanschauung*) as the middle point of this endeavor (*FF* 391). In Cassirer's interpretation of Goethe, Goethe was a transcendental idealist (Cassirer 2007a) and phenomenologist avant la lettre.[41] Cassirer's account of symbolic formation in symbolic pregnancy *is* Cassirer's interpretation of Goethe's concept of archetypal phenomenon (*Urphänomen*) as a transcendental idealism and phenomenology. As Sebastian Luft writes:

> Indeed, the whole theory supporting this doctrine [*Urphänomen*], which is not spelled out by Goethe in a coherent treatise (such was not Goethe's preferred way of working), turns out to be nothing other than Cassirer's philosophy of symbolic formation, *as imputed to Goethe* by Cassirer. According to this self-understanding, Cassirer is the executor of the basic insights in Goethe's scattered remarks into a coherent system. But Cassirer was only able to take up this role as the executor of Goethe's general outlook as a Kantian. In this role, he reads Goethe as a transcendental philosopher. (2015b, 143)

Cassirer's concept of the symbolic pregnancy has many echoes of Goethe's "archetypal phenomenon." One of Cassirer's most oft-used quotations from Goethe is this:

> The ultimate goal would be: to grasp that everything in the realm of fact is already theory. The blue of the sky shows us the basic law of chromatics. Let us not seek for something behind the phenomena—they themselves are the theory. (Goethe 1988, 307)

As Goethe himself puts it, and Cassirer cites it, "the spirit of the actual is the true ideal"; and his imagination is an "imagination for the truth of the real" (quoted in Cassirer 2007a, 571–72). Cassirer reads Goethe here as a transcendental idealist (cf. Goethe 1988, 307) and phenomenologist (cf. 308) for whom there is no deeper reality beyond that which we (subjectively) perceive. This truth of this reality, however, is not isolated facts; it is up to the subject to string together the discrete data of experience and "discover" the law that runs through them[42]—hence it is "reflective" as opposed to "constitutive" judgment:

> One phenomenon, one experiment cannot prove anything, it is an element in one great chain that is only valid in concatenation. Whoever would want to hide the string of pearls and only reveal the most beautiful one, asking us to believe all others are the same, surely no-one would enter into this deal.
>
> No phenomenon explains itself in and from itself; only many together seen in an overview, methodologically ordered, finally result in something that can count for theory. (quoted in Luft 2015b, 147)

For Goethe, the Kantian conception of cognition that orders the sensible manifold by bringing it under categories is dualistic in the same way as the Platonic forms are. For Goethe, the (functional) law that makes a phenomenal manifold meaningful, unlike the Kantian categories, is not a static concept that can be theorized apart from the phenomena in which it manifests itself. Goethe argues[43] that when phenomena are arranged through what he calls a "delicate empiricism" (zarte Empirie), the inner law connecting phenomena shines through like the melody that moves between the notes in a piece of music and can be immediately intuited. The "law" is dynamic and emergent (and so commensurable with reflective judgment). The "melody" that runs through all the different notes of experience, or what we reveal when these discrete data of experience are stringed together in this "delicate empiricism," is what Goethe calls an "archetypal phenomenon." Goethe explains "archetypal phenomenon" as follows:

> Archetypal phenomenon:
> ideal as the ultimate we can know,
> real as what we know,
> symbolic, because it includes all instances,
> identical with all instances. (1988, 303)

An archetypal phenomenon, like the melody that runs through all the notes in a piece of music, is the essential pattern or process of phenomena that symbolically represents the series as a whole (Amrine 1998, 39). Archetypal phenomena have a special pregnancy that allows them to disclose the context or series of which they are a part. An archetypal phenomenon is thus not immediately given in experience; it has to be constructed by the subject out of phenomenological experience. For Goethe, "just as the point of convergence of a mathematical series is not identical with any one of its members, so this phenomenon at the outward boundary of physics is something that has no concrete existence" (Heitler 1998, 59). Goethe's "universal" is the "*idea* of a whole group of phenomena" or "the point of convergence of a certain class of phenomena" (59).

Goethe speaks of archetypal phenomena in very different contexts, for instance, in the formations of clouds, constellations of planets, or in chromatics—where the archetypal phenomena are the primary colors red, blue, yellow—but also in primal-phenomenal human relations such as between Werther and Lotte, from his novel *The Sorrows of Young Werther*. Goethe most famously used his concept of the archetypal phenomena in relation to the "archetypal plant" in his morphology of plants. Goethe was on his Italian journey in the Garden of Palermo when he "saw" an archetypal plant that is the unitary point of all the plants that exist in the world. The *Urpflanze* is an ideal form, or symbol, of an ancestor plant that allowed Goethe to see the morphological continuities between all the varieties of plants in the world. The archetypal plant is no specific plant that exists or has existed in nature; it is a regulative principle (or heuristic) that underlies the morphological structure of all plants. When Goethe talked about this *Urpflanze* with Schiller, Schiller admonished that Goethe's *Urpflanze* is not ontologically real, but merely an idea. Goethe answered, "That may be very welcome to me, that I have ideas without knowing so and that I even see them with my eyes" (Goethe 2003, 541; quoted in Luft 2015b, 149).

The *Urpflanze* is thus not an "idea" in the Platonic sense of an entity belonging to a different realm that we never "see." Nor, similarly, is it the Kantian a priori conditions of human experience (space, time, the categories, the schemata, transcendental subjectivity). Whereas the Platonic and Kantian "forms" are beyond our sensual capacities and can only be arrived at through recollection or transcendental analysis, the

Urpflanze is observable and phenomenologically present. The archetypal phenomenon is simultaneously *sinnlich* and *geistig*: it is the concrete universal that emerges at the end of one's cognitive labors. The *Urphänomen*, or "pregnant point" in which the lawfulness of phenomena is revealed, is a pure activity that is saturated with empirical content and thus not abstract. For Frederick Amrine, Goethe's *Urphänomen* can be viewed as a kind of empirical counterpart to the "intellectual intuition" of post-Kantian philosophy, in which "universal and particular, idea and experience enter into a relationship that transcends logical subsumption," becoming instead "reciprocally determinative" and thus "a unified and organic whole" (Amrine 1998, 41). Goethe's *Urphänomen* is thus comparable to the Kantian schema.

Kant's schema like the Platonic *chora*, unites concepts with the sensuous. The Kantian schema, is, however, more than merely the medium through which the sensuous and the intellectual are brought into unity: "We are not to forget that whatever is matter of sensuous apprehension always appears in the universal form of time" (*PSF* 1:13). The schema is the synthesis of the category, the form of time as well as the sensuous content. As such, it is "no longer merely logical in character—it is 'real,' in the sense of phenomenal, of being a concrete constituent of the appearances" (*PSF* 1:14).[44] As Kant himself says, "Hence a schema is, properly speaking, only the phenomenon of an object, or the sensible concept of an object, in harmony with the category" (A146/B186; 1996, 218). It is this aspect of the schema—that the uniting medium is itself sensuous—that caught Cassirer's imagination in his own development of the philosophy of symbolic forms, and that he saw in Humboldt's philosophy of language. In Cassirer's interpretation of the Kantian schema, like Goethe's archetypal phenomena, the schema is no longer conceivable only in and through transcendental analysis,[45] it becomes an observable, phenomenal presence: the symbolic form.

Language: The Concrete Universal

As we have already seen in chapter 1, Cassirer sees linguistic structuralism as inseparable from the holistic thought of Goethe. Similarly, for Cassirer, language, like Goethe's archetypal phenomena, reconciles the sensuous particular with the universal through a structuralist, part-whole relationship as well as overcomes the subject-object dualism. Like Goethe's archetypal phenomena, language is comparable to the role that Kantian schema performs (*KEH* 106).

Cassirer thus found in language, and by extension the symbol, in an observable medium, what Kant achieved only abstractly—through his transcendental analysis—the bond of intuition and concept. If, for Kant, we cannot think without images and we cannot intuit without concepts, for Cassirer, "instead of saying that the human intellect is an intellect which is 'in need of images' ["ein der Bilder bedürftiger Verstand"] we should rather say that it is in need of symbols." For "human knowledge is by its very nature symbolic knowledge" (*EM* 57). For Cassirer, human understanding is in need of symbols as opposed to images, because his conception of the symbol is simultaneously intellectual (*geistig*) and sensuous (*sinnlich*). "Under a 'symbolic form,'" he writes, "should be understood every energy of spirit [*Energie des Geistes*] through which a spiritual content or meaning is attached to a concrete, sensory sign and is internally adapted to this sign" (2003a, 79; 2013b, 76). Words are then sensuous images, seen or heard, but, because they are used with meaning, they are "symbols" (*PSF* 1:50). Cassirer's concept of the symbol, as itself the uniting medium of the sensuous and the intellectual, renders obsolete the Kantian faculty of imagination, of which the schema is a product. If human knowledge is already symbolic, in that it already unites the sensuous and the intellectual, then one would not need a faculty for uniting images and concepts.[46] For Cassirer, it is the symbol as opposed to the schema that connects sensuous intuitions with meaning: what we *see* is constituted by the symbolic form.

I will now summarize the points that have been made in this chapter in relation to the six mutually reinforcing characteristics of a functional ontology. The hermeneutic sign—the *xiang*—at the end of this imaginative seeing operates like the Goethe's idealistic morphology and Cassirer's concept language, and by extension the symbol, in that (1) it reconciles the concrete particular with the universal (i.e., it is both a conceptual idea and also phenomenologically present); (2) it overcomes the dualism between subject and object (i.e., it is constructed by the subject in phenomenological experience); (3) the meaning of the hermeneutic sign is derived through a part-whole structuralism. As has already been mentioned, the meaning of each line in a trigram/hexagram is derived by reading the *relationship* of the line to the whole trigram/hexagram. Likewise, the meaning of each trigram/hexagram is read in *relation* to all configurations of trigrams/hexagrams.

The "innate tendencies" of things—their *qing* (情)—that we see in *Xici* 2.2 and 1.4 as well as the *Zhongyong require* the human subject, and, in the case of the *Xici*, their hermeneutic symbol, for its consummation. This consummation is enabled by placing the particular in a (structuralist) part-whole relationship within the whole of the symbolic system. This *work*, or the creativity of the sage, is a reflective judgment that does not subsume the particular under a predetermined classificatory system. The sage, like Goethe in his imaginative seeing (*Anschauung*), finds a way to do justice to the uniqueness of the particular, while creatively consummating it; the human subject consummates, like the Goethean scientist, what was already implicit. The Chinese term *qing* (情) embodies the Cassirerian and Goethean idea that the world is phenomenologically expressive to people—it is symbolically pregnant. It is only when the human actor—the sage, in this example—concretizes phenomena into a symbol (the trigram/hexagram) that *enables* the higher orders of civilization to be realized. The philosophical rationalization of the origins of the trigrams/hexagrams—which are identified with writing and civilization tout court—is thus remarkably akin to the process of symbolic formation in Cassirer's own philosophy of symbolic forms, which is also a philosophy of culture.

The Linguistic Turn of the *Xici*

Edward Shaughnessy has argued that, in making an argument (see following quotation from *Xici* 1.12) that forms a part of *Xici* 1.12,[47] "the author of . . . the *Xici* was participating in a debate about the nature of language and writing that, based on the evidence currently available, seems to have emerged within a decade or so of 300 B.C. and then became quite ubiquitous by the middle of the following century" (2001, 208). Shaughnessy goes on to call this movement, in which the *Zhuangzi* and *Mencius* participated, "the linguistic turn of the third century B.C." 211). The part of *Xici* 1.12 that Shaughnessy is specifically referring to is the following:

> The Master said: "Writing does not fully express speech, and speech does not fully express thought."
> "This being so, then how can the thoughts of the sages be seen?"

The Master said: "The sages established images in order to express fully their ideas, and set up hexagrams in order to express fully the characteristics (of things), appended statements to them in order to express fully their words, (alternated and penetrated =) caused them to change in order to fully express the innate tendencies of things [*qing* 情] and their countertendencies to spuriousness, and drummed them and danced them in order to express fully their spirit."[48] (as quoted in Shaughnessy 2001, 208; modified)

The kind of skepticism about language in the above passage is echoed in many passages of the *Zhuangzi*. In *Zhuangzi* 14.7 (外篇·天运), for example, Laozi ridicules Confucius's pride in his familiarity with the six classics by declaring them to be nothing but footprints (*ji* 迹) of the former kings. The footprints, according to the *Zhuangzi*, are ossified residuals of an original dynamism; in this instance the shoes (*lü* 履) and the act of stepping that went into making them. For the *Zhuangzi*, human freedom does not lie in the in the human creation of order/form. Order, for the Daoists, is an existing aspect of the natural world, and human ability to partake in order lies in our receptivity and sensitivity to these natural orders.

For Mark Edward Lewis[49] and Willard Peterson,[50] the way that the Master (Confucius) gets around the charge of linguistic skepticism, so rescuing the legitimacy of culture, is to say that the *xiang*, hexagrams and appended phrases do indeed capture everything that the sages intended to communicate. There are two problems with this interpretation. First, as we have already seen, the sages did not passively replicate independently existing phenomena; they consummated the symbolic pregnancy that they perceived in the world through their creation of the symbols. Secondly, if the *Xici*, as Lewis and Shaughnessy write, however, was part of a challenge to "proto-Daoist texts" arguing for the legitimacy of "writing and the scholastic" (Lewis 1999, 241)—culture (*wen* 文), in short—then this copy theory of meaning would be a weak response to the Daoists. I do not think that Lewis's (1999, 254–55) and Peterson's (1982, 98–99) explanation of this passage, that the Confucians were arguing that *this* symbolic system captures reality more than language does, would convince a hardcore skeptic. Why would the Daoists concede that this system of symbolic representation *does* capture reality when they have already laughed off the possibility of another representational system's (language) ability to do so? If the world is posited as a prior reality upon which language is merely a copy, then we will inevitably be led to an attitude of fundamental skepticism—as in Plato's banishing of the poets (the copy makers) from his Republic. What we find in the Xici, however, is an ebullient, almost hyperbolic celebration of culture and the tools that enabled culture. The only possibility remaining for convincing the Daoist that the symbols do capture reality is to ground it in a transcendent authority. Either the sage of the Xici was a human messenger receiving divine revelation, à la Parmenides and Mohammed, or the messenger is himself divine, à la Empedocles and Jesus. Grounding the symbolic system in a transcendent authority does have the advantage of explaining how the symbolic system affects reality that we saw in Xici 1.4, 1.12, and 1.10. For, if the symbolic system is grounded in the divine, then the symbolic system, as in "mythic consciousness," *can* literally claim magical powers. But this resort to transcendental authority is against the humanist spirit of the Xici (as well as Confucianism). Furthermore, the Xici does have a concept of that which the *Changes* cannot understand—*shen* (神)—which Richard John Lynn has translated as "the numinous." In Xici 1.5, we read, "What the yin and the yang do not allow us to plumb we call 'the numinous'"[51] (Lynn 1994, 54). The Xici is evidently not claiming that it knows anything about the workings of the ultimate *au-delà*.[52] *Shen* thus functions like Kant's use of noumena: it is meant to draw a boundary beyond which human experience can no longer speak meaningfully.[53]

The best riposte to the Daoist skeptic in Xici 1.12, and the only way to reconcile these seeming paradoxes is to say that symbolic systems, like language, *are* adequate for capturing reality, or, what amounts to the same thing, the reality of one's meaning, because they are the "transcendental conditions" of that very meaning. They are the transcendental conditions in the sense that they are necessary for the constitution of our experience of reality. What I am rejecting in Lewis's, Peterson's, and Puett's interpretations is that the Xici operated under a naive realism. Their interpretation and its implications go something like this: (1) There is an independently existing reality. (2) The sages were beings who had access to this reality, and copied this reality in symbols that human beings could understand.[54] (3) The reason we must be respectful, as opposed to hermeneutically suspicious, about these symbols is because the sages who created them were either divine or had access to the divine, but we are not divine and so do not have this access. (4) The symbols are thus magical and affect empirical reality. (5) Because the symbols are our guide for accessing an eternal, unchanging, independently existing reality, and because the sages no longer exist, the symbols are sacrosanct and cannot be changed.[55] None of these five implications, I believe, describes the *Xici*.[56] They describe a religious view, which, as I have shown, the *Xici* does not share. In the *Mawangdui Yijing*, Confucius himself is recorded as saying, "As for the *Changes*, I do indeed put its prayers and divinations last, only observing its virtue [*de* 德] and propriety [*yi* 义]" (Shaughnessy 1996, 241). It is only under a view where human beings are merely passive, as opposed to cocreative, in the cosmos that such store is put in divination. I do not think that the text displays an attitude whereby humans are passive in the face of the cosmos, and so their only way of achieving freedom is to subjugate themselves to the existing laws of the universe; the text is far more humanistic. The Chinese cosmological worldview is, furthermore, not one where there is a single ontologically stable order that one *can* subjugate oneself to (see chapter 1; this point will be picked up in the final chapter). On the level of the intellectual context of the *Xici*, furthermore, I think this position does not describe the Confucianism of the time of the text's composition, which was much more "humanistic."[57]

What I take the authors of the *Xici* to be getting at, when they ventriloquize through Confucius that "the sages established images in order to express fully their ideas, and set up hexagrams in order to express fully the characteristics (of things)," is that *symbolization* is necessary for exhausting one's meaning. I realize that this is quite a novel reading, but, given that the hexagrams were identified with writing and numbers (as I have already described), I think that the authors of the *Xici do* have in mind a broad category of what the sagely action of making symbols constitutes. Symbolism is a broader category than merely language, and can thus be distinguished from language; but symbolism in the Cassirerian sense is, as we have seen, necessary for the fixing and articulation of thought itself.

The only other plausible way to interpret this passage is that, because *xiang* are images, they operate in a different (and more comprehensive) way than language. As I have already said, however, I do not think this gets around the sceptic's challenge. This interpretation, however, is the way that, famously, Wang Bi (and Peterson, as we have seen) interpreted this passage:

> Images [*xiang*] are the means to express ideas. Words [i.e., the texts] are the means to explain the images. To yield up ideas

completely, there is nothing better than the images, and to yield up the meaning of the images, there is nothing better than words. The words are generated by the images, thus one can ponder the words and so observe what the images are. The images are generated by ideas, thus one can ponder the images and so observe what the ideas are. The ideas are yielded up completely by the images, and the images are made explicit by the words. Thus, since the words are the means to explain the images, once one gets the images, he forgets the words, and, since the images are the means to allow us to concentrate on the ideas, once one gets the ideas, he forgets the images.[58] (Lynn 1994, 31)

Even in Wang Bi's interpretation, we still cannot get away from the fact that it is ultimately the *xiang* that is needed in order to communicate meaning. As Cassirer writes about the symbolic form, it is "every energy of spirit by which the content of spiritual signification is linked to a concrete and intrinsically appropriate sensuous sign." The meaning of the image is established in the act of establishing the image. The meaning cannot have fully existed prior to its concretization in a material sign. Even if one can cast off the image after one has got the meaning, one could not have got the meaning in the first place without the image. The key point here is not so much the nature of the image, but the *process* of creatively exhausting meaning through a symbolic medium. My point about how *Xici* 1.12 is arguing for the importance of symbolization thus still stands.

What I have outlined in terms of the relationship between symbolic pregnancy, the possibility of thought, and the human subject will be developed in chapter 4, where we will see exactly the same relationship in other terms that express thinking in classical Chinese: *wen* (文) and *li* (理). The etymology of these words will illustrate the philosophical points that I have made in this chapter.

It will be recalled that, at the beginning of this chapter, where I introduced the problem of *xiang*, Pauline Yu had this to say about *xiang*: "It is difficult, if not impossible, to distinguish among an object, one's perception of it, its image or representation, and its significance. Indeed, the first three are all rendered by the same word" (1987, 38). As I have tried to show in this chapter, this semantic multivalence of *xiang* or the lack of distinction between the three modes of *xiang* is not due to some "primitive consciousness" unable to distinguish reality from representation. Rather, there is a recognition here that the sign is what enables our understanding of reality in the first place. It is for this reason that there is a continuum between the phenomenon, the presentation of this phenomenon through the image (synthesized by the creative imagination), and the image as the meaning of the phenomenon.

3

Shi Yan Zhi (诗言志)

Giving (Poetic) Form to *Qing* (情)

Poetry occupied a crucial position in the Confucian educational program: it was one of the Confucian six arts and was closely connected to music, *li* (礼), and moral cultivation, but there has not been a convincing account of *why* the Confucians could take poetry seriously as a morally effective force. "Poetry expresses *zhi*" (*shi yan zhi* 诗言志) is one of the two most important concepts in Chinese poetics, but there has also been no philosophical account of the significance of this concept. Notably, underlying this poetic concept is the assumption outlined in the previous chapter of (1) the relationship between symbolic pregnance, the symbol (i.e., poetry), and the human being and (2) the functional view of self as (fully) manifested in the myriad things. I argue that it is *because* of these assumptions that poetry is conceived as having a moral role. Conversely, poetry is another cultural form that displays the same assumptions we saw in the previous chapter.

In following the arch concept of *shi yan zhi*, then, we will see that this concept assumes that poetry (simultaneously) consummates the disposition of the world and the self. Poetry can do this because it is assumed that (1) both the phenomenal world and the self is by nature expressive but that (2) a *form* (poetry in this instance, as opposed to *xiang*) is needed to consummate this. Poetry, as a form, is thus comparable to the *xiang* of the previous chapter in that it is (3) a nondualistic form that describes a meaningful situation that does not have exclusively objective or subjective reference. Since the natures of things *are* how they tend towards manifestation (i.e., there is no substance behind its observable properties) and how they are in turn related to/affected by other things, the truth about the self and the world *is* to describe this process of how a disposition arose. This assumption about the relationship between the self and the world in turn becomes the moral prescription of poetry: to describe this mutual affecting. Poetry is a reflective form that gives insight into *how* the self is; it doesn't merely express the self (i.e., an automatic response like a cry of pain because one is currently hurt). Like the *xiang* (hexagrams) of the *Xici*, what is described is a relational situation, as opposed to an isolated "thing." Analogously, one can say that "poetry expresses *zhi*" is comparable to saying that *xiang* (in the sense of the hexagrams) expresses *xiang* (in the sense of the phenomena observed/creatively synthesized by the sages).

This *form*, however, because it is a reflective description of how the self came to be, can only arise in a social context. The morality of poetry thus lies in the fact that (1) the telos of poetry is to tell the truth about the self, (2) it is an inherently social medium, and (3) poetry describes how one is related to, and affected by, the world. We will also see throughout this chapter that on many of these points, Cassirer displays striking agreement.

Knowing Others: *Shi Yan Zhi* (诗言志)

The injunction for poetry to express *zhi* along with the doctrine that "literature [*wen* 文] is a vehicle for conveying the Dao"[1] (explored in the next chapter), became the two most revered and formative principles for the Chinese literary tradition (Chow 1979, 3). In the Chinese classics, the idea that poetry expresses *zhi* was canonized in the "Great Preface"[2] (毛诗序; henceforth, GP) to the *Book of Odes*, but appeared earliest in the *Book of Documents*. It also appears in the *Zuo Zhuan*, the *Zhuangzi*, and the *Shuowen Jiezi* (100–121). In the GP to the *Odes*, this idea is expressed as "Poetry is the fulfilment of *zhi* [志]: what dwells in the heart-mind [*xin* 心] is *zhi*, what comes forth in words is poetry."[3]

There are two main views on what the *zhi* (志) in *shi yan zhi* refers to: either "emotions" or "(political) ambition." For Xu Fuguan, because the poems in the *Book of Odes* are largely lyrical poems, he believes that the *zhi* in *shi yan zhi* is a *zhi* based on emotions (*qinggan* 情感) (Xu 2013a, 90).[4] As Vincent Shen tells us, from the recently unearthed *Con-*

fucius on Poetry (*Kongzi Shilun* 孔子诗论), Confucius's emphasis on *qing* is much stronger than the Mao commentaries (Shen 2014, 246–47). I will thus interpret "poetry expresses *zhi*" not as the expression of (political) ambition but as the expression of human feelings.

In the Chinese classics, one finds many examples of how it is morally exemplary to understand someone's *zhi* from their artistic compositions. In the *Records of the Grand Historian*, there is a famous passage where Confucius was not content after being told by his teacher that he has already grasped the form (曲), the technique (数), and the meaning (志) of the piece of the music.[5] Confucius was only content after grasping the kind of person (其为人也) that the composer was, whereupon he looked solemn, as if in deep thought, gazing into the distance as if in a state of beatitude. This story of Confucius's music learning resonates with the story of Zhong Ziqi's (钟子期) ability to "know the tone" (知音) in Yu Boya's (俞伯牙) *qin* playing as recorded in the "Fundamental Tastes" (本味) and "Questions of Tang" (汤问) chapters of *Lüshi Chunqiu* (239 BCE) and the *Liezi* (fifth century BCE) respectively. "Knowing the tone" has since become a proverbial expression of someone's being your kindred spirit. One's kindred spirit is one who understands what you wish to express in music.[6]

For Stephen Owen—one of the foremost scholars of Chinese poetry in the Western world—however, it is misleading to render *zhi* (志) in its most customary translation of "intention." "A moment's reflection," he writes, "will reveal how deeply the notion of 'intention' is implicated in the Western concern with free will" (1992, 28). For Owen, *zhi* "integrates *motive* and *circumstance* with those purely normative operations of signification to which the study of 'language' is limited in the Western tradition" (26; my emphasis). What Owen is rejecting, I suggest, is the (dualistic) copy theory of meaning, whereby signification involves a free will who has already a preformed, integral "intention" that selects the signifier to express this intention. He is rejecting the substance-based conception of self in which its properties (i.e., manifestations) are accidental to what the essence of that self truly is. *Zhi* communicates instead the whole situational context in which a speech utterance was made. Owen cites an example of *zhi* in *Mencius* 2A2. In answer to Gongsun Chou's question of wherein he excels, Mencius replies, "I understand language. I am good at cultivating my flood-like *qi*."[7] In further answer to Gongsun Chou's follow-up question of what he means by "understanding language," Mencius replies:

When someone's words are one-sided, I understand how his mind is clouded. When someone's words are loose and extravagant, I understand the pitfalls into which that person has fallen. When someone's words are warped, I understand wherein the person has strayed. When someone's words are evasive, 1 understand how the person has been pushed to his limit.[8] (quoted in Owen 1992, 22)

What Mencius understands from someone's words is not merely the meaning of the words or what the speaker thinks the words say. *Zhi* therefore defies the standard, (dualistic) Western philosophy of language account of meaning as an agent selecting a signifier to refer to a signified, that is, as *merely* designative and descriptive. Instead, signification and intention itself are formed in the *process* of speaking and can only arise and be understood within a context (the context being how the self is relating to the world). In the Mencian example, it is only in dialogue with Mencius, in a context, that one understands the interlocutor's *zhi*. The interlocutor's *zhi* is furthermore not a static thing. It *becomes* situationally, contextually, in relation to the dialogue's continuing evolution.

For Florence Chia-ying Yeh (叶嘉莹)—another famous scholar of classical Chinese poetry—the idea of "intentional fallacy" as famously argued by New Criticism theorists Wimsatt and Beardsley, where "the design or intention of the author is neither available nor desirable as a standard for judging the success of a work of literary art" (Wimsatt and Beardsley 1946, 468), is inapplicable to classical Chinese poetics (Yeh 1997, 19). I think Yeh rejects the intentional fallacy as applicable to Chinese poetics for the same reason that Owen takes issue with the translation of *zhi* as intentionality. The intentional fallacy as described by Wimsatt and Beardsley dualistically takes language to be separable from the disposition of the speaker. One can say that in classical Chinese poetics, there is no problem of the intentional fallacy because poetic language is *inherently* expressive of the disposition of the speaker. We cannot have *any* meaning if it were not the author's meaning. A subject is not to be inferred from its products; the self is *manifest* in those products. Just as we do not infer the presence of a mind (a ghost in the machine) from somebody's bodily actions, we do not infer an author's intent. The correspondence between one's words and what is on one's mind is an assumption, not a question; the poem *is* the poet. When Mencius hears the one-sidedness of someone's words, he can recognize that the speaker is attempting to control his language: the *zhi* of the speaker cannot be hidden. The truth about the self is not a hidden reality behind appearance; it is the appearance (in language) itself, and as such always manifest. It is for this reason that in *Analects* 2.10 Confucius said, "Look to how it is. Consider from what it comes. Examine what a person would be at rest. How can a person remain hidden?—How can someone remain hidden?"[9] In Confucian hermeneutics, someone gifted in hermeneutics is able to know the other because one is able to read the body behavior of the person, and when this is contextualized within a historical context, his or her *zhi* is fully known.

The intentional fallacy parallels the discussion in chapter 1 where Cassirer observed how in the history of physics an idea of a substantial core repeatedly takes precedence over what can be empirically observed. The antithesis to this substance model is the Confucian idea is that there is no *substantial* self hidden behind its empirically observable manifestation. The self is instead the functional self of the sage in *Xici* 1.4. There is no substance behind appearance; there is appearance, and that is all. The truth about the self is not some preformed "intention" hidden behind the welter of its expressions; the expressions of the self (through language) *is* the truth about the self. We therefore see the operative logic that was outlined in the first chapter. Once one gets rid of a substance-based understanding of things, both how the thing manifests itself (through a material medium) and a relational description of that thing comes to the fore. In the Confucian understanding of the self, then, the self *is* how it manifests itself, and how it manifests itself is always situational, in the sense that the situation describes how the self is related to the world historically. Cassirer, in a lecture on language and art gives a similar example to the Confucian and Mencian example above:

> When speaking to you at this moment I have no other intention than to communicate to you my ideas and thoughts about a general philosophical problem. But on the other hand I can scarcely forbear from conveying to you some other impressions. From my manner of speaking, from the pitch and stress, the modulation and inflection of my voice, you may feel my personal interest in special sides of the problem. You may feel my pleasure in addressing this audience; you may feel, at the same time, my discontent and my embarrassment that I have to speak here in a language that is not my mother tongue, in a foreign language of which I have only a very inadequate command. (SMC 159)

Like Mencius's interlocutor, Cassirer cannot *but* convey his *zhi*, which arises in, and can be understood in relation to, the context—in this case, his discomfort in speaking to an anglophone audience.

Cassirer would therefore agree with Mencius, Confucius, and Owen that language, especially aesthetic language "can never be defined in a mere static way as a system of fixed grammatical forms or of logical forms." (SMC 189) Language is as much *Energia* (*natura naturans*) as it is *Ergon* (*natura naturata*)—a famous Humboldtian distinction—it is "a *process* in which spiritual signification itself becomes and emerges" (KEH 119). Cassirer, like Mencius, understood language as more than a dead product, as more than "grammar, philosophical definition (which remain stable for all language users), a quasi-mathematical language of perfect 'accuracy'" (Owen 1992, 26). Language arises, in part, from the subjectivity of the speaker, and, consequently, meaning is not equivalent to the static forms of language, which is merely the *product* of (the process of) language. The meaning and form of language arises equally from the disposition (*qing* 情) of the speaker. Cassirer recognized that language was more than merely an intermediary for the designation of objects; he recognized that language is "always pervaded with the totality of our subjective, personal life. The rhythm and the measure, the accent, the emphasis, the melody of speech are unavoidable and unmistakable indications of this personal life—of our emotions, our feelings, and our interests. Our analysis remains incomplete if it does not constantly bear in mind this side of the problem" (SMC 189–90) Language is like an animate body that makes manifest what is on our minds. What is on our minds, furthermore, is constantly shifting in relation to the situations we are inhabiting.

The *expressive*[10] aspect of language that Cassirer points to here goes to the heart of the philosophy of language that is implicit in the concept of "poetry expresses *zhi*," the Mencian account of language, why Owen takes so much issue with the translation of *zhi* as intention and why Yeh argues there is no intentional fallacy in Chinese poetics. Language *manifests* the self, just as the myriad things manifests the sage in *Xici* 1.4. It is in this sense that we should understand the GP when it says that an age of disorder cannot *but* express itself in a dissonant way (乱世之音怨以怒, 其政乖). While the kingdom in ruins cannot *but* reveal its mournful fate in its music, its people are in dire straits (亡国之音哀以思, 其民困). Poetry inevitably and inalienably expresses the emotions and the context from which the poem arose, and the best poets are the ones most able to make their emotions and their context clear in their poetry. A different way of putting this, and another operative assumption in the GP to the *Odes*, is that emotions are provoked by contact and interaction with the world.[11] The self and the world are both expressive, or manifest themselves, and this manifesting causes collisions that trigger the arising of more dispositions.

The idea that poetry expresses *zhi* should be seen both descriptively and prescriptively—poetry *should* express an emotion and the context of that emotion. In the 29th year of Duke Xiang chapter of the *Zuo Zhuan*, for example, there is an account of the ambassador Ji Zha, who visited the state of Lu and asked to hear a selection of their music. He dumbfounded the audience by being able to describe the emotions conveyed by the music and so infer the historical context that gave rise to such emotional expression. From a piece of music/poetry, we can and should be able to hermeneutically read the emotions and historical context from which it sprung: literature was essentially understood as knowing others (i.e., their emotions and the context of their emotions). The Confucian view of *language* assumes that the truth about the self can be *fully* known, because the truth about the self *is* its manifestations situated in its historical context, but *poetry* is a particularly effective form for expressing this truth about the self. This is because poetry is a formalized form that communicates much more complex meanings than a simple affective interjection.

Aesthetic Forms and Morality

As we have seen, the Confucians assumed that humans are inherently emotional; the truth about the self is its emotions (*zhi*), and there is no skepticism about the ability of language to express this *zhi*. It is a certain kind of language, however, that will allow this *zhi* to become more resonant—literary language (*wen*). In the 25th year of Duke Xiang chapter of the *Zuo Zhuan*, it is said, "Language (*yan* 言) is adequate to *zhi*, and *wen* is adequate to language. If one does not speak, then who will know your *zhi*? Without *wen*, then language cannot go far" (my translation).[12] The idea that when language receives a certain patterning it is better able to effect people is paralleled in the Confucian discussion of music. The idea that only when sounds are manifested in a particular form, is it poetry/Music, and that it is *this* poetry/Music that has a morally beneficial effect on people is found in both the GP[13] and *Yue Ji* (*Record of Music*).[14]

The close relationship between Music (*yue* 乐), joy (*le* 乐), and the morally transformative effects of Music must be explained in terms of the difference between Music, music, and mere sounds.[15] As we see in *Yue Ji* 1.6, "All music (*yin*) arises in the hearts of men. Music (*yue*) is that which connects with [ethical] human relationships and principles (*lunli*). For this reason, those who know sounds (*sheng*) but do not know music (*yin*)—these are birds and the beasts. Those who know music (*yin*) yet do not know Music (*yue*)—these are the common masses. Only the superior man (*junzi*) can know Music (*yue*)" (Cook 1995, 33). Mere sound (*sheng* 声) is not yet music (*yin* 音) and music is still one remove from Music (*yue* 乐). Even animals express themselves through sounds (*sheng* 声)—in this, humans are no different from beasts: the tones rise spontaneously and reflexively from humans' inner being when we are affected by the external world, either natural or sociohistorical. The governing assumption is again the idea that we *inevitably* manifest our emotions. *Sheng* is thus a physiological and causal product of the interplay between the internal and external. It is within the realm of biological stimulus-response: it is passive and predetermined and thus limited to purely biological meaning. What does distinguish human expression from animal expression, however, is that humans have a more sophisticated repertoire of sounds—music (*yin* 音).

What differentiates mere sentimentalist (music) from a Beethoven composition (Music) is that, for Music, "the expression of a feeling is not the feeling itself—it is emotion turned into an image. This very fact implies a radical change. What hitherto was dimly and vaguely felt assumes a definite shape; what was a passive state becomes an active process" (MS 43). No matter how rich an emotional life one has, and how effusively one expresses those emotions, this alone does not make one into an artist of a high caliber. The artist knows how to turn those emotions into an image; and the ability to do so can only come about through self-conscious creative mastery of already conventional expressive forms (*yin* 音). To turn conventionalized self-expression into Music requires one to be able to remaster those self-expressions in a way that finds wider resonance. Thus, it is only when humans *consciously* reorder music (*yin* 音), when one "extends music into the realm of human affairs" (Cook 1995, 27), that it becomes Music (*yue*). Music is a higher form of symbolism, because it is subject to norms of a higher degree of complexity and richness; and this higher complexity can only come about through self-conscious creative mastery of already conventional expressive forms (yin 音).

In the 25th year of Duke Xiang chapter of the Zuo Zhuan (which we have already cited), we see a similar entelechy of meaning to the Yue Ji. There is here, as in the Yue Ji, a triadic process. First, we have zhi—what is on one's mind, and the understanding that language (yan 言) is the expression of what is on one's mind. When one finds a more sophisticated kind of language—literary language (wen), then it will endure. In a similar formulation, Cassirer writes, "The egocentric activity of speaking, as a mere self-utterance, increasingly gives way to the will to communicative understanding, and with this to the will to universality" (2013a, 352). Likewise, in the GP, this progression from mere expression of emotions to art is expressed as "Emotions come forth in sounds, and when the sounds create patterns [wen 文], they are called music."[16] Language, as we see here, is essentially for allowing others to know us. Similarly, for Cassirer, "Others can only know us only in our work, as what we do and make, as what we say and write, as πρᾶξις [praxis] and ποίησις [poesis]" (PSF 4:130). The level of praxis and poesis through which others come to know us is similar to the Yue Ji's third and highest level of expression—Music. This third level of expression is associated with culture, and thus social-conventionally derived products that endure longer than simply an expression like "ahh" in response to pain-stimulus, or an expressive burst of emotion such as of joy or grief.

In Cassirer's metaphysics, which is based upon Goethe's concept of Urphänomen,[17] there are three stages to life. The first stage is the self's experience of the ceaseless temporal process of life itself; it is "the rotating movement of the monad about itself." The second "basis phenomenon" is the active intervention of the monad in its environment, through our actions. It is within this second basis phenomenon that "we experience something that stands in opposition to us" (PSF 4:140) Cassirer identifies the "action" in this second basis phenomenon with Aristotle's notion of praxis—as the practical attempt to affect the immediate (PSF 4:183). The third basis phenomenon is called "the phenomenon of the work" (PSF 4:142). "Works" are lasting cultural products that can only be produced in a society: "Every work is as such not that of an individual, but proceeds from cooperative, correlative action. It bears witness to 'social' action" (PSF 4:159). Whereas actions, characteristic of the second basis phenomenon, are done for their effects, "work"[18] cannot be defined through merely an immediate, deliberate, or anticipated effect. For actions to become works, they must necessarily be social. In the *Yue Ji*, therefore, Music can only be self-consciously made and enjoyed when it is both a product and expression of the social realm. One can only self-consciously return to one's own creations—perhaps instinctive expressions like "ahhh"—when one becomes aware of the social significance of such expressions. It is only when music becomes a meaningful *language* that the self can return self-consciously to the sounds it utters. It is the realization of the social aspect of expressive vocalizations that renders sound into Music.[19] It is only through what Cassirer calls the "symbolic forms" that a distance from the immediacy of life is achieved, that we assert our specifically human agency. It is this aspect of music and poetry that is expressed through the earliest formulation of "poetry expresses *zhi*" in the *Shang Shu*: "Poetry expresses *zhi*, and song makes it endure" (*shi yan zhi, ge yong yan* 诗言志, 歌永言). Part of the definition of poetry is in its ability to capture the original affect in a form that would give it an endurance that it wouldn't have as mere "action."

It is because Music is formalized expression, is expression that has been given a specific form, that allows it to be meaningful across space and time to an extensive reach of people. What the *Yue Ji* describes is a process where the self begins as little more than a medium through which external things touch off certain emotions resulting in different sounds, to the point where she becomes conscious of herself, her emotions, the social meaning of the sounds she creates, and strives to effect influence in others through her creative composition of these sounds through Music. The self gives (aesthetic) form to her emotions through Music in a way that gives her freedom—from the unmeaning of her biological-affective drives. The ability to reach this aesthetic form, however, requires the social other. My ability to partake in this meaning and so achieve distance from the immediacy of my affective drives and so to share my emotions with others necessarily demands that I abide by certain rules of this social language. As Cassirer writes in the conclusion to *An Essay on Man*, "Man cannot find himself, he cannot become aware of his individuality, save through the medium of social life. But to him this medium signifies more than an external determining force. Man, like the animals, submits to the rules of society, but in addition, he has an active share in bringing about, and an active power to change, the forms of social life" (*EM* 223). In analogy to the genesis of the hexagrams that we saw in the previous chapter, then, Music is the creative product of human beings who formalize what was already an implicit process of the world (i.e., the fact that our relationship to the world touches off emotions that we need to expel/express). Unlike the hexagram example, however, instead of a single human being doing this creative synthesis, what is doing the creative synthesis is the whole of society.

The association of music with morality is thus due to three interrelated factors. (1) Music as a formalized aesthetic language can "endure" more than an expression of joy or grief, thus reaching a broader audience across space and time. This communicates the emotions of the composer in a far more multidimensional way. The aesthetic form of music is like a megaphone that transfers the composer's emotions in a way that cannot be achieved from the mere expression of emotion. As we have seen, "sounds and music enter into people deeply and transform people quickly." Music can be potent in a way that the mere expression of emotions cannot be. (2) The composer expresses herself in a way that distances her from the immediacy of her emotions by giving it a more universal meaning: her feelings gain a kind of universality through art. (3) This art form, however, is only available to her if she partakes of society in a deep and meaningful way. She cannot create universally meaningful art without using modes of expression that have universal meaning—conventional language.

We can suggest that a similar hierarchy exists for poetry. The most basic level is an automatic cry when the self is affected by something in the external world. These expressions then become folk songs or ditties that are popularly sung. The next level, Poetry proper, is to take these, by now, conventional tropes and to use them within a highly stylized system.

Music's association with morality can thus be described through the paradigm of *xing* (兴), *guan* (观), *qun* (群), and *yuan* (怨) from *Analects* 17.9, which we will see in the next section. The expression of your complaint (*yuan*) through aesthetic form allows the listener to identify and observe your emotion (*guan*). *Guan*, we could say, is the observation of the poet's *zhi*—the meaning context that gave rise to an emotion. Their observation of this *zhi* enables them to empathize with your emotion and situation (*xing*). When this aesthetic form is used as a kind of mass media by benevolent kings, it allows for social harmony (*qun*). Through this process all of us attain to the aesthetic realm, to the realm of culture, and achieve a distance from our biological natures and become truly human without ever denying that we were human (i.e., fundamentally emotional and related to the world).

Giving Form to Emotions

In the recognition that the affective-expressive nature of human experience is ineliminable, Cassirer is in clear agreement with the Confucians. For Cassirer, myth is the first symbolic form—it is the form on which language, science, religion, art, technology, and all the other cultural forms of human beings are built. Myth is the foundation of our humanity. In myth, humans objectify their deepest emotions so that their emotions have outward existence: mythical perception is always impregnated with emotional qualities. If religion is too Apollonian, then myth is too Dionysian. All sorts of affections—fear, sorrow, anguish, excitement, joy, exultation—have an external face (SMC, 173). Myth, then, is the most biological in the historical development of man, for the mythic man, like "the animal, however expressing its emotions, remains, so to speak, captured in the sphere of these emotions. It cannot exteriorize them—it cannot realize them in outward forms" (SMC 173; cf. SMC 158). It is only in the domain of art that the intuitive, experiential aspect of life can be preserved without its affective dimensions being overwhelming (SMC 191).

The Confucians, like Cassirer, were aware of the volcanic power of emotions. Similar to Cassirer's understanding of myth, for the Confucians, emotions are foundational to humanity but, if not well regulated, potentially destructive of humanity. The way to regulate emotions for the Confucians, and myth for Cassirer, however, is not to extirpate it and so take flight to that "place beyond the heavens" of which Plato speaks in the *Phaedrus* (247c–d). The Confucians recognized that "sounds and music enter into people deeply and transform people quickly"; therefore, the former kings had to carefully make "for these things a proper pattern [*wen* 文]"[20] (Hutton 2014, 219). Emotions are so infectious that their power needs to be given a proper form otherwise we will be slaves to the chaos of our emotions. Music, as the carrier of emotions, can play this role. The proper form, for the Confucians as it was for Cassirer, was not a catharsis that purges us of our emotions—it is not stoic apathy—but rather one that removes the immediacy of the original emotion and distils it in a way that allows the inner form/dynamic to shine through, allowing those who hear it, to empathize with the emotions expressed (EM 149). It is by creatively giving aesthetic form to emotions that we both confirm our affective natures and realize a freedom that is the distinguishing mark of humanity. In giving form to emotions, we turn the passivity of emotions into activity, and mere receptivity is changed to spontaneity, thus achieving a freedom specific to human beings.

In relation to this, we should remember that, when Confucius admonishes his students to learn the *Odes* in *Analects* 17.9, it is the *Odes* and not the mere expression of emotions that allows for *xing*, *guan*, *qun*, and *yuan*. It is specifically the *Odes* that can, "stimulate [people] [*xing* 兴], be a basis for observation/evaluation [*guan* 观], help one come together with others [*qun* 群], properly express complaints [*yuan* 怨]" (my translation). Poetry illuminates our emotions by giving it form. It is only after having given it form that it can stimulate others to observe/evaluate (*xing*) the emotions encapsulated in the poem. "In order to contemplate and to enjoy the work of art" (*guan*), furthermore, the spectator "has to create it in his measure. We cannot understand or feel a great work of art without, to a certain degree, repeating and reconstructing the creative process by which it has come into being" (SMC 212). This leads the spectator to empathize with the emotions of the poet leading to greater social harmony (*qun*). Our greater socialization educates us in the correct forms (poetry) in which to express our emotions (*yuan*), thereby triggering the whole cycle again. This process of social harmonization could *not* have been triggered by the mere expression of emotions. "The former kings used this means"—*poetry*—and not the mere expression of emotions, as the GP says, "to guide the conduct of husbands and wives, to inspire filial piety and generosity, to enrich social relations, to enhance education and culture, and to develop manners and customs" (Levy 2001, 920).[21] There can be no moral outcome nor foundation of culture and civilization from the mere expression of emotions.

The reason poetry, as opposed to the mere expression of emotions, can stimulate and be the basis for observation/evaluation is because poetry uses certain techniques that, like Music, are able to endure. Poetry's role is in its ability to capture emotions in a way that allows their inner *dynamic* to shine through, thus ridding the emotions of their chaotic immediacy.[22] Emotions are re-presented in a way that distils their formal structure, thus allowing it to come to the foreground. Poetry's ability to present a genetic narrative of our emotions allows the affectivity of those emotions to fade into the background. Our ability to *see* the temporal structure of our emotions as opposed to *experiencing* them allows for understanding and reconciliation. It is the poetic technique of *yijing* (意境) that, as we will see in the next section, does precisely this: it presents the historical context of how an emotion arose. But crucially, like Music, because this poetic technique is a sophisticated language (*wen*), it can likewise arise only within a social setting.

Yijing (意境): The Benevolent Continuity of Man and Nature

For Li Zehou, the dualism between representation and (lyrical) expression that governs Western art is absent in Chinese aesthetics: representation is always imbued with emotion and emotions are expressed through representation of the external world (Z. Li 2010, 29). "Crucial to this type of imitation or representation," which Li Zehou describes, "is the endowment of the scene with emotion, in order to create a *yijing* [意境], a mood or artistic idea" (29). The number of poetic techniques in the Chinese poetic tradition that describe this connectedness of emotions to the external world testifies to this.[23] It is due to the assumption that the truth about the self is how the world affects the self and touches off certain emotions that the foremost poetic concept is aimed at presenting this very continuity between self and world. If poetry is what gives a pattern to the self, then the form of poetry is not a *creation ex nihilo*; it is merely a formalized form of the implicit form/processes of things.

That the world is expressive to us is, as we have already seen, the foundational element of Cassirer's philosophy. Cassirer assumes, like the ancient Chinese, that the world has *qing* (情). The most basic human experience is of the expressiveness of the world. What the Chinese called *qing*, Cassirer calls "symbolic pregnancy." In symbolic pregnancy, the world is always already saturated with subjective/perspectival meaning, and what's more, any referent always comes within a frame of reference, a meaning context. For Confucian poetics, this tacit frame of reference should be incorporated into the poem itself; that is to say, the historical situation or context should be expressed along with the poet's emotions. When these two aspects become interfused in a seamless way, then one has the height of poetry, for it is in these virtuosic displays that one feels a *yijiing* (意境).

In *An Essay on Man*, Cassirer makes the observation that all theories of art in the Western tradition either fall under realism, with the attendant injunction towards imitation (i.e., French naturalists), or under subjectivism, with the attendant valorization of feeling, imagination, and expression (i.e., Romantics) (EM 152–70). In both theories, art is passively determined, either as a copy of the external world, or as a copy of one's emotions. Exemplifying this dualism is John Ruskin (1819–1900), who famously coined the term "pathetic fallacy" to define the "falseness in all our impressions of external things" (1998, 65) taken on by objects in the world "when we are under the influence of emotion, or contemplative fancy" (64). For Ruskin, a poet of the first order is one who even "in his most intense moods, has entire command of himself" (65), so that he can objectively describe the world. For Ruskin, therefore, the world is not symbolically pregnant, and *yijing* would be a paradigmatic case of "pathetic fallacy."

For Cassirer, the figure who harmonized these antagonistic views of art was Goethe, who "does not apprehend nature as an aggregate of physical things or as a chain of causes and effects. But just as little does he regard nature as a subjective phenomenon, as a sum of sense-perceptions" (SMC 159). Goethe overcomes the dualism of a description of merely the object or a description of one's subjective experiences. It is for this reason that in Goethe's poetry one finds instead a "real and benevolent continuity of nature and man" (Reed 1984, 15). Likewise, *yijing* (意境) was celebrated in the Chinese tradition instead of being seen as a (pathetic) fallacy because classical Chinese poetry assumed that the world was inherently expressive to people—it assumed the real and benevolent continuity of nature and man. In other words, the Chinese never thought, as Ruskin did, that one can or should "objectively" describe the world in poetry. The pathetic fallacy is the other side of the coin of the intentional fallacy. The idea that the self is a self-subsisting essence that is not related to the world, and therefore cannot be known through the world is the source of both the intentional and pathetic fallacy. Classical Chinese poetry assumed, however, as we saw in the first section, that the truth about the self is its emotions within a context, that is, how it is related to the world.

As an example of this kind of symbolism—*yijing* (意境)—let us take the Tang Dynasty poet Xu Hun's (ca. 791 – ca. 858) "Xie Pavilion Parting" (谢亭送别). This poem is a "parting poem" (a poetic genre) for marking the occasion of the poet's parting with someone of significance to him. The poem begins when the friend has already left:

A Lao song undoes the parting boat.
Red leaf, clear mountain, water rushing.
Day's end, inebriation awoken, person [the friend] is already
    far.

Wind and rain fill the whole sky, [I] descend East pavilion.
(My translation)

劳歌一曲解行舟
红叶青山水争流
日暮酒醒人已远
满天风雨下西楼

In the poem, it becomes very difficult to separate how the poet is seeing
the world from what the world is *really* like. When one reads the poem,
every part of the poem works in concert to produce a condensed image in
the reader's mind, an image of a life situation that is profoundly moving.
The chaos of the clashing colors of red and green, and the aggressiveness
contained in the verb *zheng* (争) all communicate the chaotic emotions
the poet feels about his friend's departure under a state of inebriation.
The day's end reflects the ending of a period of one's life that was shared
with a loved one. The image of a lone figure waking to find a loved one
gone and alone amid the elements communicates our existential pow-
erlessness. Just as irrevocable as the sun must set is the irrevocability of
the missed figure's increasing distance. We cannot control who remains
in our lives, just as we cannot control our own insignificance when juxtaposed against the vastness of nature and the elements. Nothing here
is "allegory"—none of the images are standing in for anything else, the
images, and their meaning, are literally *felt* as meaningful. This poem is
a par excellence example of Ruskin's pathetic fallacy.

Goethe himself picks up on this continuity between nature and
man that is described in the Chinese aesthetic concept of *yijing* in a
conversation with Eckermann:

> They likewise differ from us, inasmuch as with them exter-
> nal nature is always associated with the human figures. You
> always hear the goldfish splashing in the pond, the birds are
> always singing on the bough, the day is always serene and
> sunny, the night is always clear. There is much talk about
> the moon, but it does not alter the landscape, its light is
> conceived to be as bright as day itself; and the interior of the
> houses is as neat and elegant as their pictures. For instance,
> "I heard the lovely girls laughing, and when I got a sight of
> them, they were sitting on cane chairs." There you have, at

once, the prettiest situation; for cane chairs are necessarily associated with the greatest lightness and elegance. (Goethe and Eckermann 2009, 22)

What Goethe is referring to here is exactly the techniques of *yijing*. What Cassirer admired in Goethe's poetry, I would argue, therefore is precisely this benevolent continuity between man and nature found in Chinese poetry: *yijing* (意境). Cassirer says as much himself in the chapter on Goethe in *Freheit und Form*, "From the earliest Sesenheim poems [Es schlug mein Herz, geschwind zu Pferde!] was born a new basic relationship between 'inner' and 'outer.' Nature is no longer personal, but it is animated from within—something independent [*Selbständiges*] and wholly of its own nature [*Eigenes*], which however, moves with the ego in the same melody and in the same rhythm" (FF 190). In Goethe's poetry, therefore, "Nothing is mere allegory or mere comparison" (FF 193).

As Pauline Yu, Andrew Plaks, and Stephen Owen contend,[24] and Cassirer would agree with this, allegory is symptomatic of a dualistic worldview, and this is why allegory does not exist in Chinese poetics. (This point about allegory was already made in chapter 1, in the section "The Six Characteristics in History.") In the conclusion to *PSF 2*, *Mythical Thought*, Cassirer believes that once myth and religion are overcome, they are replaced by art. What he says, furthermore, is that, in medieval allegoresis, "the objective world loses its immediate material significance to the degree in which it is subordinated to a specifically religious interpretation. Its physical content remains only a cloak and a mask, behind which its spiritual meaning is hidden" (PSF 2:256). For Cassirer, it is only when Leibniz secularized "God" into a pantheistic vision of the harmony of the world that a new kind of symbolism could arise (PSF 2:259). This new kind of symbolism is not *allegory* but one that rests on the inherent meaningfulness of the totality of the world. It is this worldview that Goethe inherited and made possible his poetry (FF 43). In Goethe's poetry, then, one sees a kind of symbolism that is not merely allegorical—a material sign that stands in for an artificial meaning—but, rather, the world becomes *inherently* meaningful. If we remember Cassirer's definition of "symbolic pregnancy," we will realize that what Cassirer admired in Goethe's poetry is this very symbolic pregnancy of the world. Unlike allegory, the image *immediately* represents a meaning. We *live* and experience this meaning—it is intuitive—unlike the symbolism of allegory on which meaning is grafted. The meaning of allegory is an artificial one, it is *attributed* to the image. The kind of "symbolism" that Goethe admired in Chinese poetry, and that Cassirer admired in Goethe's poetry is instead a *real* and benevolent continuity between man and nature. The world *is* meaningful; it is symbolically pregnant.

For Xu Fuguan, the Confucian ideal of art was the unification of beauty (*mei* 美) with humanness (*ren* 仁) (Xu 2013b, 29). The way that this unification of beauty and humaneness manifests itself is in terms of harmony; the kind of harmony that Cheng Hao (程颢; 1032–85) calls the unification between self and object (浑然与物同体). Being a human being is like composing poetry in that it requires "exchanging his heart with my heart and exchanging the heart of all under heaven with my heart."[25] For the Confucians, as for Cassirer, the self is not a self-subsisting substance; the self is functional. It is this view of the functionality of the self that leads to the possibility of harmony between self and world, and so humaneness. For Cassirer, Goethe's poetry overcomes the subject-object dualism that dominates Western poetics. The terms in which Cassirer praises Goethe's poetry is precisely what is described as *yijing* (意境) in Chinese poetics. *Yijing* can be seen as a poetic extension of the concept of *xiang* (象). Both describe a life situation that captures an expressive meaning of the world felt by the poet/sage.[26] It is because poetry/the poetic technique of *yijing* can present this life situation, as opposed to merely expressing the emotions that this life situation gave rise to, that it is poetry. It reconciles us to our emotions by re-presenting it in an image that encapsulates the source and genesis of our emotions, and so lets us observe and understand it. The observation of this image by others enables them to empathize with our emotion and situation, and so this image becomes a pedagogic tool for cultivating empathy and, in turn, social harmony.

It is an allegorical view of poetry that leads to the "intentional fallacy" idea that the truth about the self cannot be known and that art has no moral function. Under allegory, things are not naturally related, the relation is arbitrarily imposed: the dove, for example, represents the holy spirit. On the other hand, if things are fundamentally related and so the truth about the self *is* how it is related and affected by things, then the self cannot be hidden. *Yijing* fulfils the self because it is a form that is not externally derived and imposed. The Confucians thought that poetry *does* have a part in moral education *because* they assumed that we are inherently related to the world and so experience their meaning. The poetic form of *yijing*, therefore, because it operates on this relationship of the relationality of things, can consummate this very relationality. The allegorical view of art sees morality as irrelevant to art, because it is dualistic. The artist is not saying anything *true* about ourselves by comparing our emotions to anything in the phenomenal world, and, conversely, describing the phenomenal world has no bearing on us.

In Cassirerian terms, the symbolic pregnancy of the self (*qing* 情) requires a symbolic form to be realized. In Confucian terms, the disposition (*qing* 情) of the self needs a patterning (*wen*) for it to be realized. In the context of poetry, this symbolic form can only arise in a social context. It is only in a social context that we can make use of a highly formalized language that allows us to take a metaperspective on our original emotions. There is a fundamental difference from merely saying "I am sad" to what is being communicated in "Xie Pavilion Parting." It is due to the sophistication of this poetic form that it can become so effective at consummating the self and educating others. The symbolic form of poetry, however, is not a *creation ex nihilo* (i.e., externally imposed, as in religious allegory); the form of poetry is derived from the implicit form or process of things (like the *xiang* of the previous chapter). It is assumed that we are affected by the world and then spontaneously express the emotions that are triggered. *Yijing* (意境) is this poetic form that formalizes the Confucian understanding of the human relationship to the world; it merely formalizes what is, in Cassirer's terms, a natural/biological process. In Cassirer's words, this poetry consummates the self by turning the biological process of self-expression into an active image. If we look at the triadic process of music formation, or the idea that *wen* makes language endure with an eye towards Cassirer's three stages to life, we can say that Music/poetry/symbolic form/*wen* allows our original affect to be presented in a more multidimensional way. Through this patterning, one is able to step back from the process of self-expression and turn it into a meta-image and therefore observe it.

If the ten thousand things all have their dispositions (*qing* 情) that are being manifested/expressed, then the difference about humans is that they can give form/*wen* to this self-expression. Humans can do this because in a social context we can arrive at an intersubjective form that gives us a metaperspective on this natural process. This form (which is derived from natural processes) therefore does not take us away from nature but reconciles us to it by allowing us to *understand* it. The society that allows this poetic form to arise is thus analogous to the sage of the

Xici whose creative imagination lifts out the implicit form of things and makes it into a form.

The Aesthetic Education of Man

In the ending of *PSF 2*, *Mythical Thought*, Cassirer alludes to a vision of art that overcomes the (dualistic) infancy of humanity—myth and religion.[27] In myth, man lives in the emotional immediacy of the image, believing it to be not merely representation, but reality itself. Religion, on the other hand, is too ascetic in its ban on imagery. It is only in art that this dualism between the extremes of Dionysian emotionalism-sensuousness in myth and Apollonian idealism in religion is overcome. For Cassirer, once the opposition between image and meaning necessary to religion is resolved, religion becomes replaced by art (*PSF* 2:261). Through this, a victory is won for humanism. Humans are no longer slaves to the reality of their emotions—as they are in myth; but nor do they ascribe meaning to a transcendent beyond—as in religion. In art, meaning is understood to be created by human being via the immanent means of the image.

While the Confucian tradition recognized the necessity and importance of emotions, they also believed that there is a correct form that emotions should take. We see this clearly in the GP: "Starting at emotion is the nature of the people. Halting at ritual and propriety is due to the benevolent actions of the former kings."[28] In the *Xunzi*, we similarly read, "So, people cannot be without joy [乐], and their joy cannot be without form [*xing* 形], but if it takes form and does not accord with the Way, then there will inevitably be chaos"[29] (my translation). The Confucian conception of art is thus not merely expressive. Mere expression is not in itself an aesthetic process; it is a general biological process, for animals express their emotions as much as humans. A mere utterance of emotion—of joy or grief, of love or hate, of fear or hope—is by no means art. Furthermore, because emotions are so directly connected with biological drives, if we do not give our emotions correct form, then there will be social chaos. Confucianism recognizes that, on a biological level, we are no different from animals in that external things touch off certain emotions that we instinctively need to expel through expression—we all have *qing* (情). The expression of emotions is as natural and preprogrammed as the need to eat when one is hungry. Rather than controlling such potentially disruptive biological drives through an ascetic ban on emotions or eating, the Confucians sought to channel these biological desires into forms more conducive to personal and social harmony. As in the creation of the hexagrams in *Xici* 2.2, humans create a form—which is derived from the innate disposition of the world/our innate dispositions—that allows us to be reconciled to nature/our natures. As Cassirer says, it is a chimera to think that we can have immediate access to "nature" itself. Nature without mediation, like our emotions without mediation, is chaotic. It is only the human creation of form that allows us to be reconciled to nature/our natures.

The form that is created in poetry, furthermore—*yijing* (意境)—is one that affirms the truth about ourselves—that we are fundamentally related to the world and so have emotions. *Yijing*, like myth, affirms our emotions but, unlike myth, it does not make us live it. Unlike (religious) allegory, however, its images are derived from the implicit natures of things, as opposed to externally imposed. The poetic form of *yijing* thus overcomes the dualism between expression and reflection. It is in this sense that the Confucian tradition replaced God with culture and myth/ religion with art, and thereby achieved *tian ren he yi*.

Conclusion

By following the proverbial expression *shi yan zhi* (诗言志), we have seen that implied in *shi yan zhi* is the idea that poetry has the potential to *fully* manifests the disposition (*qing* 情) of the self. Poetry is able to do so because the truth about the self—*zhi* (志)—resides in how one is affected by one's relationship to the world. Implied in *shi yan zhi* is the symbolic pregnancy of the world. When poetry expresses *zhi*, one is communicating the historical situation (*qing* 情) that led the self to have the disposition (*qing* 情) that one did. To communicate one's *zhi* is, furthermore, for others to know you. One *can* be fully known because there is no essence/substance to the self apart from how one's *qing* is affected by the world's *qing*. In other words, because there is no assumption that there is a substantial self that can be hidden (behind its properties), the cause and effect of how the poetic emotion arose is also understood as fully manifestable. This *zhi*, however, requires a particular *form* in order to be expressed—poetry—which can only arise in a social context. The mere expression of one's emotions is not art. While poetry *can* fully manifest the self, it is only a good poet and Poetry proper that *does* do this. The role of poetry/music is to give *form* to one's emotions.

It is the form of poetry that allows for the communication of *zhi*—the whole meaning context of an emotion.

The expressiveness of the world is in many ways the arch-concept of Chinese poetics, embodied in the concept of *Yijing* (意境). Once one gets rid of the idea that there is a substantial core to the self, the *truth* about the self *is* how it is related to and affected by the world. If it is recalled that in the first chapter the point was made about how overcoming a substance-based view necessarily leads to a more relational view of things, then it should hopefully be clear how Chinese poetics demonstrates this point. The truth about the self is necessarily known through portraying how a life situation gave rise to certain emotions.

The Confucians believed that people are inherently emotional and necessarily express this—they have *qing*—and that our only means for civilization must be built on the acceptance of this foundation. Humans, like all things in the world, wish to manifest their dispositions in patterns. To this end, poetry/music is needed to give proper form to these emotions. Poetry/music, furthermore, gives form to emotions in a way that transforms those original emotions, ridding them of their immediacy, and objectivizing them into a form/image. It is this kind of catharsis that allows the author of the poem to feel a kind of freedom from the immediacy of her emotions, but also frees those emotions from a passivity, so that it can initiate the socializing process of *xing, guan, qun,* and *yuan*.

This chapter serves as a hinge between the first two chapters, which are more epistemological in focus, and chapter 5, which will elucidate the Confucian view of how the self is formed through cultural forms.

4

Wen Yi Zai Dao (文以載道)

Giving (Linguistic) Form to Dao

I have already mentioned that throughout the Chinese tradition the hexagrams of the *Yijing* were identified with writing (*wen* 文); and that the hexagrams (and writing) synecdochally represented human culture (*wen* 文) itself. Accounts in the Warring States and early imperial texts of the origins of writing and the trigrams were thus often conflated with each other. We will now look to those Warring States and early imperial texts themselves and see that these accounts do indeed follow the paradigm set up in the *Xici* in accounting for the origins of *wen*. Like the *xiang* (象) of the *Xici*, therefore, these texts (1) take *wen* to mean both phenomenal patterning and an abstract symbol (i.e., writing) and (2) rationalize their commensurability in the same way as the writers of the *Xici* did for *xiang*. Like the genetic paradigm for rationalizing *xiang*, in the philosophical discussions surrounding the genesis of *wen*, the disposition (a symbolic pregnancy or *qing*) of the world—what we can in this instance call *wen* (文)—needs to be consummated through humanly created forms, which is also called *wen*.

The reason both *xiang* (象) and *wen* (文) homographically and homophonically refer to both phenomenal dispositions/patterns and the cultural artefacts of human beings is because, in both, it was a humanly created form that, by giving a form commensurate with their innate tendencies, consummates them, and thereby allows us to fully understand what was merely potentiality. Our intellectual symbols are thus tantamount to the form of things, and the fact that the same graph is used for both meanings (disposition and its consummation) captures this conceptual continuity. Operative here is again the logic of Cassirer's symbolic idealism, whereby it is the symbols of our creation that allow us epistemic access to a world that would otherwise be closed to us. As we have already seen in Cassirer's theory of the relationship between the symbol and symbolic pregnancy, we *require* symbols in order to see the symbolic pregnancy of the world. When the symbolic capacity malfunctions, we cannot *see* "patterns"; we can only see incoherent parts (i.e., a curved thing as opposed to a cup handle). The perception of a pattern necessarily entails that we recognize order (and, simultaneously, meaning). It is the recognition that the world can be ordered that is the basis of civilization; as *The Pheasant Cap Master* (He Guan Zi 鶡冠子) tells us, "Wen is for distinguishing things" (文者所以分物也). There is thus a continuum between patterns and abstract language/symbolism. It is only once we have Wen[1], in the sense of an abstract language, that we *can* see the patterns of the world; without abstract language, we would, as in aphasia, not be able to recognize the world as meaningfully patterned (ordered). Commensurable with this understanding of Wen is the paradigm that we saw in the Confucian understanding of poetry in the previous chapter. Wen as an external manifestation *inevitably* manifests the internal, and, secondly, it is morally exemplary to manifest one's patterns. In Wang Chong's (27–100) *Lunheng* (论衡) and Yang Xiong's *Fayan* (法言), for example, we read:

> The fact that humans have Wen [cultured writings] is like the beast having hair. Hair exists in five colors and all grow on the body. If one has Wen, however, but no substance, this is like the five-colored animals growing disorderedly hair.[2] (ch. 39 超奇)

> The sage is in the tiger class, his stripes [wen] are bright and distinct. The *junzi* is in the leopard class, his spots [wen] are colorful and abundant. The sophists are in the wildcat class, their markings [wen] are collected together thickly.[3] (ch. 2 吾子)

It is the morally exemplary whose patterns are clearest; and therefore manifesting one's *wen* is an ethical obligation.

The Philosophical Significance of *Wen*

Wen is a ubiquitous term in the Chinese classics and is used to describe all that is high and elevated.[4] It has a comparable status—in its ubiquity and capaciousness for embracing a plurality of meanings—to concepts such as Truth, Goodness, and Beauty in the Western tradition.[5] A definition of *wen* that captures all the different ways that it is used is "the self-presencing of a perceivable pattern/order that is simultaneously meaningful." *Wen* is thus anything that demonstrates a sensuous order; and because anything manifesting such sensuous order, form, or pattern is inherently meaningful, *wen* is a concept that transcends dualisms of mind and matter, subject and object, *forma formata* (being) and *forma formans* (becoming), nature and human artifice. In Western philosophy, of course, we see that the division between a posited transcendent arche (Being) and immanent visible phenomena has always necessitated either an ontological or epistemological bridge. In Plato's *Timaeus*, for example, the question of how universal form finds material and individual expression was reconciled through the notion of the *chora*: an interim concept or space between the universal being of ideas and the particular becoming of the phenomenal world. This dualism between form and matter persists in Kant's transcendental schema, whereby "there must be some third thing homogeneous on the one side with the category, and on the other with the phenomenon, to render the application of the former to the latter possible. This intermediate representation must be pure (free from all that is empirical) and yet intelligible on the one side and sensuous on the other" (Kant 1966, 122). Similarly, because for Kant, morality and freedom lie in the transcendental realm of forms, the purposiveness of nature became the conceptual bridge (*Übergang*) that allowed Kant to rationalize the possibility of morality and freedom in the sensible world. *Wen*, on the other hand, is a concept that, like *qi* (气), crosses the material-immaterial boundary in a way that requires no conceptual bridge. Meaning, or form/order, does not need to be imposed on a material substrate, as in a dualist framework; rather, everything material already has the potential towards form/order and thus meaning.

Wen (文), *Li* (理), and *Xiang* (象)

If one interprets *wen* as composed of lines symbolizing animal markings or other natural patterns that also have the meaning of numerals, then it is comparable to *li* (理), for *li*'s original meaning was "veins of jade" or patterns and forms in general (Chow 1979, 13). The *Guanzi* defines *li* as "the pattern that completes the pattern [*wen* 文] of things."[6] The *Er Ya* does not have the word, but the *Shuowen Jiezi* suggests that "dressing or polishing jade" and the "veins or striations within the jade" are its most fundamental meanings.[7] As Duan Yucai (段玉裁; 1735–1815) explains in the *Shuowen Jiezi Zhu*, the ancient Chinese believed that uncarved jade possessed a great quality or potency, but, to bring out that quality, crafts-men had to work on it according to its natural veins. The best lapidary is one whose craftsmanship best conforms to the possibilities inherent in the natural striations of the stone itself, and therefore maximizes those existing natural potentialities. Thus, very early on, *li* was extended to mean "order, orderly," and to "ordered (or orderly) thought," "reasoned (orderly) thinking, thought," "reason," "law," or "principle" (Chow 1979, 13). In its earliest occurrence, in the *Book of Odes*, *li* conjured up the image of "dividing up land into cultivated fields *in a way consistent with the natural topography*" to the "pathways that permit access to the fields under cultivation" (Hall and Ames 1995, 212). Operative in the etymol-ogy of *li*, therefore, is the idea of symbolic pregnancy found in Cassirer's *Linienzug* example: patterning is always meaningful, but this patterning or symbolic pregnancy requires the human subject to complete it.

In *Anticipating China*, Hall and Ames write that to adequately understand the classical Chinese idea of "thinking," we must begin from two related terms, *li* (理), most frequently rendered into English as "to reason" or "principle," and *xiang* (象), "to figure" or "image" (1995, 212). To extend Hall and Ames's point, I argue, first, that *wen* is compara-ble to *li* and *xiang*,[8] and, second, following Wang Shuren, that what is distinctive about *li*, *xiang*, *wen*, and therefore the classical Chinese idea of "thinking," can be summarized through three interrelated points: (1) None of them have an exclusively subjective or objective reference. No sharp distinction is made, for example, between "natural" coher-ence (*tianli* 天理 or *daoli* 道理) and "cultural" coherence (*wenli* 文理 or *daoli* 道理). (2) Furthermore, all three concepts are both simultaneously material and intelligible—the meanings they manifest are immanent in the phenomena themselves. As Hall and Ames write, "the most familiar use of *li* in the classical literature is to indicate the inherent formal and structural patterns in things and events, and their intelligibility" (213). (3) The meanings they manifest are not static; meaning is immanent in the becoming of the phenomena. (4) The human being is needed to bring out these patternings. These three concepts (*wen*, *li*, and *xiang*) are observable, phenomenal representational media created by the human being in accordance with the natures of things (i.e., their symbolic pregnancy) such that the sensuous and the intellectual exist simultaneously. They are comparable to Cassirer's symbol.

In the next section, we will see how the earliest rationalization for the origins of writing (*wen*) mirrors very closely the rationalization for the origins of *xiang*. In the genesis of writing (*Wen*) as well as *xiang*, the sage interpreted patterns of the phenomenal world on which is based the patterns of humanity.

The Canonization of *Wen* as the Trigrams

The *Shuowen Jiezi* is one of the Chinese tradition's oldest dictionaries; and the oldest dictionary to explain the structures of words. In its postface, Xu Shen provides an account—closely matching *Xici* 2.2—of the origin and early development of writing:

> When in ancient times Lord Baoxi [accession ca. 2852 BCE] ruled the world as sovereign, he looked upward and observed the images [*xiang* 象] in heaven and looked downward and observed the models [*fa* 法] that the earth provided. He observed the patterns [*wen* 文] on birds and beasts and what things were suitable for the land. Nearby, adopting them from his own person, and afar, adopting them from other things, he thereupon made the eight trigrams in order to pass on to later times the model symbols [*xiang* 象].
>
> Later on, Sheng Nong [神農氏; accession ca. 2737 BCE] made knots in rope to direct and regularize activities. Thus, all kind of professions were multiplied, and artificial and refined things sprouted and grew.
>
> Cang Jie [仓颉], scribe for the Yellow Emperor [黄帝; accession ca. 2697 BCE], on looking at the tracks of birds and animals, realizing that certain patterns and forms [*fen li* 分理] were distinguishable, started to create graphs [or carving of graphs; *shuqi* 书契], so that all kinds of professions could be regulated, and all people could be kept under scrutiny. This he probably took from [the hexagram] "Break-through" [*guai* 夬]. "*Guai* exhibit in the royal court"—means that the patterns [or the cultured, *wen* 文] proclaim education [*jiao* 教] and manifest

civilization in the king's court. "Thus the gentleman bestows emoluments upon his [cultured] subordinates, but if he lives on virtue [de 德], all these may be avoided." [All quotations are from *Book of Changes*.]

When Cang Jie first created writing [shu 书], he probably imitated the forms [xiang xing 象形] according to their categories [lei 类]; so the figures were called "patterns" [wen 文]. Later, when the writings were increased by combining the form [pictographs, xing 形] and phonetics [sheng 声], the results were called "compound graphs" [zi 字]. "Patterns" [wen 文] here means the root of the forms of things [wuxiang 物象]. "Compound graphs" means reproduction and gradual increase. When they are put on bamboo and silk they are called "records" [shu 书]. (quoted in Chow 1979, 5–6; modified)

In this postface, the trigrams are not only perceived as the origins of writing, each successive advancement of writing, from knots in rope to the archaic graph to writing, closely follows the paradigm of the creation of the trigrams. Both Shen Nong and Cang Jie followed Baoxi in being inspired by an implicit order phenomenologically perceptible in the world, and then invented human symbols based on these insights, so that this original order might be amplified and put to greater use in human affairs. In modeling the creation of writing on the *Xici*'s account of the invention of the trigrams, therefore, Xu Shen linked *Wen* with (1) the sense of patterns on birds and animals, (2) the trigrams, (3) the idea of culture, which implies education (jiao 教), enlightenment, and civilization, and (4) written language. In Xu Shen's postface, we can see all the elements that made the later adage "Literature [wen] is a vehicle for conveying the Dao" (wen yi zai dao 文以载道) so canonical.[9] There is a very established tradition of relating wen with Dao in the imperial tradition, and we will see two of these examples.

The Literary Mind and the Carving of Dragons (文心雕龙) and "The Origins of Wen" (文原)

Liu Xie (ca. 465–ca. 520) was one of the first to associate *Wen* with the Dao, and writes that "the Dao is handed down through the sages via *Wen* and the sages are able to enlighten Dao because of *Wen*."[10] Han Yü's

(韩愈; 768–824) disciple Li Han (李汉; d. ca. 847–860), in the Classical Prose Movement (*Guwen yundong* 古文运动), gave a more succinct expression to this association: "Literature is a tool for interconnecting the Dao. One who does not get to the bottom of this Dao and reach it will not be able to achieve anything in literature."[11] The most famous expression of this view comes from the *Tong Shu* (通书), by Zhou Dunyi (周敦颐; 1017–73), in which he writes, "*Wen* is meant to be a vehicle for conveying the Dao."[12] Su Shi (苏轼; 1037–1101) quoted Ou-yang Xiu (欧阳修; 1007–72) as saying, "The Literature of which I speak must accompany the Dao."[13] Although recognizing that the Dao is the root and literature is the branches and leaves, Zhu Xi (朱熹; 1130–1200) remarked, "Literature *is* the Dao" (Chow 1979, 3–4).[14]

In the first comprehensive work of literary criticism in Chinese, Liu Xie's (465–522) *The Literary Mind and the Carving of Dragons* (文心雕龙)—the first to systematically associate *Wen* with the Dao—one finds a conception of *wen* that shares many of the characteristics of *xiang* in the *Xici*. Liu Xie's rationalization of *Wen*[15] is persistent throughout the imperial era. As an example from the Ming dynasty (1369–1644), let us take Song Lian's (1310–1381) "The Origins of *Wen*" (*wenyuan* 文原). In both these works, *wen* is discussed as (1) a spontaneously arising pattern. (2) The human *Wen* is essential in completing the processes of the universe. (3) Finally, human civilization or order is indebted to the earliest forms of human *Wen*—the trigrams of the *Yijing*. These three points will be explored.

(1) In the opening chapter of *The Literary Mind*, "The Source" (原道), *wen* is described as the spontaneous expression of the world (Dao). Anything material inherently tends toward formal expression, and so displays its *wen*. *Wen*, like the *xiang* (象) of the *Xici* thus contains the sense of a naturally arising pattern:[16]

> 1.1 *Wen*, or pattern, is a very great virtue [*de* 德] indeed. It is born together with heaven and earth. Why do we say this? Because all color-patterns are mixed of black and yellow, and all shape-patterns are differentiated by round and square. The sun and moon like two pieces of jade manifest the pattern [*xiang* 象] of heaven; mountains and rivers in their beauty display the shape [*xing* 形] of the earth. These are, in fact the *wen* [文] of Dao itself. And as one sees above the sparkling heavenly bodies, and below the manifold forms [*zhang* 章] of earth, there is established a difference between high and low

estate, giving rise to the two archetypal Forms [yin and yang].
Man, and man alone, forms with these the Great Trinity,
and he does so because he alone is endowed with spirituality. He is the epitome of the five phases[17] and completes the
heart-mind of heaven and earth. With the emergence of the
heart-mind, language [yan 言] is instantiated, when language
is instantiated, Wen is brought to light—this is spontaneous
and natural. . . .

    1.2 . . . When we extend our observations, we find that
all things, both animals and plants, have patterns [wen] of
their own. Dragons and phoenixes portend wondrous events
through the picturesqueness of their appearance, and tigers
and leopards recall the individuality of virtuous men in their
striped and spotted variegation. . . . Can these features be due
to external adornment? No, they are all self-soing. Furthermore, the sounds of the forest wind blend to produce melody
comparable to that of a reed pipe or lute. . . . Therefore, once
physical form [xing 形] is established patterns [zhang 章] arise,
when sound arises, wen [文] is born. Now if things which are
unknowing can express themselves so extremely decoratively,
can that which is endowed with a heart-mind lack a pattern
[wen] proper to itself? (Hsieh 2015, 8; modified)

The myriad things all have a form appropriate to themselves and are not
externally imposed. Form is manifested whenever there is diversity—that
is, contrasting patterns of different colors. The human being as a continuum of the natural world also manifests his own wen. Wen, as pattern,
is the external manifestation of some latent or internal order. From the
primal configurations of heaven and earth to plants and animals, all
phenomena manifest the wen that is appropriate to them.

    We see the same statement about natural wen arising from the
Dao in Song Lian's "The Origins of Wen": "In changing, it [the Dao]
achieves free-flow, and its vitality cannot be exhausted, thereby becoming
the spontaneous Wen of heaven and earth."

    (2) For Liu Xie, when the heart-mind of the universe is completed
by humans, human Wen—language (言 yan)—is instantiated: "Man, and
man alone, forms with these the Great Trinity, and he does so because
he alone is endowed with spirituality. He is the epitome of the five
phases and completes the heart-mind of heaven and earth" (Hsieh 2015,

8; modified). In the last paragraph of *The Literary Mind*, we see a more explicit restatement of this idea that it is the human being (with his language) that completes the universe:

> Both [Baoxi and Confucius] observed the pattern [*wen*] of the heavens in order to comprehend their changes exhaustively, and both studied the pattern [*Wen*] of human activity in order to transform them [for the better]. It was in this way that they were able to legislate for the universe and to establish the principles governing human society, to achieve gloriously in fact, as well as to beautify literary forms and ideas. From these things we know that the Dao is handed down through the sages via *Wen* and that the sages are able to enlighten Dao because of *Wen*. . . . The *Book of Changes* says, "The stimulation of all movements under heaven depends upon the phrases [*ci* 辭]. The reason why the phrases [*ci* 辭] can stimulate all under heaven to movement is because it is the *Wen* of Dao itself. (Hsieh 2015, 10–11; modified)

Human *Wen* is both a manifestation and a broadening of the Dao. *Wen*, like the appended phrases of the *Book of Changes*, can stimulate all under heaven, *because* it is both a manifestation of the Dao itself and the work of human beings.

We see the same understanding of *Wen* as completing the work of the universe in "The Origins of *Wen*": "By itself it is both that which initiates and that which brings things to completion"; "it [*Wen*] supports heaven and earth without trespassing, illuminates the sun and moon without excess, and helps coordinate the four seasons without transgression."[18] It was due to this that *Wen* was needed to illuminate the principles inherent in things:

> Ah! The *Wen* of which I speak is born of heaven, conveyed by the earth, and propagated by the sages. Once its roots are established, then its ends are set in their proper channels. Once its form is ascertained, then its use becomes manifest. These are what have control over the great transformation of *yin* and *yang*, regulate the three most important social relationships, and order the six social relations. It is that which traverses the terminus a quo and terminus ad quem of the universe,

orders the myriad things, and completes the eight corners of
the world.[19] (All Song Lian translations are my own.)

Wen, it is stated here, *required* the trinity of heaven, earth, and man to
be completed. It is this completion that allows *Wen* to, in turn, effect *yin*
and *yang* and order the myriad things, and complete the eight corners
of the world. What Song Lian seems to be saying here—if we use the
language of universals and particulars—is that *Wen*, as the expression or
representation of the universal source (Dao), goes in the other direction,
and comes to affect the universal itself.

(3) In both *The Literary Mind* and "The Origins of *Wen*," one finds,
furthermore, the same statement that human order owes itself to the
principles inherent in the earliest form of *Wen*—the *xiang* of the *Yijing*.
In *The Literary Mind*, we read that "Both [Baoxi and Confucius] took
images [*xiang* 象] from the Yellow River Map and the Luo River Writing,
and both divined by means of milfoil stems [the divinatory tools for the
Yijing] and tortoise shells" (Hsieh 2015, 10; modified). In fact, like the
postface to *Shuowen Jiezi*, the creation of writing is traced to the sages'
creation of the hexagrams.[20]

Baoxi, we read in "The Origins of *Wen*," observed the world and
laid down its principles in the hexagrams, and this was the beginning
of the *Wen* of humanity.[21] Civilization *could not* have arisen directly out
of the Dao itself, for as Song Lian explains, although the Dao is the
inexhaustible source of all things, without something to effectively *capture*
the Dao, the Dao would be opaque to humanity: "It is not solely because
the utmost Dao encompasses all and neglects nothing that in fashioning
implements it follows the images [*xiang*] as the supreme guide," he writes,
for "without *Wen*, indeed nothing would have be accomplished."[22] Song
Lian thus takes several hexagrams from the *Yijing* to show that the technologies and social regulations which constitute civilization were gained
through applying the principles (*xiang* 象) of the hexagrams:

> For example, governance through the adoption of robes was
> inspired by the hexagrams of *Qian* and *Kun*. The idea of put-
> ting a ridgepole at the top and rafters below was taken from
> the hexagram *Dazhuang*, . . . [Song Lian goes on to list more
> inventions that were inspired by the hexagrams.] *Which of these
> are not the brilliant* Wen *itself?* . . . It [*Wen*] is the expression
> of natural order and the common law of the people. The

carrying out of ceremonial form, [ritual] music, punishment, and governance; the normative model of regiments, battalions, and punitive expeditions; the differentiation of units in the well-field system; the difference between civilization and barbarism; *all conforms to and symbolizes [xiang 象] it* [Wen of humanity]. *Thus, all that which has to do with the victuals of humankind and the provisions of life are within the bounds of Wen.*[23] (my emphasis)

Wen, as we can see here, has come to encompass the hexagrams of the *Yijing*. Civilization—human order—arose out of human *Wen*, but this human *Wen* (the *xiang* and trigrams) itself is both *completely natural* and *completely human*. They are the "expression of natural order and the common law of the people." In accessing and communicating the essential principles of the Dao, *Wen* allowed humans to harness its principles in the service of techne and social regulation. Technology is thus the physical aspect of *Wen*. It is the physical hermeneutic tool with which we both engage in and creatively partake of the world. Again, we are reminded of *Xici* 1.12: "Therefore what is above physical form [*xing* 形] pertains to the Dao, and what is below physical form pertains to concrete objects [*qi* 器]." Furthermore, because of this commensurability between human and natural *wen*, and because, as Liu Xie writes, "*Wen*, or pattern, is the utmost virtue [*de* 德]," *Wen* comes to bridge nature and man's moral vocation. *Wen*, as a sign of natural phenomena and humans' tendency toward recognizable order or form, is virtue per se.

We find exactly the same paradigm in 1.5 of *The Literary Mind*. Liu Xie posits here that the model humans at the beginning of Chinese history "drew their literature [*zhang* 章] from the heart-mind of the Dao." The text then goes on to explain how they made use of the milfoil stems, tortoise shells, and "observed the pattern [*wen*] of the heavens in order to comprehend their changes exhaustively, and how both Baoxi and Confucius studied the pattern [*Wen*] of human activity [*renwen* 人文] in order to transform them [for the better]" (Hsieh 2015, 10; modified). We see a paradigm here that should now be familiar to us, if the sages already had access to the Dao, why do they need to consult natural signs such as the Luo River Writings and make divinations? Similarly, if the sages already had access to the numinous secrets of the universe, why do they need to study its *wen*? Liu Xie goes some way to providing an answer by concluding that signs such as the hexagram phrases (*ci*

辞) are the *Wen* of the Dao itself.[24] We are still left with this question, however: If the sages had access to some prelinguistic meaning, why do they then need the linguistic signs later at all? We can only conclude that it is because these seminatural, semihuman signs are what complete the heart-mind of the universe. The reason this is the case is the same reason the *xiang* of the *Xici* allows the sage greater access to reality and completes the work of nature that we saw in chapter 2.

The Boundedness of Spirit and Form

The discussion on how nature and human beings manifest patterns has a bearing on Cassirer's contention with *Lebensphilosophie*. For Cassirer, Heidegger along with Nietzsche, Schopenhauer, Bergson, and Max Scheler represent a dominant trend in nineteenth- and twentieth-century philosophy. Broadly characterized as the philosophy of life (*Lebensphilosophie*), philosophies that fall under this category posit a metaphysical source— life—that precedes cognitive or cultural rationalization. True authenticity lies below the threshold of forms, variously conceived. In Nietzsche, this would be the Dionysian, and in Heidegger, this would be Being/Nothing. Cassirer would argue against the *Lebensphilosophie* in vogue during his time. For Cassirer, the idea of "nature" or "life" is an absolute prior to all mediation, or a pure "life" prior to its distortion in culture, is a (dualistic) chimera. Like the concept of substance, it is a metaphysical assertion. As Cassirer puts it, his view is that the source (*Geist*)—one can use the Chinese vocabulary of "Dao" as an equivalent—*necessarily* manifests itself in a material form. Like the Confucian understanding of language in chapter 3, the self *necessarily* manifests itself in its speech acts. To posit that meaning and its outward form are separate is an intellectual abstraction; in reality we always experience their inseparability:

> We must not understand the term "Geist" or spirit as designating a metaphysical entity opposed to another called "matter." If we accept the radical dualism between body and soul, matter and spirit, between "substantia extensa" and "substantia cogitans," language becomes, indeed a continuous miracle. In this case, every act of speech would be a sort of trans-substantiation. Speech is meaning—an incorporeal

thing—expressed in sounds, which are material things. The term "Geist" is correct; but we must not use it as a name of a substance—a thing "quod in se est et per se concipitur." We should use it in a functional sense as a comprehensive name for all those functions which constitute and build up the world of human culture." (Cassirer 1945, 113–14)

For Cassirer, this view of the boundedness of language to thought or the boundedness of cultural forms to *Geist* overcomes the dualism found in *Lebensphilosophie*. In saying that *Geist* necessarily manifests itself, Cassirer is, I think, taking on the Herderian idea that, "generally, all life is determined as a drive to and urge to 'express' itself" (FF 132). Cassirer agrees with Herder that language should not be understood as a copy and imprint of what exists, but as the "unfolding and expression of spiritual energies [*seelischer Energien*]" (FF 133).

For Cassirer, the antinomies between life as a force and its outward form was historically reconciled by Leibniz. In Leibniz's philosophy, life itself has an inner lawfulness that sets limits on itself (i.e., gives form to itself). In setting limits to itself, it is unfolding its own individuality; in contrast to the mechanical view in which the law is externally imposed (FF 256–57, 262). For Cassirer, Leibniz's view of life anticipates that of Goethe (FF 54). In Cassirer's view, Goethe saw the life of spirit and the life of nature as rooted in the same source: "A constantly becoming, restless activity, which however sets for itself measure and limits: for Goethe this is henceforth the life of Geist, as it was the life of nature" (Ein stetig Werdendes, rastlos Tätiges, das jedoch sich selbst Maß und Schranke setzt: das ist für Goethe nunmehr das Leben des Geistes, wie es das Leben der Natur war); FF 256).

The idea that nature or a natural force tends towards external manifestation, or physically observable behavior is seen in the works of both Goethe and Herder.[25] We thus see a view of how culture comes to materialize that is highly comparable to the view of the genesis of *wen* that we see in the Chinese tradition. Both natural and human *wen* are expressions of a life force—in the German tradition we can say *Leben* or *Geist*, in Chinese instance, one can say Dao or *qi*. This view of an immaterial source as necessarily manifesting itself (in a form), and thereby extending the source itself is shared by these two traditions. For Cassirer, this necessary manifestation of thought in a concrete form—what I have called the boundedness of spirit and form—overcomes the dualism between a posited metaphysical source (of freedom) such as "life" and its external manifestation, which is understood as mere limitation.

In *The Spell of the Sensuous*, David Abram (2017) attempts to envision a more ecologically sustainable relationship between selves and the natural world. One that overcomes the dominant Cartesianism of the Western tradition that views the natural world as merely a passive, inert mechanical mass to be exploited by human agency. In this endeavor, Abram takes inspiration from the phenomenological works of Merleau-Ponty, in which meaning is ultimately grounded in the body's engagements and interactions with the animate world. For Abram, there are two key assumptions in Merleau-Ponty's work on embodied cognition. (1) The human ability to perceive meaning is because the human being, as a porous organism, is in constant engagement with the external world (49), and (2) the experience of the external world is not passive; it is dynamic, animate, and expressive. Under these two assumptions, the act of perception, unlike its dualistic Cartesian counterpart, is understood to be one of a sentient self and sentient world entering into a sympathetic, reciprocal relationship of communication. As Abram writes, under the Merleau-Pontian view, perception "is an attunement or synchronization between my own rhythms and the rhythms of the things themselves, their own tones and textures" (54). Abram finds much consonance between the embodied nature of perception in Merleau-Ponty's work with indigenous, oral cultures whose lack of written language predisposes them towards a heighted attunement to the "language" of the earth. Absent in Merleau-Ponty's and that of oral cultures' account of perception is the Cartesian view that the human being, alone in nature, is possessed of spontaneity and the rest of nature is a dead (mechanically determined field), inert mass. Perception and thus meaning is fundamentally a result of our ability to participate in and read the "language" of the world.

Abram's account of a more ecologically sustainable relationship to the land is thus pivoted around the idea of language. His assumption—informed by Merleau-Ponty and indigenous oral cultures—of the expressiveness of the earth and the openness of the human being to understanding what the earth expresses, has much relevance to our discussions. In our discussions of *wen*, we have similarly seen that *wen* is the expressive pattern that is common to both human beings and the earth itself. The *wen* of the earth, in the Confucian-Chinese view, testifies to

Abram's account of language in which all things are "styles of unfolding," are "potentially expressive" (Abram 2017, 81). The Confucian-Chinese view of language is consonant with Abram's statement that "we find ourselves in an expressive, gesturing landscape, in a world that *speaks*" (81). That *wen* is a term that applies to both the natural and the human testifies to Abram's insight that language "'belongs' to the animate landscape as much as it 'belongs' to ourselves" (82). In a passage that describes precisely the Chinese concept of *wen* as the patterns of the land, Abram writes:

> The earthly terrain in which we find ourselves, and upon which we depend for all our nourishment, is shot through with suggestive scrawls and traces, from the sinuous calligraphy of rivers winding across the land, inscribing arroyos and canyons into the parched earth of the desert, to the black slash burned by lightning into the trunks of an old elm. The swooping flight of birds is a kind of cursive script written on the wind; it is this script that was studied by the ancient "augurs," who could read therein the course of the future. Leaf-miner insects make strange hieroglyphic tabloids of the leaves they consume. Wolves urinate on specific stumps and stones to mark off their territory. (95)

As Abram himself notes, quoting Jacques Derrida, who in turn quotes Jacques Gernet, the "multiform meanings" of the Chinese term for writing evidences this precise "interpenetration of human and nonhuman scripts":

> The word *wen* signifies a conglomeration of marks, the simple symbol in writing. It applies to the veins in stones and wood, to constellations, represented by the strokes connecting the stars, to the tracks of birds and quadrupeds on the ground (Chinese tradition would have it that the observation of these tracks suggested the invention of writing), to tattoos and even, for example, to the designs that decorate the turtle's shell ("The turtle is wise," an ancient text says—gifted with magico-religious powers—"for it carries designs on its back"). The term *wen* has designated, by extension, literature." (Derrida, quoted in Abram 2017, 96)

The designs that decorate the turtle's shell that Gernet refers to is the Yellow River Map (河图). The idea that nature bodies forth such profound symbols is consonant with the idea that nature can itself be read for meaning. Abram's anthropological account of human writing as arising from the human ability to read the patterns of the land is consonant with the *Xici*'s view of the origin of language. The sages observed the expressive patterns of the land and was thereby inspired to create human writing.

That the Confucian-Chinese view of language finds so much resonance in Abram's account of an ecologically sound relationship of engagement to the earth is because the Confucian-Chinese view of language operates under the very participatory relationship between human beings that Abram aspires to: *tian ren he yi*. Under the Confucian-Chinese view, all things express their natures: human beings are not unique in having language, all things have a will-to-expression. The meanings that human beings have and wish to express are touched off by the myriad things expressing *themselves*. Our human meanings do not arise internally and ex nihilo; the very meanings that we have within ourselves are a product of our being in the world, that is, engaging in reciprocal communication with a natural world that is, *sponte sua*, alive with its own expressions. It is this particular assumption of the nature of the human being, the world she resides in and the relationship between them that leads to the *Xici* expressing the similar anthropological view of the arising of writing. Writing is a continuum shared by all the myriad things of the earth, and the human creation of *wen* partakes of this continuum.

In the next chapter, we will see that the same paradigm of a material form, which is the human expression of herself, in turn extends herself. Giving form to the self is not understood as a limitation on some metaphysical source of the self (an essence of the self)—form is not understood as limiting freedom—but, rather, as creatively extending the self. As we will also see, this particular understanding of *education* has its counterpart in the German tradition of *Bildung*, which is also rooted in organic conceptions of growth.

Zhi You Wen Ye (质犹文也)

Giving (Human) Form to the Self

This chapter is the culmination of the chapters of this project so far. We have already seen that potentiality requires form for its consummation with regard to *xiang* (as phenomenal patterning) and *xiang* (as the hexagrams) in chapter 2, *qing* (情)/*zhi* (志) and poetic form in chapter 3, and *wen* (as pattern) and *Wen* (as linguistic form) in chapter 4. Conversely, and put differently, the operative assumption is that "things"—be they the dispositions of people (emotions) or phenomena—tend toward externalization: the "natures" of things necessarily become manifest. It is *because* the natures of things manifest themselves that it is conceivable to speak of an (external) form consummating what was on the "inside." There is no essence of things separate from their manifestation (no ontologically separate "reality" behind appearance). In this chapter, we will see that human potentiality—human nature—for the Confucians, similarly requires form for its consummation. If there is such a thing as "human nature," then it is only ever potentiality.[1] This potentiality requires education through cultural forms for its consummation. It is *because* the essence of the self (human nature) is identified with its potentiality,[2] that it is conceivable to speak of the *forms* of humanity consummating the essence (i.e., potentiality) of human beings. If we assumed a substantial essence of the self, on the other hand, the forms of culture can, logically, only be seen as cosmetic upon a preexisting self. This view of cultural forms as mere external embellishments to a preexisting self, like the view of language as merely copying a preexisting truth, leads naturally to a skeptical attitude.[3] This chapter is the culminating point of the previous chapters, as the paradigm of the hexagrams, poetic form, and language we have already explored could not logically be feasible without this particular understanding of subjectivity. Conversely, the previous cultural systems we have explored serve the role of giving *form* to the self.

Wen in the Analects

Confucius, as portrayed in the *Analects*, holds *Wen* in the utmost regard—*Wen* being a byword for Confucius's ideal of humanity and acting as the bedrock of his philosophical vision. In passage 9.5, one reads:

> The Master was surrounded in Kuang. He said, "Now that King Wen [文] is gone, is not culture [*Wen* 文] now invested here in me? If heaven intended this culture to perish, it would not have given it to those of us who live after King Wen's death. Since heaven did not intend that this culture should perish, what can the people of Kuang do to me? (Slingerland 2003, 87; modified)

This has been interpreted as showing Confucius's faith in having the Mandate of Heaven (Bol 1992, 1). What can be further inferred is the importance of *Wen* for Confucius's ability to partake of heaven. In Slingerland's translation that I have cited, *Wen* is translated as "culture": Confucius's perceived unassailability is thus attributed to his participation in the *cultural* forms passed down by King Wen.[4] There is a religious fervor in this sentiment; the idea that the blessing of some power renders one invulnerable to the arrows of mundane fortune is usually a theological one. What is different in this instance is that the *Wen* that safeguards Confucius are the cultural forms of humanity.

In *Analects* 3.14, we read, "The Master said, 'The Zhou gazes down upon the two dynasties that preceded it. How brilliant in culture [*Wen* 文] it is! I follow the Zhou" (Slingerland 2003, 23). What Confucius is usually taken to mean by *Wen* here are the ritual and music of the Zhou dynasty. Zhu Xi, for example, comments that "what manifests the Dao is *Wen*, presumably it is ritual and music which is referenced"[5] (Zhu 1983, 110). Xu Fuguan, following *Analects* 14.12,[6] argues that the content of

Wen in the *Analects* is ritual and music (Xu 1996, 122). Some have even taken *Wen* to refer to ritual per se (B. Liu 1990, 233–34). For Hall and Ames, in the *Analects, Wen* stands for the historical and cultural documents on which Confucius placed such emphasis, as well as social institutions, ritual, and music. It refers, furthermore, to the Confucian "six arts" (六艺), which comprised ritual, music, archery, charioteering, writing, and calculations (1987, 45). Similarly, Chad Hansen writes that the Confucian notion of Dao is of a rule-governed practice enabled by a "literature curriculum designed to shape character" (1992, 86). The Archaeologist and historian Li Feng writes that because Confucius was historically recorded as one of the most learned men of his times, and is traditionally understood to have compiled or commented on the *Book of Documents, Book of Poetry, Spring and Autumn Annals,* and *Book of Changes,* it is not too speculative to conjecture that Confucius might have had a "Confucian curriculum" (F. Li 2013, 212). Regardless of what Confucius regarded as the exact content of *Wen,* it is evident that *Wen* is contrasted with "substance"—*zhi* (质). In *Analects* 12.8, we are told that substance is tantamount to *Wen* (质犹文也):

> Ji Zicheng said, "Being a gentleman is simply a matter of having the right native substance, and nothing else. Why must one engage in cultural refinement [*Wen* 文]?"
>
> Zigong replied, "It is regrettable, Sir, that you should speak of the gentleman in this way—as they say, 'a team of horses cannot overtake your tongue.'
>
> "A gentleman's cultural refinement [*Wen* 文] resembles his substance, and his substance resembles his cultural refinement. The skin of a tiger or leopard, shorn of its fur, is no different from the skin of a dog or sheep." (Slingerland 2003, 129)

I want to suggest that Confucius held *Wen* in such a high regard for two reasons. (1) The Confucian understanding of the self is functional: the self is immanent in the structures it creates. Put negatively, there is no self apart from its manifestation and participation in culture. Put positively, the essence of the self is its ability to participate in, and creatively transform, culture. It is in this sense that *zhi*—in the sense of substance—is tantamount to *Wen.* (2) *Wen* itself is understood by Confucius (and the Confucians) as the historically evolving, pluralistic and socio-conventional *function.* As in the sage of the *Xici,* the self *is* the hermeneutic law that can order and give meaning to experience. Hall and Ames, as I interpret it, have a similar understanding of Wen when they write that Wen in the Analects "is the human *organization* and elaboration of the stuff of existence, the articulation of human values and meaning captured in symbol and then transmitted from generation to generation" (1987, 45; my emphasis). Wen, like the Cassirerian symbolic form are *systems* for organizing experience and thus making experience meaningful. The "objective exercise of learning"—(*xue* 学)—furthermore, is the appropriation, embodiment, and transmission of a cultural tradition (Wen 文) (Hall and Ames 1987, 44–45). One learns to acquire these cultural traditions not out of any utilitarian calculus,[7] but in order to appropriate the terms in which one can become human,[8] in which we can become free for our humanity. Like the other virtues that Con-fucius taught, Wen is an end in itself, as we see in Analects 7.25: "The Master taught four things: cultural refinement [Wen 文], comportment, dutifulness, and trustworthiness" (Slingerland 2003, 72). Confucius's great concern with education and the acquisition of Wen through this education—the German Bildung (which we will go on to discuss) is perhaps a more accurate term—shows the value Wen has in realizing our humanity. The self is thus a human *becoming*, the self *is* inasmuch as it is situated within the process of increasing Bildung, the process of which is an end in itself.[9] As opposed to the familiar understanding of the Mencius as subscribing to an Aristotelian idea of development in which cultivation teleologically fulfills the formal essence of the self, self-cultivation and Bildung are not meant in this teleological sense of fulfilling a (utilitarian) end. The Confucian concept of self-cultivation and the classical German concept of Bildung escape any merely causal conception of the self.

For Cassirer, the essence of the self can similarly only be revealed through the mediation of diverse cultural forms. As in Zigong's statement that *zhi* is tantamount to Wen, similarly for Cassirer, as we have already seen, "The term 'Geist' is correct; but we must not use it as a name of a substance—a thing. . . . We should use it in a functional sense as a comprehensive name for all those functions that constitute and build us the world of human culture" (1945, 114). It is because the human being or human spirit is functional, that it is able to be tantamount to the world of culture. For Cassirer, from a merely ontological or metaphysical point of view, it would be very difficult to refute the thesis that there is a discontinuity and radical heterogeneity in human culture:

But for a critical philosophy the problem assumes another face. Here we are under no obligation to prove the substantial unity of man. Man is no longer considered as a simple substance which exists in itself and is to be known by itself. His unity is conceived as a functional unity. Such a unity does not presuppose a homogeneity of the various elements of which it consists. Not merely does it admit of, it even requires, a multiplicity and multiformity of its constituent parts. For this is a dialectic unity, a coexistence of contraries. (EM 222)

It is *because* the self is a functional one—one that merely organizes the facta of experience—that there is no antinomy between the "substance" or "essence" of the self and the cultural forms in which the self partakes. Repeatedly, Cassirer stresses that a human can only be known, can only become a self through his or her partaking of culture. The essence of the self, like the Confucian *zhi* (质), lies in its potential—growth through embodying culture:

The philosophy of symbolic forms starts from the presupposition that, if there is any definition of the nature or "essence" of man, this definition can only be understood as a functional one, not a substantial one. We cannot define man by any inherent principle which constitutes his metaphysical essence—nor can we define him by any inborn faculty or instinct that may be ascertained by empirical observation. Man's outstanding characteristic, his distinguishing mark, is not his metaphysical or physical nature—but his work. It is this work, it is the system of human activities, which defines and determines the circle of "humanity." (EM 67–68)

Cassirer's functional understanding of the self is thus in contrast, and stands as a corrective to, the prevalent essentialist, "substance" or ontological model of human nature.[10] To put things into perspective, this functional understanding of subjectivity is radically at odds with the Freudian conception of the self, where the *true* self is threatened and repressed by civilization.[11] Relatedly, one could say that this essentialist understanding of selves partly explains why Western philosophy has, historically, rarely taken culture seriously. If the self, like meaning, is understood as preexisting before language and culture, then one cannot *but* be skeptical about the medium of its (re)presentation. Culture, under this paradigm, becomes *merely* a phantasmagoric distortion and is associated with authoritarianism and social oppression of the individual. For the Confucians, the sociocultural does not exist at the expense of the self; it fulfils the self, just like its understanding of the relationship between meaning and language.

It is this "functional" understanding of the self that leads to a corresponding emphasis on self-cultivation or *Bildung* in the two respective traditions. Transformation through cultural education takes ontological primacy before "substance" or "human nature." As Yang Xiong—one of the foremost Confucians of the Han dynasty—writes in *Fa Yan* (法言), "The sage is the one who acculturates [people's] substance."[12]

Even for the more "biological"[13] understanding of *xing* (性) that Mencius arguably subscribes to, this *xing* is only ever a potential that cannot grow unless it is within culture. The *Mencius* expresses this idea in 4A27:

> Mengzi said, "The core of benevolence [*ren* 仁] is serving one's parents. The core of righteousness [*yi* 义] is obeying one's elder brother. The core of wisdom is knowing these two and not abandoning them. The core of ritual propriety is ordering [*jie* 节] and the adornment [*wen* 文] of these two. The core of music is to delight in these two.
>
> "If one delights in them, then they grow. If they grow, then how can they be stopped? If they cannot be stopped, then one does not notice one's feet dancing to them, one's hand swaying to them." (Meng and Van Norden 2008, 101; modified)

For Mencius, although benevolence and righteousness are part of human nature—whether we understand this to mean that humans have the potential towards benevolence and righteousness or that these qualities always already define human nature—one still needs ritual propriety and music to nourish these aspects of human nature. Ritual acts as an ordering and adorning influence, whereas music allows one to delight in benevolence and righteousness. Music and poetry has this pedagogic aptitude, for, as we saw in chapter 3, the form of music/poetry is not externally imposed, but, rather, it is merely a formalization of our own implicit form/processes and how we are related to the world.

The idea that it is human culture that consummates our innate tendencies towards humanity is also expressed in the *Zhongyong 1*:

> What *tian* commands (*ming* 命) is called natural tendencies (*xing* 性); drawing out these natural tendencies is called the proper way (*dao* 道); improving upon this way is called education (*jiao* 教).[14] (Ames and Hall 2001, 89)

That humans achieve their humanity by participating in and creating forms can be similarly seen in the *Xunzi*. Xunzi's view on ritual are most succinctly put when he writes: "What is the reason for the three-year mourning period? I say: It takes measure of people's dispositions [*qing* 情] and establishes a proper form [文] for them"[15] (Hutton 2014, 213). *Wen* for Xunzi is a humanly created pattern that orders existing phenomena.[16] Much like the Confucian attitude towards *qing* (情) and poetic form, ritual is needed to stabilize affective dispositions so that these affects gain a form that is conducive to order, and in turn the realization of our humanity.

Freedom and Form

If we understand *Wen* as the systematic ordering of our world, then culture is prior to, or simultaneous with, both subject and object. It is prior in the epistemological sense that culture is necessarily antecedent to the development of the self; it is simultaneous in the genetic sense that, obviously, culture did not historically antedate the existence of people. It is only within culture that we come to know what a subject and object is. The importance of the acquisition of *Wen* as the telos of study is thus because it is only once we are conversant with cultural forms that the world can be disclosed to us, that the world can be ordered in a meaningful way, and that we can, in turn, become partakers of meaning, that we can have *substance*, be *substantial* subjects in any meaningful sense. In this instance, a tiger and a leopard cannot *essentially* be a tiger or a leopard without its external expression. Cassirer is famous for positing that what distinguishes us as human beings is our symbol making capacity: we are *animal symbolicum*. What elevates us from being merely biological beings is that we can comprehend the world through (intellectual) tools—symbols—of our own making, which we could equally call *Wen*. Without the symbolic forms (or *Wen*), "the variations which realize themselves in individual specimens within the sphere of the plant and animal world remain biologically insignificant; they emerge, only to vanish again" (*LCS* 126). Without the symbolic forms, we remain on the level of biological beings. As Thora Ilin Bayer writes, for Cassirer, "an animal does not organize its world by making shared, nontemporal interpretations of it" and therefore is purely determined according to what one might call "fate" (Bayer 2001, 43). With *Wen*, however, "man discovers and proves a new power—the power to build up a world of his own, an 'ideal' world" (*EM* 228). For Cassirer, the human being is that animal that needs culture in order to flourish. Just as a fish requires an environment appropriate to it in order to flourish—water—so does the human being require its own appropriate environment. The difference between the human being and all other animals is that humans *create* the environment they need to flourish: culture. In the Confucian instance, a gentleman could not feasibly be a gentleman without the cultural forms that shaped him, which is why there is an emphasis on the simultaneity of native substance with *Wen*. This partaking of cultural forms and the partaking of "freedom" is not an either/or choice between having freedom and not having freedom. In the Confucian conception, freedom exists on a continuum. As expressed in *Analects* 2.4, in Confucius's biography, Confucius's increasing freedom came with increasing learning and attendant agency.

The Confucian stress on culture can be elucidated through a contrast with Daoist skepticism toward culture.[17] Historically, the Daoists have straw-manned the Confucians as prudes who do not have the imagination to go beyond ossified rules. In my interpretation, the Confucians are not unconcerned with a "free and easy wandering"—they just have a different understanding of how we achieve this same "freedom." Whereas spontaneity (and freedom) lies under the threshold or before the determination of (humanly created) forms for the Daoist, for the Confucians, it is only once we have created form, that we can begin to be free and spontaneous. As Hall and Ames put it, "A physical notion related to the Confucian way (*dao* 道) in expressing the classical Confucian concept of natural order is *wen* 文" (1998b, 33).[18] It is only with humanly created form—*Wen*—that we can access a spontaneity that is appropriate to us as human beings. Our human, civilized world may always be informed by the spontaneous natural sources of the world—just like the *xiang* of the *Xici*, and our emotions, as in poetry; but it is *because* we have these symbols (*Wen*) that we can remake our *ideal* world on our own terms. Human *Wen* is not an arbitrary arising—it is instead, as Song Lian wrote, "born of heaven, conveyed by the earth, and propagated by the sages." *Wen* is derived from the nature of things, but it is human *Wen*—"propagated by the sages"—that allows for moral *order*. Human order, because it is more consciously *made*, because we have a more deliberate role in the creation of our own *Wen*, must also be more consciously maintained; and it is our reflection on the role we have in maintaining this order that is the beginning of ethical reflection. The humanism underlying this stress on the importance of culture is the same for the Confucians as it is for Cassirer. As one Cassirer commentator puts it, "Culture is *made*, not encountered, and its works, its *facta*, are where we can be ourselves, where we can *only* be ourselves. Heaven or the kingdom of ends is not in another world, but here, insofar as heaven on earth can only be a world of culture" (Luft 2015b, 15). Similarly, Confucius's veneration of the sage kings was because they were the ones who gifted unto progeny *Wen*,[19] thus allowing us the possibility of freedom and meaning that is denied to the physical world of things and the animal world of mere impulses and instincts: it is only with the *Wen* forms that we can have the enlightenment of culture (文明) and realize a freedom unique to us.

Like other Cassirer commentators, such as Sebastian Luft and Massimo Ferrari, Martina Plümacher, in her article "The Ethical Impulse in Ernst Cassirer's Philosophy of Symbolic Forms" sees the ethical moment in Cassirer's philosophy in his Kantian emphasis on the spontaneity of spirit (*Geist*) and the creative activity of consciousness (Plümacher 2008, 111). Humans do not passively receive the world as given; the "given" world is a result of human freedom—the freedom of humans as symbolic animals to construct a world of form and thus meaning. Plümacher goes on to say, however, that Cassirer's "explications of human freedom and creativity are characteristically reserved. They describe new creations in the context of the questions and problems which older creations throw up, as well as the relevance of reflection on the axiomatic attitudes and postulates which define the framework for theory formation and action. They illustrate the unfolding of human reflexivity in the history of culture and knowledge" (112). This is why "Cassirer does not argue for *creation ex nihilo*. Nor does he overstretch the ideal of creativity by giving primacy to the production of novelty" (112). Likewise, the Confucians, contra the conventional stereotypes, are not unconcerned with freedom and personal realization. They believe, however, that this freedom does not come *ex nihilo*; this freedom is dependent upon a robust nexus of cultural forms. The conservatism attributed to Cassirer here, and with which Confucianism is famously stereotyped, is thus a logical consequence of their understanding of personal realization. Once we realize that we couldn't have meaning if we all spoke our own private languages, then we are naturally led to a conservative attitude whereby we emphasize the stability and continuity of a linguistic tradition. The kind of radical freedom that is a counterpart to *creation ex nihilo* is incommensurable with the understanding of the self as realized through cultural forms, and thus dependent upon the continuity of cultural forms.

The ethical dimension of this thought follows from the epistemological dimension: my positive, practical freedom extends only so far as these *Wen* forms exist, which in turn motivates me to uphold these cultural forms. It is therefore the creation and maintenance of this community of meaning from which we gain our first sense of normativity and social obligation. The very possibility of meaning, because it is predicated on the other, compels us to uphold these norms (for, otherwise, we ourselves could not *meaningfully exist*), and because it is these very cultural norms that can establish our *meaningful existence*, these two dimensions—the subject and the cultural medium/civilizing process (*Wen*)—become a self-completing, closed circle. To partake in culture thus becomes *itself* the ethical ideal. In this, we can use Cassirer to speak for Confucius: "The moral aspect of this philosophy of culture is to be a human, to join the communal work of culture. The more culture, the more freedom" (Luft 2015b, 15). Civilization (the Confucian Dao) is the goal that motivates us towards the civilizing process; the Dao, as a *terminus ad quem*, is not a place to be arrived at; civilization is something towards which we, as our self-cultivations, are constantly striving. It is in this sense that we can understand Confucius when he says, "Learn as if you could not reach your object, and were always fearing also lest you should lose it" (8.17). Learning is not the mere acquisition of information: learning is an activity whose goal cannot be *acquired*, the goal is the *process* itself, whose very activity upholds the space of cultural and thus ethical action. Learning is the beginning of the process of self-realization, of positive freedom. It is the beginning of ethical consciousness, and the opening up of a space for the realization of human culture. By learning these cultural forms, my own subjective realization is simultaneous with the realization of the other. The Confucian stress on the acquisition of culture can be put into dialogue with Cassirer's view on the relationship between language and normativity:

The more the child progresses in his linguistic development, the more there awakens and strengthens in him the awareness that there is a common general standard, an objectively correct usage. It appears that the consciousness of *this* correctness, which prevails in the norm of language, is, for the awakening of spiritual life, one of the most important and earliest examples of the sense of the norm *in general*. It is in the linguistic bond, in the devotion to the general meaning of words, that the child experiences perhaps the best and most immediate of the basic character of the social bond, the normative as such. It weaves and works itself constantly into the web of language. Yet, it is not able to spin this web simply out of itself but has to rely on the steady and continuous work of the whole. The work of language arises in this uniform collaboration of all and, at the same time, turns it into the strongest bond between all who collectively create it and acquire it, with and for one another. The ever-stronger-growing tendency of children to *ask* the names of things illuminates this state of affairs. For the question that needs, demands, and awaits an answer is perhaps the finest form of "social" interconnection, not only a practical but also an intellectual and psychological interconnection. (Cassirer 2013a, 352–53; from the essay "Language and the Construction of the World of Objects," originally published 1932)

We are perhaps used to thinking of Confucius as a bland moralist, but in the Confucian conception of *Wen*, as I construe it, we are supposed to derive existential joy from upholding a civilizing structure in which we are realizing our own freedoms.

In this context, it bears remembering that the "rites and music, which for Confucius constitute the basis for much of what is beautiful and refined (*wen* 文)" (Brindley 2012, 99), are so valued by Confucius because *Wen* as an expressive conduit, as the *proper* expression of one's emotions, allows my native substance (*zhi* 质) to be guided through the appropriate (*Wen*) forms. *Wen* forms such as music are the *proper* and *appropriate* forms, because these forms put us into communicative union with the other in a way that generates aesthetic pleasure. *Wen* forms such as music and ritual are so cherished by Confucius, as it is through them that the moral *ought* can become a source of *pleasure*. It is the socially beneficial nature of these *Wen* forms that for Xu Fuguan is the Confucian ideal of art: "It [the Confucian ideal of art] is the absolute epitome of the harmonizing union of benevolence [ren 仁] and beauty [mei 美]" (Xu 2013b, 29). And, further, it is why, "yue functions indisputably as a means by which one unifies and integrates one's moral knowledge" (Brindley 2012, 95). In this sense, Confucius's philosophical system is premised upon insightful observations about human interaction or social psychology. Confucius's great veneration for Wen is, under this reading, due to the *very fact* that they are a source of *pleasure*. The individual possesses her uniqueness through participation in the ethical-social world that she in turn helps to shape, and Wen, because they put my desires as a human being into a mutual-reciprocal exchange with the other, act as the lubricant for this self-realization through the other. Furthermore, because the joy I derive from these forms—an existential joy in which I am simultaneously experiencing the joy of my own meaningfulness—requires upholding the norms of a community (of which I am a member) to make this meaningfulness possible, my acting in accordance with the rules of these forms becomes a prerequisite for my own subjective fulfilment. As Mencius says, "The core of music is to delight in these two [ren 仁 and yi 义]. If one delights in them, then they grow. If they grow, then how can they be stopped? If they cannot be stopped, then one does not notice one's feet dancing to them, one's hand swaying to them" (4A27; Meng and Van Norden 2008, 101; modified). These are the forms, then, that are most conducive for moral-social behavior as such. It is through Wen that the utmost virtue of ren—realizing the other while realizing myself—becomes easiest. The thought that I cannot take pleasure in music without abiding by the rules of expression that make a particular style of music meaningful can be extended into an ethical system tout court. In *Analects* 6.30, we see the ethical manifestation of such a social understanding of the self: "The man of ren, in wishing to establish [li 立] himself, seeks also to establish others, wishing to realize [da 达] himself, seeks also to realize others." As we have seen, it is impossible to realize oneself outside of a social context, which is why it becomes integral to also realize the social other, as my own self-realization is premised upon the existence and competence of the social other in upholding these intersubjective communicative systems.

Ancient Wen Graphs

The relationship between epistemology, morality, and the self can be seen from the ancient graphs for *wen*. The early Chinese graph for the character *wen* (文) consists of a person with patterns across their body.[20] Following our previous discussion, we can say that it is the insignia on our own world and selves that allows us to identify ourselves as self-conscious human beings. The patterns we make on the world assumes a comprehension of that world as something reducible to a certain order of meaning. Furthermore, we can contribute to the meaning of that world through meanings of our own creation: our patterns. It is these patterns that demonstrate our self-conscious elevation from the unreflective order of nature. Further, this very self-conscious elevation requires a form of meaning that others also recognize. I cannot know that I am self-conscious unless there is another who recognizes me as self-conscious; and the only way of reaching this accord is through these patterns.[21] The apparent visual meaning of the pictograph *wen* is commensurate with its original meaning: (distinctive) "marking" of any kind (Boltz 1994, 139). Witness the way it is used in the *Zuo Zhuan*: "When Zhongzi was born, she had a *mark* (*wen* 文) in her hand."[22] There are many further examples of markings (*wen*) on a person being associated with their personality traits or eventual greatness.[23]

Wen, *Bildung*, and the Aesthetic Education of Man

In *An Essay on Man*, Cassirer writes, "If the term 'humanity' means anything at all it means that, in spite of all the differences and oppositions existing among its various forms, these are, nevertheless, all working toward a common end" (EM 70). In relation to this passage, Donald Phillip Verene writes that Cassirer "likely has in mind the connection between *Humanität* and *Bildung*" (2011, 95). In *Truth and Method*, Gadamer argues that the knowledge that the humanities offered is less one of objective knowledge of the world than of knowledge that pertains to the cultivation of the self (*Bildung*). I think that Gadamer's project of restoring dignity to the humanities, also characterizes Cassirer's project. This *Humanitätsideal* of *Bildung* is, furthermore, comparable to the Confucian stress on self-cultivation.[24]

In both the German humanist and Confucian traditions, what most essentially defines humans is that there is no fixed essence. The human essence is its ability to become human through cultural forms; in the unceasing development of our capacity for becoming (more) human, there is no *end* to growth: "To be human is to have no such algorithmic notion of oneself. Humanism is rather an unending quest for civility in

138 A Philosophical Defense of Culture

human affairs that can only be achieved or exercised in the process of culture and the cultivation of one's own talents" (Grondin 1995, 118).[25] It is for this reason that Confucius is so famously reticent about *defining* what *ren* (仁) (cf. *Analects* 9.1) or human nature is. Instead, we only hear about his discussing what learning is:

> We can hear our Master's views on culture [*Wenzhang* 文章], but we cannot hear his views on human nature [*xing* 性] and the Way of Heaven [*tiandao* 天道]. (*Analects* 5.13)

Likewise, in reply to a question on why Kong Wenzi (孔文子) was accorded the title "cultured" (文), Confucius replied that it was because "he was diligent and loved learning, and was not ashamed to ask advice from his inferiors. This is why he was accorded the title, 'Cultured'" (5.15). As with the *Bildung* tradition, one does not speculate about a final essence that determines what one is; that is both unknowable and not useful. One concentrates instead on the process of learning and thus growth itself. One does not focus on a reality behind appearances; one focuses on the appearances themselves.

The humanist conception of *Bildung* is beautifully expressed by Jean Grondin:

> For humanism, it is precisely the "essence" of mankind not to have an essence since it is able to surpass any fixed essence one could assign to it.
>
> This is also the lesson that Gadamer draws from the humanistic tradition. If man never ceases to learn, then there is nothing fixed about his essence. Furthermore, if one has to "build" or "form" oneself through *Bildung*, one will naturally be open to other points of view, to different perspectives than one's own. . . . What distinguishes our humanity, is not a rational capacity that would catapult us into a divine world of pure ideas. Rather, it is the ability to go beyond our own particularity by taking into the account the heritage that can help us grow above and beyond our limited selves. (1995, 119–20)

The knowledge of the humanities allows us to realize ourselves by embracing the world as opposed to sinking into introspection. The broadening of horizon that this brings about enables us to reflect on our own limited perspective, thus elevating us to a more universal form of knowledge that Gadamer deemed specific to the humanities. This is the unique task of the humanities, which could not be appreciated by the paradigms of the exact sciences.

In the "Naturalistic and Humanistic Philosophies of Culture," Cassirer asks, "In addition to this threefold combination of physics, psychology, and metaphysics, is there another possible standpoint from which to gain leverage capable of guaranteeing independent significance and worth to the being and the actions of the individual?" (*NHPC* 19). Cassirer answers that the best means for securing the sovereignty of the individual, and not to reduce it to the positivism of the sciences or to subsume it under metaphysics, is to look to the classical era of German humanism, to the *Goethezeit*.[26] For Cassirer, the Kantian subject was divided between the determinism of the sciences, and metaphysical freedom: "Kant's doctrine rests upon a dualism between nature and freedom, between the '*mundus sensibilis*' and the '*mundus intelligibilis*.' But Herder and Goethe have not followed him here. What they comprehend under the idea of *humanitas* they view not so much as a unique [state of] *being*, but, instead, as a unique *achievement*" (*NHPC* 22–23).[27] Creating and maintaining the forms in which we achieve this liberation is the task of humanity. Cassirer follows Herder and Goethe in taking the *telos* or definition of the self as our capacity for civilization, and the enabling condition of civilization is the symbol. It is in this sense that Cassirer famously said that man is a symbolic as opposed to rational or biological animal (*EM* 26). The symbolic as meaning, which is created by and dependent on human beings, replaces *logos* as truth (which exists independently of human beings):

> This desire and capacity for giving form to experience is what Herder and Humboldt show to be the essence of language, what Schiller points to as the essential nature of play and art, and what Kant shows us to be true of the structure of theoretical knowledge. For them, all this would not be possible as outgrowth, as sheer product, if unique modes of formal construction [spheres of possibility] did not underlie [the working out of] these creations. The very fact that man is capable of this type of productivity is precisely what stands out as the unique and distinguishing characteristic of human nature. "*Humanitas*," in the widest sense of the word, denotes that completely universal, and, in this very universality,

unique—medium in which "form," as such, comes into being in which it can develop and flourish. (NHPC 22)

The symbol as a meaning created by human beings overcomes the Kantian dualism between nature and freedom; and in this regard, for Cassirer, "it was not Fichte, Schelling, nor Hegel, but Wilhelm von Humboldt who succeeded in erecting this bridge [between nature and human nature]" (NHPC 23). It is because the definition of being human lies in the creation of forms that enable meaning that the distinguishing feature of humans does not lie exclusively in morality:

> We are particularly habituated to studying the eighteenth century's "ideal conception of humanity" [Humanitätsideal] from an ethical point of view; we are accustomed to looking upon it, if not exclusively, at least for the most part as an ethical ideal. But this interpretation is clearly too narrow. For Winckelmann and Herder, for Goethe and Humboldt, even for Schiller and Kant, the truly concrete significance of this concept of humanity lies elsewhere. To be sure, they are convinced that a specific form of morality and a specific order of social and political life flow from the idea of "humanitas" and that, in a certain sense, these represent its ripest and noblest fruit. But this is not the only object of their vision. For, beyond this, they are confronting, in addition, a far more universal theme, a far more comprehensive problem.
>
> What concerns them in the concept of humanity does not lie completely within the limits of moral order. It extends to every creative act whatever, regardless of the particular sphere of life within which it realizes itself. Here there emerges, as the *fundamental feature of all human existence*, the fact that man is not lost within the welter of his external impressions, that he learns to control this sea of impressions by giving it *ordered form*, which, as such, stems in the final analysis from himself, from his own thinking, feeling, and willing. (NHPC 21–22)

"Of all *natural beings* only man is capable of this achievement [*Leistung*]"—"What the human being thus completes [*vollzieht*] is the *objectification*, the apperception, of the ground of all theoretical, aesthetic, and ethical creation of form [*Formung*]" (*NHPC* 23). Cassirer puts the stress here on "natural beings," as we are irrefutably the biological animals of the one side of the Kantian dualism. We are unique among natural beings, however, in that our actions [*Leistung*] have a creative role in shaping our world. Freedom can thus be seen in any domain—and thus not limited merely to morality—in which the human being creatively shapes her lifeworld. The fact that we understand the world in different ways through the various cultural forms (and according to different national cultures) means that we are freer than the Kantian system gave credit for.

In explaining the concept of *Bildung*, Gadamer notes that before it was associated with the idea of culture and the "properly human way of developing one's natural talents and capacities," it referred to external appearances such as the shape of the limbs, the well-formed figure, and, in general, to nature shapes such as mountain formations (*Gebirges-bildung*) (2004, 9). Herder gave *Bildung* its most canonical definition in the idea of "rising up to humanity through culture" [*Emporbildung zur Humanität*], which was later filled out by Hegel and Humboldt (9). For Herder, the most basic meaning of *Bildung* is formation, molding, but it also takes on meanings such as development, education, culture, cultivation, civilization (Herder 2002, 272n3).[28] *Bildung* cannot be captured by a means-end spectrum. One cultivates oneself not for the purpose of a utilitarian end. No naive teleology can describe *Bildung*, for, like nature, *Bildung* has no goal outside of itself, the process of *Bildung* itself *is* its purpose. "Bildung is not achieved in the manner of a technical construction but grows out of an inner process of formation and cultivation, and therefore constantly remains in a state of continual Bildung" (Gadamer 2004, 10). For Gadamer, therefore, the Greek idea of *physis* captures the idea of *Bildung* particularly well—a constant state of becoming (10).

In the Chinese equivalent for *Bildung*—Wen (文), or *Wenjiao* (文教)—we find the same etymological genesis from an external material form to the proper form of humanity, and the cultivation of this form. *Wen*, like *Bildung*, stands for the ideal of education, culture, cultivation, civilization, as well as the unending processual nature of this cultivation/acculturation of an inner potential. The term *Wenhua* (文化), literally "educative transformation through *Wen*," occurs first in the "Zhi Wu" (指武) chapter of the *Shuo Yuan* (说苑; 17 BCE).[29]

Cassirer's Aesthetic Individual

For Cassirer, the freedom *for* individuality stands in stark contrast to the religious mysticism that preceded the Leibnizian philosophy. In the Protestantism of Luther and Calvin, it is by surrendering to the passiveness of man in the face of the divine that the individual establishes his relation to the infinite and experiences salvation and freedom. In the philosophical interpretation of this religious view—Spinoza's *Ethics*—the self is not confronted by an inexplicable divine decree, but by the immutable eternal, rational law of the universe itself. The lawfulness of the self can only be understood when its individuality is subsumed and thus distinguished by the rational law of the universe. In Leibniz's *Monadology*, however, each individual subject, like a monad, by fulfilling and completing the circle assigned to it, is at the same time free and bound. It is bound because everything that arises from it proceeds in a strictly lawful manner; it is free because it is only the law of one's own being that is expressed in its works (FF 42). Leibniz's *Monadology* thus overcame the dualism between the particular and the universal. Whereas in Spinozism, "it is necessary for the ego to undergo a *self-renunciation if it is to have a vision of the whole*, if it would participate in full knowledge of God and nature," in the neo-humanism of Goethe, Herder, and Humboldt, on the other hand, there is a different paradigm for relating the individual with the whole.

> To them, the Spinozistic thesis, that a definition is limitation, is valid only where it applies to external limitation, such as the form given to an object by a force not its own. But within the free sphere of one's personality such checking heightens personality; it truly acquires form only by forming itself. . . .
> Every universal in the sphere of culture, whether discovered in language, art, religion, or philosophy, is as individual as it is universal. For in this sphere we perceive the universal only within the actuality of the particular; only in it can the cultural universal find its actualization, its realization as a cultural universal. (NHPC 24–25)

In the Spinozistic thesis, the uniqueness of personality—determination in space and time (*omnis determination est negation*)—is limitation and is the antithesis of the infinite being of God and nature. For Cassirer, under this thesis, there is no possibility for the affirmation of individual personality, as personality is merely being bound up in the limitation and determination of the universal, is merely a delusional anthropocentrism and anthropomorphism. Under "neo-humanism," however, the individual is, like the monad, completely unique but still partakes of a greater whole: "A form is only a real form, when it also has a shape [Gestalt], a structure in which the freedom of creativity is reconciled with the dynamic context that coordinates and organizes the manifold" (Ferrari 2003, 53).

On the political level, Cassirer sees the reconciliation of the general with the individual as manifested in Wilhelm von Humboldt's liberalism. Humboldt's liberalism is usually known through John Stuart Mill, who acknowledged that his own concept of liberty is derivative of Humboldt's. On Liberty begins with a quote from Humboldt promoting the two requisites for individual liberty—"freedom, and variety of situations." For Cassirer, however, the true nature of Humboldt's liberalism was lost in translation to British world. The "harmonious development of powers" in the Humboldtian aesthetic individual was informed by Leibniz and not Locke. The concept of the individual at play was not an atomistic individual "derived from the state of nature or presumed by common sense, but the infinite monad that was always coextensive with its environment" (Moynahan 2013, 181).

Humboldt's "aesthetic individual" thus follows Leibniz: (1) the individual/particular is of central importance, but (2) the individual can only meaningfully exist through participation in a whole; and (3) the greatest good is established through the individual, but this is accomplished through transformations of form, through changes in law, art, or mores (FF 329–30). For Cassirer, it is thus form and not pure individuality that defines Humboldt's liberalism. Humboldt's liberalism thus does not rest simply on the defense of individual rights as it arguably was in Mill's reception of Humboldt. Humboldt focuses on the medium through which individual self-realization can take place, for, unlike other animals, humans are not social in that they owe sociality to reasons of "protection, help and procreation. Humans are social in the deeper sense, that it is only through others that one is raised to consciousness of oneself and an 'I' without a 'Thou' is for this understanding and perception an absurdity [ein Unding]" (FF 352). Form and spiritual energy [geistiger Energie] are thus at the center of Humboldt's thought as opposed to individuality, as the forms of sociation are in a sense prior to the individual and the collective definitions of reality. It is the intersubjective medium from which the individual and the collective definition of reality is derived. To think otherwise would be a "retrospective fallacy," to use a Deweyan term. Greater emphasis is placed on the means for, the form of, self-actualization than the defense of individual rights—of freedom in a negative sense. Humboldt's "aesthetic individuality" thus goes beyond the legal and political protections of spiritual belief and freedom of thought in the Reformation and Enlightenment. Cassirer writes, "The basic and primary right of the individual, which is to defend itself against both [state and society], is no longer the right to freedom within a specific walled-off [abgegrenzten] individual sphere, such as was the case in freedom of consciousness or freedom of thought. It is the right to peculiarity [Eigentümlichkeit] as such" (FF 346).

For Humboldt and Schiller, Cassirer argues, the aesthetic individual provides a happy medium (Mittelglied) to the idea of the individual in Hobbes's "state of emergency" and the individual defined by the "state of reason" (FF 344). The aesthetic particularity of the individual cannot be reduced to the delimitations either of nature or ideas, because in aesthetic experience the individual finds a form of experience that is "at once free and bound, which belongs to nature even as it is free [gelöst] from it," and that as such can form a "new unity of real and ideal, of sense and spirit" (FF 345). Like Confucius at seventy, when he was able to follow his heart's desires without overstepping the bounds of propriety, the aesthetic individual reveals the *freedom* of her individuality through creative engagement with the rule-forms that conditions human thought/action. Humboldt is arguing, Cassirer writes, that the individual is "symbolic in the sense of Goethe" in that she or he only "works through connections which arise from the essence of one's being and that makes the well-being of others conditional upon one's own, and in this manner, indirectly realise the totality of humanity" (FF 347). Like the *ren* of *Analects* 6.30, the realization of the self is contingent upon the realization of the totality of humanity.

The affinities between the Confucian conception of education as creative development of oneself through the rule-forms of a society has been well noted in previous scholarship. As Geir Sigurðsson notes, this Confucian understanding of education is more akin to *Bildung* as opposed to *Ausbildung*. *Ausbildung* connotes formal vocational education and corresponds with the latin *educare* as "rationally ordered education," whereas *Bildung* corresponds with the latin *educere*, which, as Hall and Ames note, suggests that one extend "one's inner tendencies through a mode of *self*-cultivation that is, in fact, self-*creation*" (quoted in Sigurðsson 2015, 83). Sigurðsson notes that this conception of *Bildung* received its first formulation with Hegel, who attempted to reconcile the Enlightenment antagonism between tradition and reason. Hegel, that is, attempted to reconcile the authority of tradition—*Sittlichkeit*—concretely embodied norms, with the Enlightenment stress upon individual reason and liberation from tradition. The Hegelian *Bildung*, like Cassirer's aesthetic individual thus provided a *Mittelglied*. In Cassirer's case, this *Mittelglied* was between Hobbes's "state of emergency" and the "state of reason," whereas in Hegel's case, this *Mittelglied* was between tradition and individual reason/liberty. As Sigurðsson notes, this "aesthetic" conception of Confucian education resonates with the Gadamerian and Deweyian understanding of education due to their common source in Hegel (91). Cassirer's "aesthetic individual" does not thus bear merely superficial similarity to the Confucian idea of education; there are historical reasons for their similarity.

What we have been describing as an "aesthetic individual," Charles Taylor has related to an expressive view of human life and the self. What is worth remarking is that this expressivist view of the self is related to an organic worldview:

> My claim is that the idea of *nature* as an intrinsic source goes along with an expressive view of human life. Fulfilling my nature means espousing the inner élan, the voice or impulse. And this makes what was hidden manifest for both myself and others. But this manifestation also helps to define what is to be realized. The direction of this élan wasn't and couldn't be clear prior to this manifestation. In realizing my nature, I have to define it in the sense of giving it some formulation; but this is also a definition in a stronger sense: I am realizing this formulation and thus giving my life a definitive shape. A human life is seen as manifesting a potential which is also being shaped by this manifestation; it is not just a matter of copying an external model or carrying out an already determinate formulation.
>
> This conception reflects the return in force of *biological* models of growth, as against the mechanistic ones of association in the account of human mental development, models which Herder articulated so well and so effectively in this period. (1989, 374–75; my emphasis)

What Taylor has described here is the (Herderian) idea of *Bildung*. In this chapter, we have pointed to the affinities between this idea of education as growth with the Confucian ideas of self-cultivation. Taylor, very interestingly, asserts that this model of growth is related to a biological worldview. As we will see in the next chapter, for Cassirer, a key figure in conceiving this "biological" model in Western philosophy was Leibniz (other key figures being Herder, Goethe, and Humboldt). Leibniz's *Monadology*, as we will see, bears striking resemblance to the organicist worldview of Chinese "correlative cosmology." It is this source in the organic that is the root of the commonalities between the philosophical similarities between ideas about education and, as we will see, ideas about pluralism.

In Defense of Culture

In the conclusion to *Ernst Cassirer: The Last Philosopher of Culture*—the first English biography of Cassirer—Edward Skidelsky dismisses Cassirer's project as a failed one and unviable for the modern world. As I understand it, Skidelsky's problem with Cassirer is that because there was no Archimedean anchorage in his philosophy of culture, it necessarily redounds to mere (historicist) description:

> It was not just that many individual aspects of his system had fallen into disrepair, but that the whole thing was no longer obviously *philosophy* at all. Cassirer's thought is inductive, not deductive in its method. Setting out from the variety of human culture, it attempts to comprehend it as an organic whole. But most twentieth-century philosophy, analytic and continental, has sought a standpoint *beyond* the variety of culture—an absolute conception of consciousness, meaning, or the world. Viewed from this angle, Cassirer does not so much mediate between analytic and continental traditions as fall foul of them both. His "reconciliation" is on terms that neither can accept. (2008, 5–6)

Skidelsky's assessment of Cassirer is a familiar one that has often been levelled at Cassirer.[30] Against Skidelsky, I would argue that culture *must* be seen as a priori, there is no standpoint beyond this. To take culture as a priori is merely to affirm that there is no unconditional beyond culture. To think that there is such a "standpoint beyond the varieties of culture"—"an absolute"—necessarily entails essentializing: we will inevitably take a part of (one culture) to characterize the whole.[31] To wish for an Archimedean point of certainty, or view from nowhere, is to escape from our world, as well as the nature (in sense of Mencian optimism about human nature) and thus task of being human. Skidelsky's reproach against Cassirer is that he ultimately doesn't give us the ethical and intellectual certainties of a "God" principle, or its secular variant such as Truth or Reason.[32] But, as Cassirer has repeatedly emphasized, the *impossibility* of absolutes opens the way for the distinct dignity of human beings—that of creating the forms in which we realize ourselves: "The ethical world is never given; it is forever in the making" (EM 61). Instead of pining for an unavailable absolute, we should see our human predicament in a positive light, and embrace it:

> And if we return from the Hegelian notion of *idea* to the Kantian, from idea as "absolute power" to idea as "infinite problem," we must, of course, give up the speculative optimism of the Hegelian view of history. But, by doing so, we also give up fatalistic pessimism with its prophecies and visions of decline. With this, human action again has an opportunity to determine itself by its own power and through its own answers, knowing full well that the direction and future of civilization are dependent upon this kind of determination. (NHPC 38)

As Cassirer writes, while the possibility of an absolute might seem like a comforting promise, it is also simultaneously a fatalism. It is to return to a substance view of the world, where all is already determined, and all freedom comes from subjecting ourselves to this given. For Skidelsky, because Cassirer has a functional conception of the human being as "raising up to humanity through culture," this results in an inability to defend a human essence, that is, "human rights." Relatedly, because Cassirer understands religion from a secular perspective—as a mere expression of human culture, there is no transcendental authority, and thus external tribunal against which to judge our action (Skidelsky 2008, 232–36). However, as Richard Rorty writes, "From a pragmatist's point of view, the notion of 'inalienable human rights' is no better and no worse a slogan than that of 'obedience to the will of God'" (1999, 83). We only evoke final vocabularies such as "human rights" and "God" when we have given up the humanist faith that the Other *is* ultimately human, and we can and therefore should empathetically talk to each other. Cassirer's ethical project is, I think, a reformulation of the Vico formula:[33] "All that can be said on this score is that culture will advance just to the extent that the truly creative powers, which in the final analysis are only brought into play by our own efforts, are not forsaken or crippled" (*NHPC* 37). We will survive for as long as we have faith in our human capacities. We should bring ourselves to remember, however—and this was, in part, what this project has strived to do—that Confucianism had always been anti-foundationalist in a way that I think is comparable to Cassirer's vision.

If there is no view from nowhere, no universal, to guide our actions, then the only possible measure comes in the form of comparing our own actions and practices with those of others. Under this paradigm, it is in our own interest to preserve the diversity of cultures, for it is only when alternatives exist that we can understand ourselves. We can become kinder, more considerate, and freer only by observing the practices of others. As Confucius tells us in *Analects* 7.22, in the company of two other persons, we are bound to learn something from among them; we can learn from their good actions as well as their bad.[34] Operative here, of course, is the assumption that the faults of others *are* of relevance to oneself; after all, we are all human, and subject to the same failings. Confucius could not have become a moral exemplar living on his own in a desert, deducing universal ethical principles from foolproof first premises or waiting for some divine revelation (like the early Church fathers); it is only among the company of others, and what's more, others different from himself, that he learns. This is why Confucianism embraces harmony and holism as opposed to universalism. To know that one's perspective is *not* universal is to realize the (Gadamerian) point that the universal is not a given; it must—like Goethe's *Urphänomen*—be reached through the broadening of one's perspectives, through the stringing together of *diverse* phenomena. It is something to be *arrived* at as a result of an intellectual labor that creatively orders a myriad of phenomena. It is only through empathetic understanding of other perspectives that we can come to a meta or reflective understanding of our own positions. Once we give up the idea of universals, we are pushed toward empathy as opposed to prejudice, dialogue as opposed to dominance. Historically, the condescension against (other) culture(s), if not outright intolerance, comes from the view that one already has Truth. Once one has Truth, what need has one of culture or of learning from other cultures?

The project of being human is much like an architect's project of world-making: it is not a contemplative science, and there can be no formulaic absolutes that will relieve us of the actual task of making our world (i.e., determinate, constitutive vs. reflective, regulative judgement). The job of the architect does not consist in refining a formula that would be applicable for all contexts. It is childish to think that *the* "solution" to good environments lies in the discovery (or perfection) of a universally applicable magical formula. Only the utilitarian calculus of building developers takes such a formula to be sufficient for the "problem" of building environments; and in so doing they impoverish our lived environments (as our environments are multifaceted and cannot be measured through one standard). No formula can be a substitute for the imagination that both goes into harmonizing a whole swathe of (often conflicting) demands, and also simultaneously makes the product of those utilitarian demands into a *meaningful* form. Nor, therefore, does the job of the architect consist in eradicating the ugly parts of a building (e.g. mechanical servicing).

Just as the making of our physical world lies in imaginatively harmonizing a heterogeneity of human needs, the making of our cultural world lies in imaginatively harmonizing the human being's various spiritual expressions. The fact that there are better and worse architects means that the imaginative power of the architect is something that is hard-won and requires effort. As Skidelsky has written, Cassirer's project is to comprehend the varieties of culture as an organic whole. The next chapter will provide a philosophical defense, with an eye towards the Confucian tradition, of how this idea of culture as an organic whole can be intellectually tractable. This holism will, contra Skidelsky, be a robust alternative to the idea that we need a standpoint *outside* of culture(s).

6

Wu Yi Wu Wen (物一无文)

Organic Harmony

This chapter argues that Cassirer's philosophy of symbolic forms and Confucianism share a similar philosophical model for reconciling the part with the whole: the harmony found in the organic world.[1] Cassirer's dissatisfaction with both the mere heterogeneity of empiricism and the homogenizing unity of dogmatic rationalism led to his valorization of, and taking inspiration from, Goethe's idealistic morphology, Humboldt's account of language, and Herder's account of history. The "organic universal" that underlies the project of all three figures is, for Cassirer, rooted in Leibniz's *Monadology* and Leibniz famously studied the *Yijing*. The nature of Cassirer's own project of "harmony in contrariety" among the symbolic forms as well as that of his four forebears is elucidated via the Confucian project of harmony. Confucian harmony is premised on the idea found in the *Monadology* and the organic world that, although all things uniquely follow their internal dictates, this does not redound to conflict and chaos.

This last chapter will also pick up the idea introduced in the first chapter that many of the characteristics of Cassirer's philosophy and Chinese philosophy can be understood as rooted in a nonsubstance ontology. A different way of understanding this nonsubstance philosophy is to understand it in terms of the paradigm of the organic. Historically, Cassirer traces the genesis of this paradigm to Leibniz. Leibniz, in turn, had a formative influence on the philosophers of the *Goethezeit*—Goethe, Humboldt, Herder—of whom Cassirer can be seen as a legacy. Leibniz is a crucial figure in this story, as the "organic" philosophy that he is understood to have introduced to Western philosophy bears striking similarities to a worldview conventionally understood as distinctively "Chinese"—correlative cosmology—which is another way of describing an organicist worldview.[2] The ideal of education in *Bildung*, the idea that a material manifesting consummates an implicit potential, the idea of the relational connectedness of all things, and finally the idea of harmony as a midway between chaos and sameness, can all be understood as characteristics of an "organicist" worldview.

Cassirer and "Harmony in Contrariety" between the Symbolic Forms

In the closing paragraph of *An Essay on Man*, first published in 1944—a summary of his *Philosophy of Symbolic Forms*—Cassirer writes:

> Philosophy cannot give up its search for a fundamental unity in this ideal world. But it does not confound this unity with simplicity. It does not overlook the tensions and frictions, the strong contrasts and deep conflicts between the various powers of man [the different symbolic forms]. These cannot be reduced to a common denominator. They tend in different directions and obey different principles. But this multiplicity and disparateness does not denote discord or disharmony. All these functions complete and complement one another. Each one opens a new horizon and shows us a new aspect of humanity. The dissonant is in harmony with itself; the contraries are not mutually exclusive, but interdependent: "harmony in contrariety, as in the case of the bow and the lyre."[3] (*EM* 228)

For Cassirer, the "search for a fundamental unity" that does not reduce to mere identity with a "common denominator" is not merely a scholastic question; it is the ethical task of philosophy.

Cassirer's dilemma can be put as follows: How can we do justice to the uniqueness of each particular without redounding to a (irreconcilable) heterogeneity: to "accidents" that are merely accidently next to each other? How can the uniqueness of the particular be preserved while simultaneously seeing it as part of a larger, meaningful (coherent) whole? Cassirer's question is ultimately about the relationship between the particular and the universal. The ideal "harmony" among particulars after which Cassirer is seeking is captured by Goethe: "Fortunately, we have the conviction that many things which would like to replace each other, can and must exist side by side, the world spirit is more tolerant than one thinks" (Goethe 1981, 741; also quoted in Cassirer 2004, 134). How can this poetic optimism about a harmonious order among heterogenous particulars become intellectually tractable? Relatedly, in *The Confucian Philosophy of Harmony*, Chenyang Li claims that, "if we were to choose just one word to characterize the Chinese ideal way of life, that word would be 'harmony.' Harmony is the most cherished ethical and social ideal in Chinese culture, particularly in Confucianism" (Li 2014, 1). A canonical expression of this harmony among difference occurs in *Analects* 13.23: "The gentleman harmonizes [和], and does not make himself identical [同]. The petty man makes himself identical [同], but he does not harmonize [和]" (my translation). A comparably confident assertion of harmony in contrariety can be found in the *Zhongyong*: "All things are nurtured together and do not cause injury to one another; the various ways [*dao* 道] travel together and do not harm each other [*xiang-bei* 相悖]"[4] (my translation). Cassirer's solution to the dualism between the universal and the particular, I argue, is modelled on the reciprocal relationship between the part and the whole found in the organic world,[5] and thus bears comparison with the Confucian understanding of harmony—which has been called "correlative thinking."

In an organicist paradigm,[6] heterogenous particulars can coexist without threatening the law of the whole. The relationship between the part and the "whole" under the model of the "organic universal" is one where each part is internally driven (*ziran* 自然) but requires for its completion the other parts of the whole. The "whole" is understood to be the functional law[7] derived from all the parts; but it is more than merely the sum of its parts. The whole is thus not a substantial "thing" but a dynamic and evolving law. What characterizes the organic universal is the constancy of change and, relatedly, the spontaneous arising of novelty from the interaction of the parts.[8]

Conversely, because it is the constancy of change that characterizes the organic universal, there are no static laws that can determine/describe the causal relations that exist within its parts. Each thing is self-causing, and so causes are impossible to describe in a unilinear way. The coherence among the parts is instead explained through an attunement (*ganying* 感应) between the parts. The Aristotelian view of nature, on the other hand, is that all motion in the world is set into motion by an unmoved mover (*Physics* 258b10–259a20; Aristotle 2018, 154–55). Nothing in the physical world moves of its own accord, as its movement must be caused by something external and necessary (*Physics* 258b26–33; Aristotle 2018, 155). Things that are more powerful are higher up in this hierarchy and move the lower, "for that which exceeds in power, i.e. the more powerful, is prior; and such is that according to whose choice the other—i.e., the posterior—must follow, so that if the prior does not set it in motion the other does not move, and if it sets it in motion it does move; and here choice is a beginning" (*Metaphysics* 1018b19–1018b25; Aristotle 1984, 1608). This hierarchical idea of causality is alien to the organicist paradigm, whereby movement and "cause" is explained through the mutual responsiveness of all the self-soing parts and is thus impossible to map out in terms of static laws.

A characteristically Confucian element in this correlative thinking is the thought that it is ethically correct human behavior that allows this organicist harmony to continue (i.e., humans forming a triad with heaven and earth, *ren can tian di* 人叄天地). This subjective turn in Confucianism can be paralleled with the subjective turn of the *Critique of Teleological Judgement*, which similarly reconciles the simultaneous necessity and conventionality of our way of knowing Nature. Cassirer read Goethe, Humboldt, and Herder as critical idealists (especially after the fashion of the third Critique). This subjectivism-perspectivism necessarily entails intellectual humility and, relatedly, pluralism.[9] In sum, the (organic) whole is the *functional* law that is derived from the totality of *all* particulars, and so there is an inherent mutual dependence of the whole on *all* particulars. Furthermore, the Confucian tradition's stress on harmony and disparagement of identity (*tong* 同) elucidates the ethical point implicit in Cassirer's unrelenting assault on the dogma of substance (which he identifies with "the myth of the given") and is continuous in his entire oeuvre: the Confucian and Cassirerian (ethical) ideal is harmony as opposed to identity.

In *The Confucian Philosophy of Harmony*, Chenyang Li argues that the conventional Western understanding of harmony is in terms of a naive, passive agreement (and, worse, oppression) (Li 2014, 7–8).[10] The West has ironically (mis)understood Chinese harmony in terms of its opposite—identity. For Li, this "innocent harmony" or identity (exem-

plary of which are the Platonic forms and Pythagorean numbers) is contrasted, for Western interpreters, against its more preferable counterpart
"justice," whereby each person asserts their own rights, even if it leads
to continuous conflicts. The Western (mis)understanding of Chinese
harmony is tellingly symptomatic of a deep-seated dualistic metaphysics
that Cassirer tried to overcome (through what I take to be a Chinese
conception of harmony). As Li has shown, the only rubric the West
has for understanding accord is in terms of identity, which is contrasted
with its dualistic antithesis, an anarchic heterogeneity. This dualism is, I
would argue, following Cassirer, the result of a metaphysics of "Being."
Li points out that, because Chinese metaphysics never presupposed a
preestablished order—Being—it is characterized by a dynamic process that
seeks to harmonize a plurality of heterogenous elements (1). As we will
see, I think Cassirer agrees with this assessment about the relationship
between Being, identity, and homogeneity.

For Cassirer "Being" possesses an "absolutist character"; it cannot
tolerate difference, because difference falls into its opposite, nonbeing,
as we see in the philosophy of Parmenides. "Being" leads to dualisms:
either identity or nothingness (Cassirer 1949, 872).[11] A functional "order,"
however, is marked by "differentiation and inner multiplicity" (Cassirer
1969, 8). Order *requires* diversity, because unity/sameness does not need
ordering—unity/sameness is already identical with itself.[12] The concept
of order is tolerant of difference because order is a functional law that
is comprised by the parts that compose it. Pluralism is inherent in the
idea of order (i.e., a functional law) and is synonymous with harmony:
it is only when there is diversity within a manifold that we talk about
harmony; if the manifold was homogenous, then we speak merely of
identity—the characteristic of Being. The functional law as the concept
of order is thus synonymous with harmony or "organic harmony."

There are six interrelated characteristics of this "organicist" paradigm. (1) Structuralism, the order of things is the "resonant" relationship
between the parts (*yin-yang*; *yang/yin* trigrams; the 64 hexagrams—all of
these aspects of Chinese philosophy are similar to the symbolic relationship
talked about by Cassirer). (2) Hermeneutic laws are avowedly merely
conventional. (3) Understanding a situation is based on a subjective
judgment arrived at through consultation with hermeneutic laws in
relation to a given situation. (4) Pluralism-perspectivism is assumed. (5)
Change or causality is not understood as due to a hierarchy of causes, but
rather due to particulars mutually affecting each other. (6) The utmost

knowing manifests itself in allowing life itself to continue. The governing ethos behind the Confucian model of knowledge is that there is no
form of knowledge that can take us to that "place beyond the heavens"
of which Plato speaks in the *Phaedrus* (247c–d; SMC 53) and thus no
unmediated access to truth.[13] This leads to an emphasis on pluralism in
the modes of knowing, and an emphasis on subjective judgment. The
Confucian and Cassirerian ideal of knowledge is an affirmation of life.
In Cassirer's eyes, the "insight into the finitude of human existence" for
both Kant and Goethe "is not identical with the idea of the nothingness
of that existence" (2007a, 558); and we can perhaps say the same for
the Confucians. Human understanding is *merely* discursive understanding,
but the very discursiveness of that knowledge means that it has no final
telos. And this is its virtue: there is no ultimate knowledge that will put
an end to knowledge itself; knowledge is a living process of growth and
regeneration and is, furthermore, pluralistic.

These six characteristics are found in both Cassirer's thought, his
assessment of Goethe, Humboldt, and Herder, and in Chinese philosophy.
First, let us look to Cassirer's assessment of this organic paradigm in the
thought of his intellectual forebears.

The Dogma of Substance versus
(Critical Idealist) Unity as Function

Cassirer starts from an empiricist (or phenomenological) position in
affirming the particularity of the various manifestations of spirit but
does not rest content with mere heterogeneity. For Cassirer, we cannot
be content with a relativism whereby different particulars are merely
quantitively next to each other; but nor can we be content with a
dogmatic metaphysics that would seek unity via an absolute identity
among all the particulars to a "substance." The dogmatic metaphysics
that Cassirer has in mind is demonstrated by his critique of Aristotelian
substance ontology and the logic of concept formation that accompanies
it. There are two principal problems Cassirer associates with it: the
concept is either an empty descriptor or it is an arbitrary descriptor;
both of which does injustice to the richness of our world. (1) In traditional, Aristotelian logic, we ascend from the species to the higher
genus through increasing abstraction, by abandoning certain characteristics, and, in this process, we draw a larger range of objects into the

circle. The increasing extension of the concept, however, is inversely proportional to its intension, so that in the most general concept of all—Being (*ousia*)—there is no definite content. The most universal of all concepts, the concept that can be applied to all particulars would thus be empty (*SF* 6). (2) Cassirer also criticizes the Aristotelian theory of concept-formation because the essential properties (the species and genera), which are presumed to be shared by a set of individual substances, are only *arbitrarily* chosen from a manifold of potential relations. When we select "similar" properties from a manifold, we merely take a *part* to characterize and be representative of the whole. The property that we select as explaining the whole is understood to be the "essential" moment by which the whole is determined, but there is, in fact, nothing to assure us that the common properties that we select include the truly typical features, which characterize and determine the members of the group (*SF* 6–7). Cassirer would be in accord with the pragmatists about "the philosophical fallacy"—that is, "the abstracting of some one element from the organism which gives it meaning, and setting it up as absolute" and then proceeding to revere this one element "as the cause and ground of all reality and knowledge" (Dewey 1969, 162).

For Cassirer, we cannot define, and we cannot explain, the world's unity through any system of metaphysical determinism. For this unity is not a given thing and thus cannot be made *certain* as in a correspondence theory of truth whereby we appeal to a corresponding "thing" (or transcendent prototype) that underlies our representations. This unity is an idea and an ideal, and, as such, it "must be understood in a *dynamic* sense, instead of conceiving it in a static sense. It must be produced, and in this production consists the essential meaning of culture and its *ethical value*" (*SMC* 90; my emphasis). Our ethical task is to produce a unity among particulars that simultaneously does justice to their particularity. This unity cannot be a "thing" (and must instead be dynamic), for this would imply, as we have seen, that either (1) this "thing" would be so empty of content that it becomes an empty descriptor ("Being") or (2) it would have a limited number of characteristics that we arbitrarily take to represent the whole, and these characteristics cannot change and thus becomes anachronistic in the face of an always emergent reality. In (neo-)Kantian terms, the "universal" is to be arrived at through *reflective* as opposed determinative judgment—the universal has to be "produced." Relatedly, it is *regulative* as opposed to constitutive judgment, because the unity is subject to change, and as such "dynamic."

In the philosophies of Leibniz, Goethe, Humboldt, and Herder, Cassirer sees a relationship between the part and the whole unavailable to either empiricism or dogmatic rationalism. The paradigm of organic harmony, which is ultimately derived from Leibniz, overcomes the dualism between mere heterogeneity and homogeneity; and in so doing reconciles the particular and the universal (whole). The next sections will look at the part-whole problem in Goethe's idealistic morphology, Humboldt's theory of language, and Herder's view of history. Each figure rejected the Aristotelian relationship of part-whole in terms of genus and species: no static part can characterize the whole. The whole is, furthermore, not empty of content (unlike Being)—it is the totality of (but greater than the sum of) the parts: it is a functional/organic whole. The reality of nature, language, and history is a continuous whole (both spatially and temporally) and can only be understood from the totality of their partic-ular manifestations. Spatially speaking, no static part can be prioritized as more essential than any other part, and thus taken to characterize the whole. Temporally speaking, the parts are constantly evolving, so that the whole is also constantly evolving; it therefore makes no sense to freeze a characteristic to describe the whole (for all time). The relationship of the part and the whole must be seen as a constantly evolving one that the human subject produces, through simultaneous attention to the particulars (*guan* 观), and via their own creative imagination.

At a time when a wealth of information was pouring into Europe, it is significant that rationalists like Descartes and Spinoza take no interest in other cultures. The thought goes that, if we all used our reason cor-rectly, we would all arrive at the same opinions or knowledge, so there would be no need to engage with other cultures. Herder posited against these rationalist philosophers that there exists radical spiritual (*geistig*) differences between different historical periods and nations. Against the dogmatism of the rationalists, Herder recognized a plurality of "reasons" and is often seen as the founding father of the view that each of the world's nations has a specific and unique character (Sikka 2011, 1). Truth lies in the whole. Similarly, Goethe's ideal of "world literature" is embodied by the idea that one can conceptualize all the literatures of the world as a symphonic whole while maintaining the individuality of each work (Said 2003, xviii). Wilhelm von Humboldt is famous for the view that different languages create different worldviews (Cassirer 2013c, 120–21). The embrace of cultural pluralism in these thinkers, in contrast to the rationalists, is because their worldviews are informed by a different philosophical paradigm: the organic. We will first see how the paradigm of the organic operated in Leibniz, before seeing how Cassirer saw similar (Leibnizian) characteristics in Goethe, Humboldt, and Herder.

Leibniz and Organism

For Cassirer, the *Monadology* eliminated all dualistic separation between the particular and the whole, and Leibniz did this through the revolutionary idea of the monad. In the philosophy of the monad, the general [*Allgemeine*] does not make particular disappear; rather the general allows the particular to lay the foundation for its own meaning (FF 26). What allowed the *Mondalogy* to provide this reconciliation, as against the mechanistic-physical naturalism of Spinoza, was the organicist worldview that it entailed. In the *Monadology*, the "foundation for a new philosophy of the organic was laid" (PE 84).[14] In this organic (qualitative as opposed to quantitative) relation, the whole can only be conceived through the particular, and the particular can be determined and defined only in its relationship with the whole. The relational law that binds the elements together, as opposed to the mechanical-spatial conception, is not merely incidental and adds nothing to the definition of the parts; the relational law instead defines the elements.

In Leibniz's *Monadology*, each monad is unique and self-existent in that it is cut off from all external influence and follows its own law. Each individual apprehends the whole from a different point of view and thus gives to its representation a particular distinctness and a unique stamp. These "unique perspectives" of the universe are bound to one another, however, by a fundamental coherence that pertains between them all (*KLT* 287). Each individual part is unique, furthermore, in the sense that every monad cannot be reduced to the sum of its merely static qualities. The monad manifests itself in its effects. The monad is what it *is* in virtue of its activity, in virtue of the continuous transition from one state to another, which it produces out of itself. Its present state is a consequence of its preceding state and is also pregnant with the future. The monad is a thing evolving in time (SMC 101). This change is change into greater variety. This view of time leads Leibniz to be "a pluralist, not a monist" (101).

For Cassirer, this new conception of substance in terms of force and change "lends an entirely new significance to the problem of the individual entity" (PE 32). Whereas in analytical logic, the logic of identity, the individual can only be determined and understood when it is subsumed under a general concept and when it renounces its individuality, the Leibnizian monad no longer functions as merely an instantiation of a general concept. It expresses something essential in itself. This is because the monad, as in organic life, exists only so far as it evolves in time. Life is not a thing but a process (EM 49). The relationship between parts can thus no longer to be reduced to the properties of substances, to analytical identity, but must be understood dynamically. There is a dynamic mutually defining relationship between the parts and of the part with the whole. The idea of a thing evolving in time and in reciprocal exchange with the whole overcame the antinomy between the particular and the universal.[15]

Cassirer's Interpretation of Goethe's Idealistic Morphology

In the fourth volume of Das Erkenntnisproblem, Cassirer argues that, since Aristotle, there had been "an inner bond between logic and biology" (PK 124). Aristotle's logic was one of class concepts:

> The biological species signifies both the end towards which the living individual strives and the immanent force by which its evolution is guided. The logical doctrine of the construc- tion of the concept and of definition can [for Aristotle] only be built up with reference to these fundamental relations of the real. The determination of the concept according to the next higher genus and its specific difference reproduces the process by which the real substance successively unfolds itself in its special forms of being. Thus it is this basic conception of substance to which the purely logical theories of Aristotle constantly have reference. (SF 7)

The essence of the organism is the end toward which it is teleologically striving. For Goethe, however, "Nature and art are too great to aim at ends, and they don't need to either. There are relations everywhere, and relations are life" (Goethe, in letter to Friedrich Karl Zelter, January 29, 1830, as quoted in Cassirer 2007a, 548). The relation between the particular and the universal (life), was, according to Goethe, not one of (Aristotelian) logical subsumption nor one of induction but of ideal or "symbolic" representation. Goethe once defined life as "the rotating movement of the monad about itself" (*die rotierende Bewegung der Monas um sich selbst*; *Maxims and Reflections* 391 in Goethe 1949, 135; *PSF* 4:127). Because life *is* dynamism and change, it cannot be defined according to Aristotelian logic. For Goethe, the part and the whole are mutually defining, and dynamically evolving. To see this reciprocal relationship, however, requires the subject to be inwardly mobile to the flux of phenomena, and through their own "reflective judgement" pull the part and the whole (momentarily) together in an act of imagination (Goethe 1988, 31, 64).

The dominant biological paradigms of Goethe's time followed Aristotelian class concepts: Carl Linnaeus's[16] (1707–78) concept of "species" and Georges Cuvier's (1769–1832) idea of "type." In the generic Linnaean system, nature was understood by arranging it in the pigeonholes of our concepts such as species and genera, into families, classes, and orders (Cassirer 2007a, 549). It should be highlighted that Linnaeus's taxonomy of *Systema Naturae*'s, published in 1735, included human races: he was in fact the first to scientifically divide people up into large distinct groups (Marks 1995, 50). Neither sufficed for Goethe in understanding nature. Goethe inveighed against abstracting a single part from the flow of experience, as it destroys the continuity that is an integral dimension of reality. For Goethe, all of nature forms a whole, and *all* parts partake of the whole. Statements about the inseparable wholeness of nature abound in his writings on nature. "The things we call the parts in every living being are so inseparable from the whole that they may be understood only in and with the whole" (Goethe 1988, 8; in the essay "A Study Based on Spinoza"). "Ultimately we will see the whole world of animals as a great element in which one species is created, or at least sustained, by and through another" (Goethe 1988, 56; in the essay "Toward a General Comparative Theory").[17] "An individual cannot serve as a standard for the whole, and so we must not seek the model for all in any one" (*PK* 144; Cassirer is quoting from Goethe's essay "Entwurf einer vergleichenden Anatomie").

For Goethe, the "type" could not be understood merely spatially and statically; it had to be understood dynamically—for otherwise what we understood would be merely dead matter. "To be sure, what is alive can be dissected into its component parts, but from these parts it will be impossible to restore it and bring it back to life" (Goethe 1988, 63). "But if we look at all these *Gestalten*, especially the organic ones, we will discover that nothing in them is permanent, nothing is at rest or defined—everything is in a flux of continual motion" (63). For Goethe, Cuvier's classificatory logic, by erecting rigid and insurmountable barriers, would sharply separate the continuity of nature and reduce it to *disjecta membra*, which are merely accidentally next to each other. Life *is* inasmuch as it is dynamic and an integrated whole. Neither Linnaeus's concept of species nor Cuvier's idea of type could capture the dynamism and holism of life.

For Goethe, the Linnaean system and Cuvier's concept of type were misguided in that they arbitrarily took the part or a static relation to represent an always continuous and dynamic whole. Although Goethe did not reject the idea of types, as he regarded the description of nature as impossible without it, for Goethe, the type is that which is only perceived dynamically. Goethe described it as a "Proteus" (1988, 121). In Goethe's idealistic morphology, the relationship between the part and the whole is neither inductive nor deductive: "This whole is no longer attained by the gradual progress from the particular, but appears and pulls itself together at the same moment in a point, in a concrete symbol" (*FF* 212). This symbol, furthermore, requires the (creative imagination of the) human subject to come into existence. This "symbol" is Goethe's concept of *Urphänomen* (archetypal phenomenon).

Goethe thought that in the archetypal phenomenon he was able to take viewing (*Anschauung*) into a higher form. Goethe's way of seeing (intuitive observation—"*Anschauung*") cannot be reduced to the hypothetico-deductive method, as Goethe saw life as perpetually in flux. Instead of reducing reality to static schemas, the Goethean scientist must remain inwardly mobile in her observations through participating in the metamorphosis of the phenomena themselves so as to cultivate the mode of representation that the phenomena, which is in perpetual flux, demands. The self is thus transformed in its ability to see the *natura naturans* of phenomena; and this transformed self is in turn "co-creative" in the construction of phenomena. It is only in the dynamic, dialectical relationality between the subject and phenomena that we can talk about an inner law. We must become inwardly mobile so as to become acquainted with the manifold variability of phenomena so that we may be ready to pursue the *protean* type through all its changes such that it never slips away from us. The archetypal phenomena have a particular pregnancy that enables them to disclose the context or series of which they form a part. The archetypal phenomenon is thus not immediately given in experience; it has to be constructed by the subject out of the phenomenological experience. It is because of the emphasis on the dynamism and holism of reality and the role of the human subject in creating a "symbol" that momentarily represents the relationship between the part and the whole that "there prevails in his [Goethe's] writings a relationship of the 'particular' to the 'universal' such as can hardly be found elsewhere in the history of philosophy or of natural science" (*PK* 145).[18] For Cassirer, Goethe's idea of "morphological idealism" was enabled in a formative way by Leibniz.[19] It was Goethe who first coined the word *morphology* (Cassirer 2007a, 549),[20] and in it we can see all the traces of Leibniz's *Monadology* (*FF* 33). Goethe's idealistic morphology abandons the naive teleology of Aristotelian physics; the organic object is not defined through a formal essence toward which it will teleologically and deterministically fulfill. In a highly illuminating passage in the fourth volume of *Das Erkenntnisproblem*, Cassirer traces the connection between Leibniz, Herder, and the idealistic morphology of Goethe and Jakob von Uexküll (1864–1944).[21] While in Aristotle's teleology, nature ultimately serves the ends of human beings,[22] Uexküll's biology, in its struggle against materialism and mechanism, holds fast to the idea of inner purposiveness. Here every organism has its center of gravity within itself; it is *ziran* (自然). "This basic conception . . . goes back to the philosophy of Leibniz" (*PK* 203), and it "is remarkable to see how exactly the plan and development of Uexhüll's biology conformed in every particular with this view of Goethe" (205).

Humboldt and Language

Statements to the effect that language is a living organism abound in Humboldt's writings. In his famous Kawi Introduction, for example, he writes that "language, in direct conjunction with mental power is a fully-fashioned *organism*" (Humboldt 1999, 90), and "under no circumstances can a language be examined liked a dead plant. *Language* and *life* are inseparable concepts" (93). Elsewhere he writes that language has an "organic nature, and that must be treated as such" (1968, 4, 10). In sum, as Michael Losonsky writes, "Humboldt by nature is a holist about human beings" (2006, 85). Since language is not the "dead skeleton" (Humboldt 1968, VI, 147) of an inert collection of words and grammatical laws but is instead a living and dynamic organism, we cannot merely understand language mechanically, through its mere products—*Ergon* (*natura naturata*)—but must also see it as an activity: *Energia* (*natura naturans*) (Humboldt 1999, 49). As a living organism, language cannot be sufficiently described through static laws, just as organic life cannot be described through an enumeration of its parts: language is dynamic and constituted by its relationships. The unity of the vocabulary of each language is instead a whole, resting on "*connections*, guided by the affinity of concepts" (Humboldt 1999, 94). As Cassirer writes on Humboldt's behalf, "the content of the spirit can be conceived only in activity and as activity" (*PSF* 1:160). In the organic world, the mutual influence of the parts constantly create novelty. In the organic conception of language, each particular speech act stands in a *reciprocal* relationship to "the" language as a universal. The universal here is not a self-contained, already integral, independent, substantial "thing" that is juxtaposed to its individuals; rather, the universal exists as the functional law of the totality of specific individuals. There is a spontaneity and dynamism to the organic that cannot be exhaustively captured through universal and necessary laws; it *is* inasmuch as it is active and changes. Inasmuch as organic "being" is constantly becoming, it cannot be universally and necessarily determined for all time, and therein lies its *freedom* (from causal necessity). Language "as an organism, which situated the organic process *between* nature and freedom, hence subjected it to no absolute necessity but left a certain amount of free play between the different possibilities" (*PSF* 1:169). The "essence" of language is its livingness, growth, birth, vitality. "It was through this fusion of the idea of organic form with the idea of totality that Wilhelm von Humboldt arrived at his philosophical view which implied a fundamental new approach to the problem of language" (155). The true "essence" of language, unlike the concept formation of Aristotelian syllogism is not arrived at through abstraction of all differentiation of the mere products—its *Ergon*; but because it is constantly becoming, its "essence" must be disclosed through the totality of (ongoing) differentiations whose source is the *Energia* of language. A language is like an organism in that it is like a "web," "meshwork," or "net," and each uttered expression "intimates [*antönt*] and presupposes the whole of language" (quoted in Glock 2015, 382).

Furthermore, because Humboldt saw language as a spontaneous organ for *creating* reality—human language is "divinely free" (Humboldt 1999, 24); there is a "*creative principle*" or "*artistically* creative principle"

(214, 91). Each language is objective in relation to the speaker. Accordingly, it is only the totality of these different views that constitutes the universal of "language," and it is the totality of these different views that constitutes the "objectivity attainable by man" (*PSF* 1:159). "Since all objective perception is inevitably tinged with *subjectivity*, we may consider every human individual . . . as a unique aspect of the world-view" (Humboldt 1999, 59). "Each language is a note in the harmony of man's universal nature" (*PSF* 1:159). In his conception of individual languages as "monads" representing the whole from their individual points of view, and the harmony and whole of these perspectives constituting the reality of the phenomenal world, Humboldt expanded the "universal-idealistic view implicit in the general principles of the Leibnizian philosophy" (159).

Herder and History

In Cassirer's view, the results of the new relationship between the part and the whole of Leibniz's organicist philosophy "are discernible in the interpretation of history and the philosophy of history prior to its influence in biology. Here it was Herder who helped the idea to achieve its ultimate victory" (*PK* 203). As a means of emphasizing the radical nature of Herder's breakthroughs, Cassirer contrasts the antithetical attitudes to history in Herder's forbears: the rationalists and the Enlightenment philosophical historiographers like Bayle, Montesquieu, and Voltaire. Herder's revolution consisted in that (1) he overcame the rationalistic ideal of knowledge that denigrated history because it could not provide necessary truths. This is to be paralleled with Cassirer's first critique of Aristotelian concept formation whereby "Being" is an empty descriptor. (2) He overcame the (Enlightenment) "unhistorical history" that used history as the raw data in which to find permanent, uniform, and constant properties of human nature. This is to be paralleled with Cassirer's second critique of Aristotelian concept formation whereby we commit the philosophical fallacy of taking a part to characterize an always emergent reality. Because Herder rejected these two points, (3) he (after Vico) was the first to break from the Enlightenment narrative of universal history that saw the values and interests of eighteenth-century Europe as universal. Herder "fought the naïve belief of the Enlightenment in

progress and the view of man as the goal of creation, and of the educated
man of that century particularly as the goal of all humanity" (PK 203).
Herder is instead guided by the pluralistic belief that "each nation has
its *center* of happiness *in itself*, like every sphere its center of gravity!"
(Herder 2002, 297). Herder thus gave place to the uniqueness of particulars and could thereby affirm history, as well as different epochs and
cultures (cosmopolitanism).

    For Cassirer, when Herder writes, "But not a thing in the whole
of God's realm, am I able to persuade myself though!, is *only* means—
everything *means* and *purpose* simultaneously, and hence certainly these
centuries [are so] too" (Herder 2002, 310), Herder transposed Kant's
kingdom of ends to the human, historical world. There is no final *telos*
under which all particulars are subsumed. Our values are to be found
within the immanent particularity of humanity, which is inherently
plural and heterogeneous: Herder makes no attempt "to capture the
ever-flowing life of history in the circular movement of metaphysical
thought" (LCS 12). For him there is no fixed course, predetermined and
prescribed by the nature of spirit (12), and thus the "meaning and value
of the development of humanity could be comprehended only in the
totality of all its forms" (PK 203–4). Herder broke the spell of "analytical
thinking and of the principle of identity," for history "dispels the illusion
of identity; it knows nothing really identical, nothing that ever recurs
in the same form" (PE 231). Herder, like Hume, was able to preserve
the individuality of particular events and peoples; but, unlike Hume,
he was able to do so within a *unity* that draws all these particularities
together with no loss to their individuality. But the individual events in
history, although not identical, are also not merely scattered fragments
(*disjecta membra*). The course of history is thus the course of *life* itself.
Like life, each moment is unique, but its uniqueness does not thereby
render it meaningless. Each unique moment of life can be framed within
a narrative whole without obliterating its individuality. The unity that
emerges—which does not reduce to mere simplicity or identity—arises
from the relational law that all the particular facts, in association with
each other, compose. Herder gets around the antagonistic dualisms of
rationalism and empiricism by neither seeing the particular fact as a
mere instantiation of a general law nor letting the empirical particular
rest merely in its particularity. The particular gains significance by virtue
of the relationships it enters; it takes place as a member of a course of
events in a narrative nexus.

Like Humboldt's view that the truth about language lay in its liv-ingness, its becoming (*Energia*), and like Goethe's view that the reality about nature lay in its fluctuations, similarly for Herder, history is the exact opposite of its temporal separateness. History only has meaning if and as it refers back to a past and forward to a future. History only has meaning in a living, relational nexus. For Cassirer, the Herderian conception of history is integrally indebted to Leibniz's *praegnans future*: "It was this new metaphysical concept of time and this metaphysical valuation of individuality that proved to be decisive for the evaluation of historical thought" (SMC 102). Apart from the idea that a "thing" must be defined dynamically, in relation to its past and future, we can see the Leibnizian influence clearly in Herder when he writes that "all dissections of sensation in the case of *Buffon's*, *Condillac's*, and *Bonnet's* sensing human being are abstractions; the philosopher has to neglect one thread of sensation in pursuing the other, but in nature all these threads are a single web!" (Herder 2002, 107). Reality cannot result from the subsumption of the individual; it must be understood through the totality of all individuals.

In sum, the *Goethezeit* figures were the forefathers of the view that there is no universal for understanding the truth about human beings. What universal there is lies in embracing a pluralism of different per-spectives through which we rise above our provincialism to a relatively higher universalism. The normative moment of the idea of harmony is not, as is it usually mistaken to be, an anything-goes relativism. It is, instead, to *creatively* seek for a solution that overcomes the antinomies of chaos/particularism and identity.

Needham, Whitehead, and Correlative Cosmology

Like Cassirer, Joseph Needham thinks that "the part played by Leibniz in the history of philosophy was that of a bridge-builder. The antago-nistic viewpoints of theological idealism on the one hand and of atomic materialism on the other hand had been an antinomy which European thought had never succeeded in solving" (Needham 1956, 498)—until Leibniz's *Monadology*. For Needham, "It might almost be said that the monads were the first appearance of organisms upon the stage of occi-dental philosophy" (499). Leibniz's metaphysical system seems to arrive in European intellectual history fully mature, and without either religious or philosophical antecedents. Leibniz was also the first major Western thinker to seriously and sympathetically study Chinese philosophy. Such striking coincidences led Needham to take it for granted that Leibniz was influenced by Chinese (neo-Confucian) philosophy.[23] Needham points to three similarities between the *Monadology* and Chinese correlative thinking: (1) there is no dualism between Being and non-Being, only Becoming; (2) there is a mutually defining relationship between the part and the whole; and (3) there is what can be understood as the organic conception of influence. The difference between the mechanical and the organic lies in the fact that the organic parts influence each other, not through the mechanical cause of anything else, but according to the preestablished harmony of a larger plan. And this is characteristic of the "correlative thinking" of Dong Zhongshu (Needham 1956, 499–500).[24] In contrast to Western-style "subordinative thinking," which relates classes of things through substance and emphasizes mechanical causation, in Chinese correlative thinking, "conceptions are not subsumed under one another, but placed side by side in a *pattern*" (280). "The key-word in Chinese thought," for Needham, "is *Order* and above all *Pattern* (and, if I may whisper it for the first time, *Organism*)" (281). In the organic paradigm, *form* arises from particulars following their internal dictates, and is not externally imposed.

Whitehead credits Leibniz as the father of the philosophy of the organism (1948, 155–56). Whitehead himself characterizes his own process philosophy as "the philosophy of the organism," which approximates more to "some strains of Indian, or Chinese, thought, than to western Asiatic, or European thought" (1978, 7).

What I have been saying so far about the six interrelated characteristics of the organicist paradigm as exemplified in the thought of Leibniz, Goethe, Humboldt, and Herder is thus also to be found in Confucian metaphysics. Confucian metaphysics assumes that each particular is *ziran* and constantly changing, and so it is impossible to define a "thing" for all time. What knowledge one can have of things is like the knowledge offered by Goethe, Humboldt, and Herder: the relationships between things that requires the creative imagination of the subject to be arrived at. If we were to use Kantian vocabulary, we could say that it is akin to the reflective and regulative judgment of the third Critique. What this knowledge allows us, in turn, to do is to help the processes of life to continue.

Organicist Thinking in Confucianism

The kind of knowledge that Confucianism seeks is not a metaphysical determinism that gives us truths that, as in the mechanistic model, can apply in all contexts. Due to the (organicist) assumption that one needs to validate all particulars, and by extension the infinite ways in which these particulars can change, under this view, it is impossible to offer determinate truths. The Confucian model of knowledge rests instead on: (1) the affirmation of different perspectives; (2) the understanding of the relations that obtain between things, which is situational and thus always in need of reinterpretation; (3) the realization that the "truth" about things always requires personal judgment.

Within an organismic framework there is a constant production of novelty, so that our categories and classifications are always running short of a ceaselessly changing reality. *Xici* 2.8 expresses this as follows:

> As a manifestation of the Dao the *Changes* involves frequent shifts. Change and action never stand still but keep flowing all through the six vacancies. Rising and falling without any consistency, the hard and the soft lines change one into the other, something for which it is *impossible to make definitive laws*, since they are doing nothing but keeping pace with change.[25] (Lynn 1994, 89; my emphasis)

The only permanence is change and transition, and so the lawfulness of the whole is only ever momentarily grasped, before it loses its applicability in the face of a newly risen (or evolved) whole.[26] The constant evolution of the combinations means that from a given set of conditions, unpredictable orders of complexity might occur. It would be impossible to predict how "things" might change, because with enough change, the "rules" that govern "things" might mutate to a different order. Another way of expressing the idea of the unpredictability of change is to emphasize the absolute particularity of each thing or event (and its future evolution). It is because the particularity of things leads to unpredictable change, that the *Xici* says, that it is "impossible to make definitive laws." The *Zhongyong* expresses the connection between change and radical particularity: "The way of heaven and earth can be captured in one phrase: Since events are never duplicated, their production is unfathomable"[27]

(Ames and Hall 2001, 107). In the physical-mechanistic model, on the other hand, change is described in terms of external causation where one identical object acts on the other; and these laws can be described as eternally universal and necessary. More poetically, the organic idea of change is expressed in *Analects* 9.17, where standing by a river, and in a Heraclitian manner, the Master said, "Look at how it flows on like this, never stopping day or night!"[28] (my translation). It is this recognition of the inadequacy of human knowledge in the face of the overwhelming dynamism of reality that perhaps partly motivated Confucius's famous reticence about the metaphysical.[29]

Despite this intellectual humility, however, the Confucians were clearly not anti-intellectualists, nor skeptics about the value of knowledge (especially with regard to its role in informing action). Whereas the idea of ceaseless change would instruct the Daoists in the futility of making any laws to understand change, the Confucians affirm a certain virtue in "knowledge." In the *Daxue* (大学), there is a passage that states that effective rulership of a kingdom rested on an internesting series of conditions: the ordering of the state, the regulation of one's own family, one's own cultivation, the rectification of one's heart-mind, the sincerity (*cheng* 诚) of their thought, and, ultimately, the utmost extension of one's knowledge (*zhi* 知), which in turn requires the investigation of things (致知在格物). In *Analects* 6.27, "The Master said, 'Someone who is broadly learned with regard to culture [*Wen* 文], and whose conduct is restrained by the rites, can be counted upon not to go astray'"[30] (Slingerland 2003, 62). Zhu Xi comments on this passage: "When it comes to learning, a gentleman desires broadness, and there is therefore no part of culture that he does not examine."[31] This appeal to broad learning, however, does not seem to endow even the most exemplary among us with a certainty in knowledge (necessary truths). In *Analects* 9.8, the Master said, "Do I possess knowledge [*zhi* 知]? No, I do not. But if a simple peasant puts a question to me, and I draw a blank, I chisel at it from both ends until the question is dried up [*jie* 竭]"[32] (my translation). The exhaustion of a problem seems dependent upon the exhaustion of the different perspectives from which it can be viewed. The same idea occurs in *Zhongyong* 6, where the Master said, "This man, Shun, was a person of the greatest wisdom. Shun loved to ask questions and loved to examine familiar words, passing over what was unhelpful to expand upon those ideas that had merit. Grasping these ideas at both ends, he would exercise impartiality (*Zhong* 中) in governing his people. It was this that made him a Shun"[33] (Ames and Hall 2001, 91). Shun's wisdom lies in his inquisitiveness, which leads to his desire to see an issue from different perspectives. It is this pluralistic attitude towards understanding that leads to the ethical virtue of impartiality.

The closest approximation to the ideal of "necessary truths" in the Confucian classics is perhaps the *Yijing*. Confucius himself speaks of being adequate to studying its contents in *Analects* 7.17: "If I were granted more years, and could devote fifty of them to the study of the *Yi*, surely I would be free of major faults"[34] (my translation). In the *Records of the Grand Historian*, it is recorded that "in his old age Confucius delighted in the *Changes*. He wrote the *Tuanci, Xici, Xiangci, Shuogua, Wenyan* [i.e., "Ten Wings"]."[35] He loved reading the *Changes* so much that the leather binding broke several times. He said, "If I were granted more years I could be adequate to the *Changes*"[36] (my translation). In the "Essentials" (*yao* 要) chapter of the *Mawangdui Yijing*, there is a famous passage where Confucius answers Zigong's rebuke that Confucius's interest in the *Yijing* in his old age contradicts his earlier injunction that it is only those without virtue who tend toward spiritualism and those without wisdom who prognosticate.[37]

> The Master said: "As for the *Changes*, I do indeed put its prayers and divinations last, only observing its virtue [*de* 德] and propriety [*yi* 义]. Intuiting the commendations to reach the number, and understanding the number to reach virtue, is to have humaneness and to put it into motion properly. If the commendations do not lead to the number, then one merely acts as a magician; if the number does not lead to virtue, then one merely acts as a scribe. The divinations of scribes and magicians tend toward it but are not yet there, delight in it but are not correct. Perhaps it will be because of the *Changes* that sires of later generations will doubt me. I seek its virtue and nothing more. I am on the same road as the scribes and magicians but end up differently."[38] (Shaughnessy 1996, 241)

For Confucius, one studies the *Yijing* not for its "prayers and divinations" but to observe the virtue [*de* 德] and propriety [*yi* 义] that it embodies. What is the virtue that Confucius sought in the *Yijing*? If one looks to the ordering[39] of the trigrams, one notices that what are considered the *yang* trigrams have quantitatively more *yin* lines in them. Likewise, the *yin* trigrams have quantitatively more *yang* lines. As *Xici* 2.4 puts it, "The yang trigrams have more yin than yang lines, and the yin trigrams have more yang than yin lines" (Lynn 1994, 80). The determination of the character of a trigram or hexagram is not mechanical or quantitative. *Xici* 2.4 goes on to explain why this is the case: "The yang trigrams consist of one sovereign and two subjects; this denotes the Dao of the noble man. The yin trigrams consist of two sovereigns and one subject; this denotes the Dao of the petty man" (80). The rationale for this classificatory logic is thus an analogy taken from social situations; it is a socioconventional hermeneutic based on an understanding of human situations. Similarly, when one looks to the eight basic images (*guaxiang* 卦象), the association between the configurations of the lines and the metaphorical association seems very much *merely* metaphorical.[40] The character of the trigram/hexagram is thus based on a manifestly human understanding. There are no claims being made about the intrinsic natures of the trigrams/hexagrams.

When one looks to the *Shuogua* ("Explaining the Trigrams"; 说卦), one finds that there is an overabundance of hermeneutic laws at work in deciding why a certain natural or social phenomenon falls under a certain trigram. The classificatory logics appear, furthermore, *merely* conventional. It's conceivable to see how the same phenomenon understood from a different perspective (or by a different person) might have the character of a different trigram.[41] Furthermore, one sees how a similar phenomenon can fall under different categories. *Qian*, we are told, "has the nature of the horse,"[42] but it is also specified that *Qian* "is a fine horse, an old horse, an emaciated horse, a piebald horse."[43] We are later told that the kind of horses that corresponds to the trigram *Zhen* (震) are those that "excel at neighing, those that have white rear legs, those that work the legs [i.e., run fast], and those that have white foreheads"[44] (Lynn 1994, 123). Similarly, the kind of horse that corresponds to the trigram *Kan* (坎) are those "with beautiful backs, those that put their whole hearts into it, those that keep their heads low, those with thin hooves, and those that shamble along"[45] (124). None of the characteristics mentioned are intrinsic properties. A horse is "good" at neighing only relatively speaking. We can envision that the same horse, under different contexts, can be either *Zhen* or *Kan*. There are no natural kinds, all categorizations are *merely* conventional, and contingent upon the context. The kind of imaginative seeing at play here is far closer to Goethe's intuitive observation than Aristotelian concept formation.

It is for these reasons that it is only in old age that Confucius feels adequate in studying the *Yijing*. Someone too intellectually immature might go to the *Yijing* with the attitude of mere "magicians" and believe that the *Yijing* provides a determinate map of all space-time. For someone too intellectually immature, the *Yjing* might bear the illusory promise of an intellectual panacea: should we but properly grasps its recondite laws, then we can unlock the causal laws that explain all phenomena. The philosophical exegesis given in the "Ten Wings" dispels any fanciful thinking that such knowledge is possible. The truth about the world lies in its relations (which are constantly changing); there is nothing that can be simply defined in and of itself and can therefore simply stay defined forever. Relations are so numerous as to be beyond enumeration or classification and, what's more, because relations are dynamic and evolving, they are exponentially numerous; it is thus futile to try to characterize all relations. The *meaning* of these relations is also up to personal judgment and contingent upon context (i.e., relational). There is no knowledge possible that can definitively tell you the meaning of a phenomena, as the phenomena in question has many different meanings (according to different perspectives), and it would be up to one's own judgment as to how to interpret the phenomena. This is the case when it comes to reading the hexagrams in a prognostication. There is such an overabundance of hermeneutic laws[46] that the "correct" reading devolves to the judgment of the prognosticator in choosing which hermeneutic law to use. *Xunzi* chapter 17, "Discourse on Heaven," [天论] summarizes this difference between intellectual maturity and immaturity: "The myriad things are but one facet [*pian* 偏] of the Way. A single thing is but one facet of the myriad things. Foolish people take a single facet of a single thing and think themselves to know the Way—this is to lack knowledge"[47] (Hutton 2014, 181).

Like Goethe, Humboldt, and Herder, then, Confucianism does not subscribe to a view of knowledge as offering determinate truths. The natures of things are inherently relational and thus subject to change. To think that one can offer determinate truths is inevitably to take a part as representative of the whole. Instead, Confucianism affirms holism and perspectivism. Knowledge is inevitably perspectival and ad hominem, so that the closest we can get to objectivity is to exhaust the number of perspectives that exist.

The Continuation of Life

Why then, we might ask, do the Confucians put any faith in knowledge? In the *Xici*—which is traditionally attributed to Confucius—the harmonious, or proportional, alternation between two ("opposed") principles,[48] *yin* and *yang* is the Dao, is life. *Xici* 1.5: "In its capacity to produce and reproduce we call it 'change'"[49] (Lynn 1994, 54). The most arcane source of the world—the *yi*—which we might equate with the concept of noumena in Western philosophy—is change, is life. And what brings the harmonizing process to completion is the human subject. *Xici* 1.5: "The reciprocal process of yin and yang is called the Dao. That which allows the Dao to continue to operate is human goodness [*shan*], and that which allows it to bring things to completion is human nature [*xing*]"[50] (53). The role of the human subject in the *Xici*—and by implication, the role of human knowledge—is the maintenance of a certain harmonious proportion, which, because it is dynamic, cannot be formed for all time. It is a dynamic relationship between parts that, if maintained properly, sustains the propagation of life. The terminus ad quem of knowledge is not a Laplacean vision that possesses complete knowledge of the universe at any given moment,[51] but that which allows life to continue.[52] Likewise, this knowledge is not the static order of numbers in the Pythagorean conception of harmony. The *Zhongyong*, for example, talks about how the correct ethical behavior is to affirm the uniqueness of particulars, as the affirmation of particularity *is* the affirmation of change and thus life.[53] In *Zhongyong* 30, the "way" of the sages—which Confucius continues—is nature itself. This nature, because it cultivates all particulars, is radically pluralistic and tolerant.[54] The utmost virtue spoken of in the *Zhongyong*—*cheng* (诚)—has the effect of sustaining life in a comprehensive manner like nature.[55] This (regulative) end is not incomparable to Nietzsche's[56] eternal recurrence (2001; 2006, 178) or *amor fati* (2001, 157) in the sense that the terminus ad quem is not a transcendent realm (Being) that overcomes life (Becoming) itself, but a confirmation of that very life (and so ceaseless becoming). The ideal of knowledge is not an absolute knowing that will have determinate knowledge of all space-time, thus simultaneously eradicating the possibility of future novelty. What is affirmed is a mere becoming that, because it has the potential to create novelty, will be also be merely perspectival, particular, and contingent, but also pluralistic.

Harmony and Mutual Responsiveness (*ganying* 感应)

If we remember Needham's list of the three shared characteristics between the *Monadology* and Chinese correlative thinking, the third was the organic conception of influence. Whereas in the mechanistic model nothing in the physical world moves of its own accord, under the organic paradigm, things are internally driven—they are *ziran* (自然). Confucian metaphysics thus sees the world as a heterogeneous manifold (*wan wu* 万物) of fully individualistic self-soing (*ziran* 自然) potencies. There is no stark dichotomy between nature and freedom—there is already self-willed action in nature—and the order or form we find therein thus *cannot* be a static, eternal one. Because each particular acts according to its inner dictates, and these inner dictates are constantly changing, it is impossible to definitively map out the web of all these interconnecting relationships.

To capture the fact that things are radically particular but that this does not redound to chaos, Confucian metaphysics speaks of harmony and "resonance" (*ganying* 感应). The *Shuowen* defines harmony as "responding to each other."[57] Some of the earliest analogies used in explaining harmony were culinary and musical metaphors.[58] We see this understanding of harmony as mutual responsiveness in *Zhouyu* C (周语下) of the *Guoyu* (国语), in terms of a musical metaphor:

> When instruments are played in accordance with their natures, there is equilibrated music [*yueji* 乐极]. Bringing such equilibrated music together is called tones [*sheng* 声]. When tones mutually respond [*ying* 应] and promote one another [*xiangbao* 相保], it is called harmony. When low and high do not mutually trespass, it is called balance [*ping* 平]."[59] (my translation)

The reason culinary and musical metaphors serve the Chinese idea of harmony so well is that the unity in diversity is not achieved by following a preestablished formula. The particulars responding and mutually complementing each other *is* order. The musical metaphor serves very well the idea that diverse particulars can be affirmed without redounding to chaos. It is for the same reasons, we can suggest, that Goethe, for example, famously chose the metaphor of a symphony to describe his vision of world literature.[60]

In *Zhengyu* (郑语) of the *Guoyu* (国语), Shi Bo (史伯) in conversation with Duke Huan of the state of Zheng explains the importance of harmony—the lack of which led to the decline of the Zhou dynasty:

> Harmony [*he* 和] indeed leads to fecundity [*shengwu* 生物], identity [*tong* 同] means barrenness. Things accommodating each other on equal terms [*ping* 平] is called harmony, and in so doing they are able to flourish and grow, and other things are drawn to them. If identical things [*tong* 同] are used to supplement identical things then, once they are used up, nothing will remain.[61]

Shi Bo goes on to counsel how the former kings attained the utmost harmony by harmonizing the five phases, the five flavors, the four limbs, the six musical notes, the seven orifices, instituting harmony among diversity within social and political institutions, taking consorts from different clans, and allowing for a plurality of different opinions. The passage ends with the injunction, "There is no music in a single note, no refinement/culture-civilization [*wen* 文] in a single item, and no taste in a single flavor, no comparison with/reconciliation [*jiang* 讲] in a single thing."[62]

The Confucian view of harmony is, I argue, well expressed by Aimé Césaire's when he writes that

> I'm not burying myself in a narrow particularism. But neither do I want to lose myself in an emaciated universalism. There are two ways to lose oneself: walled segregation in the particular or dilution in the "universal."
>
> My conception of the universal is that of a universal enriched by all that is particular, a universal enriched by every particular: the deepening and coexistence of all particulars. (Césaire 2010, 152)

The Confucian view of harmony is not an abstract universal imposed onto the particulars themselves. Nor, however, is it the chaos of mere particularity. The *coherence* that obtains between the particulars in Confucian harmony overcomes this dualism. *Order* cannot be understood as something static (an abstract universal). Order is understood to arise through the mutual responsiveness (*ganying* 感应) or resonance of all things with each other, so that, in Césaire's words, there is a deepening of all particulars. This mutual responsiveness and coexistence between all particulars *is* the Chinese universal—it is "harmony." Order *is* the mutual complementarity between all things. This, we might suggest, is a model of harmony that would have been of interest to Cassirer when he said that our task is "to gather the various branches of science with their diverse methodologies—with all their recognized specificity and independence—into one system, whose separate parts precisely through their necessary diversity will *complement* and *further* one another" (*PSF* 1:77; my emphasis).[63]

By contrast, in the *Logic of the Cultural Sciences*, Cassirer writes that

the Greek concept of being and the Greek concept of truth are to be compared, according to the simile of Parmenides, to a "well-rounded sphere" that rests firmly on its own center. Both are complete and perfect in themselves; and between them exists not only a harmony but genuine *identity*." (*LCS* 5; my emphasis)

Identity is also antithetical to change and thus *life* itself. Inasmuch as life is change, and change into greater diversity, the idea of being, identity, and something "firmly resting in its own center" (and thus not changing) is antithetical to life. The Chinese tradition also picks up on this connection between harmony, diversity, and life. Once one assumes, on the organic paradigm, that things are radically particular (because they are ceaselessly changing) then one needs another way to describe order. Order cannot be understood as something static; order is instead understood as emergent from the radically heterogeneous particulars acting on their own terms but *cooperating* and *responding* to each other. What is harmonious comes from a dynamic mutual relationship between the diverse particulars and needs to be constantly reachieved. It is this model of harmony, as the affirmation of diverse things, that also leads to the flourishing of life.

Symbolic Forms for a New Humanity

Scholarship on Cassirer has not paid enough attention to how the concept of the organic influenced Cassirer's thinking about the relationship between the various symbolic forms. Donald Philip Verene, for example, discusses Cassirer's reference to harmony in his Heraclitus quotation in *An Essay on Man* (Verene 2011, 95–102). Verene, however, does not pay attention to how Cassirer's conception of harmony is informed by his understanding of the organic relationship between part and whole, nor Cassirer's indebtedness to thinkers whose thought, in Cassirer's own account, exampled this "organic" paradigm. Nor have scholars taken seriously Cassirer's idea of harmony as an intellectually or morally compelling ideal. Edward Skidelsky expresses an orthodox assessment when he dismisses Cassirer's project of comprehending "the variety of human culture" as an "organic whole" as a failure, and thus unviable for the modern world. Likewise, Leo Strauss criticizes Cassirer's "aestheticism," and so weak defense of Kantian moral principles, and suggests that he should have rewritten his *PSF* with a focus on morality (Strauss 1947, 128). Habermas thought that the "the normative foundations [of the *PSF*] remained entirely unclear" due to Cassirer's "perspectivism" (Habermas 2001, 23). Likewise, Birgit Recki writes that "the moment of its [*PSF*] normative orientation remains conceptually vague"[64] (Recki 1997, 72). Like Skidelsky, the problem Cassirer's critics had with his system was that, as there was no Archimedean anchorage in his philosophy of culture, it necessarily redounds to mere (historicist) description and thus lacks any normative moment (Skidelsky 2008, 5–6).

This chapter has argued that scholars have overlooked the idea of (organic) harmony as the ethical moment of Cassirer's philosophy. Cassirer may never have explicitly written an ethics, but his stress on harmony is his ethics. What's more, this ethics is of relevance to our contemporary world. To seek for a position "beyond" the varieties of culture is to return to a dogmatic metaphysics that posits one aspect of human experience as prior to the others. Contra Cassirer's critics, the kind of reconciliation through harmony that he tried to effect is something we have to accept. As Cassirer himself pointed out, it is in the realm of the organic that we can best see the solution to the antinomies of particularism and identity, arche (single order) and anarchy (mere particularism). It is the concept of the organic that offers a viable paradigm for coherence among particularities: harmony as such. This organic harmony will be a robust alternative to the idea that we need a standpoint outside of culture(s).

If the reader casts their mind back to the last section of the previous chapter where I defended the Cassirerian (and, by implication, Confucian) project of culture against its detractors, I argued that I will show how culture(s) as an organic whole does have intellectual traction. Against Cassirer's detractors, then, we could argue that the Confucians had a similar conception of culture(s) as an organic whole. Once we *assume* the particularity of things, we are pushed toward the idea that order is *created* through the functional law that emerges from the whole of the parts. The idea that order is *created* as opposed to given leads to two more important ideas. First, order rests on the particulars mutually responding to each other. Second, what order we see is a subjective judgment of the totality of the parts. In both, the human subject becomes inextricable from the concept or existence of "order." Order is not an ontologically stable reality that we have to discover; order is instead always a (creative) work in progress. In the case of human cultures, order is something we create through mutually cooperating with each other, or through the creative imagination that finds order among the parts.

In Foucault's reading, Kant's *Anthropology* reveals the historical specificity of our a priori categories and so contains the seeds of its own radical transformation into the historical a priori (Foucault 2008, 55). It is mere provincialism that convinces itself that there are universal and necessary a prioris;[65] familiarity with other cultures cannot but disabuse us of this notion. Once we understand that there are many diverse particulars in the world we cannot but dispatch with the idea of universally valid universals.

In *Symbolic Forms for a New Humanity*, Drucilla Cornell and Kenneth Michael Panfilio write that we,

> must learn to respect the inevitable plurality of symbolic forms. Such respect demands that we view symbolic forms from within their own logic and not unilaterally condemn them as irrational through comparison. In our post-colonial world we clearly need the enlarged mentality that inheres in the work of Ernst Cassirer. (2010, 93)

As Cornell and Panifilio write, we have to affirm the particularity of each symbolic form from within and not impose a universal on them that is not internally derived. This affirmation of particularity *is* Cassirer's paradigm of organic harmony. Similarly, in "The A Priori of Culture: Philosophy of Culture between Rationalism and Relativism—the Example of Lévi-Strauss' *Structural Anthropology*," Luft argues that Cassirer's idea of a universal basis among all cultures is always a work in progress, dependent upon empathy (2015a, 398) and mutual understanding (Luft 2015a, 399). This empathetic understanding can only be a result of a first person, and never third person, perspective, and is, furthermore, always historical and fallible, and can make no claims to finality.[66] Like the Confucian conception of harmony, then, the universal—harmony—is something to be arrived at from the affirmation of all particulars. The mutual responsiveness and complementarity between particulars *is* the universal, *is* order. In other words, order, or the universal, rests on empathetic understanding that we must work at for its realization. This universalism, like the Confucian *ren* (仁), is thus a task, a regulative ideal, a terminus ad quem (as opposed to a terminus a quo) that we never fully reach, but toward which our efforts must constantly be aimed. It is a universal that, unlike Kant's a priori categories, cannot be given for all time. It is instead historical—situational and always subject to change. As Cassirer writes in *An Essay on Man*, "The ethical world is never given; it is forever in the making" (*EM* 61). Because reality is always changing, the harmony among contrariety must be constantly (re)achieved by us.

Against Cassirer's detractors then, we cannot wish for an Archimedian point outside of culture itself. This will inevitably become a philosophical fallacy, as we will take a part to be representative of the whole. As Xunzi told us, "The myriad things are but one facet of the Way. A single thing is but one facet of the myriad things. Foolish people take a single facet of a single thing and think themselves to know the Way—this is to lack knowledge." We *must* affirm the totality of all particulars. The totality of cultures, however, need not redound to chaos, as the particular cultures can mutually respond to each other and create a harmonious order. To wish for an Archimedean point outside of culture(s) itself is to forget that we are responsible for the mutual empathy that goes into creating a harmonious order, or the creative imagination necessary for seeing order among the parts, and so to forget and neglect the task of ordering our world.

Organic Harmony as an Ethics in Cassirer's Oeuvre

Cassirer left Germany in 1933 and spent his remaining career in exile. In this period, Cassirer reflected greatly on how the phenomenon of Nazism became a possibility. In "The Technique of Our Modern Political Myths,"[67] a lecture given on January 18, 1945, Cassirer gives a summary of the main argument of his last book, *The Myth of the State*. The symbolic form of myth became central to Cassirer's analysis of the rise of Nazism. Throughout his oeuvre Cassirer repeatedly emphasizes that myth *is* a symbolic form. Cassirer rejects the conventional idea that myth is just the dualistic antithesis to rationality. Myth is, in fact, the first symbolic form—it is the form on which all other symbolic forms are built. Myth is the foundation of our humanity. Myth is also the most immediately affective of all the symbolic forms. In myth, humans objectify their deepest emotions so that their emotions have outward existence: mythical perception is always impregnated with emotional qualities. In myth, all sorts of affections—fear, sorrow, anguish, excitement, joy, exultation—have an external face (SMC 173). Coherent with his previous account of myth, in this lecture, Cassirer reiterates the two essential characteristics of myth: its inalienable function in the human being's sociocultural life[68] and its emotional nature[69] (SMC 254–55). As part of his argument that myth is an ever-present aspect of human cultural life, Cassirer quotes the anthropologist Bronisław Malinowski[70] favorably against Lévy-Bruhl (SMC 249). Malinowski emphasizes (along with Franz Boas[71]) that there is genuine cultural diversity in the world. Contra Lévy-Bruhl, for whom myth is a primitive stage of humankind, for Malinowksi, different cultural forms (including mythic forms) exist contemporaneously. As Michael Forster writes, Malinowski was "an implacable and trenchant critic of evolutionism" (Forster 2010, 215). Cassirer's message in contrasting Malinowski favorably against Lévy-Bruhl is clear: myth is not a stage of humankind that European man has left behind, it is an ever-present aspect of human existence.

For Cassirer, the problem is *not* that Nazi political myth-making *exists* but rather that this kind of political myth has dominated and overwhelmed the other symbolic forms of sociocultural existence. As each symbolic form is a self-sufficient medium for understanding the world, there is a tendency for them to assume a dominant or hegemonic position with respect to the other symbolic forms. It is the task of humanity to create equilibrium between these different cultural expressions of humankind. Cassirer is explicit that the solution to Nazi myths is not to extirpate myth from our social existence (just as, for Cassirer, one cannot castrate the emotions just because they are sometimes the enemy of reason[72]). Cassirer's antidote to Nazism is instead couched in terms of an "equilibrium" (SMC 246), "counterbalance" (SMC 247), and "harmonious equilibrium" (SMC 254) between the various symbolic forms:

> The organism of human culture does not eliminate the mythical elements root and branch, but it learns to control them. It develops new constructive powers of logical and scientific thought, new ethical forces and new creative energies of artistic imagination. By the appearance of these new forces myth is not entirely vanquished, but it is counter-balanced and brought under control. (SMC 246)

Cassirer's attitude toward myth (and the emotions) belies his humanism. Cassirer's ethical project is, in a sense, informed by the Vico formula, "The criterion of the truth is to have made it (Veri criterium est id ipsum fecisse)."[73] For Cassirer, nothing that is created by human beings can become completely alienated from human beings; we can always understand (and so have mastery over) the culture we have created.[74] For Cassirer, spontaneity *always* lies with the human subject, and human spontaneity realizes itself in its work. As an expression of human spontaneity, nothing that is the work of the human being can become incomprehensible to human beings. None of the expressions of Geist—the various cultural forms—are inherently coercive or bad. The problem is when any one symbolic form dominates. Cassirer's embrace of myth should be understood in this spirit of the pluralistic embrace of the whole cultural gamut of the "will to formation." Given this affirmation of *all* cultural manifestations of humankind's Geist, for Cassirer, the ethical project of philosophy "is the great effort of thought to embrace and unify all the different activities of man—to bring them into a common focus" (SMC 219). The ethical project of philosophy is to bring the pluralistic cultural expressions of man into a harmonious equilibrium.

Cassirer's criticism of the "preponderance" (SMC 243; MS 3) of political myths under Nazism is coherent with his criticism of the dominance of Lebensphilosophie[75] and logical positivism[76] in the philosophical milieu of his day. In both, Cassirer saw a return to a dogmatic metaphysics that posited one aspect of human experience as prior to all others. What should have been a healthy ecosystem of the different ways people understand and experience the world is leveled to homogeneity. In Cassirer's eyes, both Lebensphilosophie and (logical) positivism gave way to the dogma that there is an a priori beyond the fact of culture itself. This intellectual homogeneity cripples our critical powers as the monopoly of one symbolic form anaesthetizes us to the fact that order is created, and so pluralistic, as opposed to found and so singular and totalistic.[77] Attendant upon this fundamentalism is an anti-humanistic suppression of the human being's critical powers and so her passivity in the face of a (posited) monolithic law.[78] When all other philosophical perspectives can be reduced to a posited hegemonic principle or logic, such as verificationism on the basis of a protocol sentence or *Geworfenheit*, we regress to a metaphysical determinism/fatalism whereby the human being is determined by one aspect of her cultural life. On this point, it is instructive to remember that although religion has totalistic claims to being the ultimate explanation, under Cassirer's critical, anthropological gaze, it is understood as just another symbolic form. There is nothing wrong with these philosophical positions in themselves, the fault lies with the field of philosophy and society at large in surrendering to just one symbolic form or narrative. In this way, the philosopher, as well as humanity at large, forsake their ethical duties in safeguarding the ecosystem of culture. It is in these terms that, at the end of his lecture "Philosophy and Politics" in 1944, Cassirer criticized academic philosophy for not having kept watch over the space of culture. Here he quotes Albert Schweitzer's charge at the failure of academic philosophy to have been a "watchman" "in the hour of peril" (SMC 232).

Cassirer's critique of Hegel, Spengler, Heidegger, and Arthur de Gobineau in *The Myth of the State* also centers around this same critique of dogmatic, single-cause explanations. In Cassirer's eyes, Gobineau's racial determinism (224–47), Heidegger's existential philosophy (293), Hegel's identification of history with "the development of Spirit in time" and the state with the "divine Idea" on earth (263–76), and Spengler's historical determinism (289–92) belie a common characteristic. They all posit an absolute law to which all other human phenomena can be reduced; they are forms of metaphysical determinism (which Cassirer rejected in the Aristotelianism that was already described). As Cassirer observed, Gobineau's racial ontology—metaphysics dressed up in the tangible empiricism of science—came to fill the void left by traditional metaphysics (MS 230–31). Gobineau convinced himself and his readers that the law of gravity of the human world was race (MS 225–31). Under this law of race, no human being is free to change their fate; their fate value and moral worth are, instead, sealed for all time by their race.[79] It is the dominance of the kind of single-cause explanation/metaphysical determinism/fatalism found in Gobineau, Hegel, Spengler, and Heidegger that Cassirer connects with the rise of Nazism:

> There is an indirect connection between the general course of ideas that we can study in the case of Spengler or Heidegger and German political and social life in the period after the First World War. As soon as philosophy no longer trusts its own power, as soon as it gives way to a merely passive attitude, it can no longer fulfil its most important educational task. (SMC 230)

As already shown, what Cassirer greatly admired about Kant's third Critique is the idea of reflective judgment; the order that we see in nature is ultimately attributed to the creative powers of the human subject. Cassirer's answer to the phenomenon of Nazism is that society (including philosophers) *allowed* certain discourses to dominate the space of culture to the extent that we forget how, ultimately, order is created and not found. To be critically aware that order is created is to be cognizant of the *pluralistic* ways in which human beings do order the world (through the diverse symbolic forms). Furthermore, it is to be aware that the metaorder that pertains between the symbolic forms is never given (as it is in organic life, order is dynamic and emergent). Culture/civilization/ the balance among the symbolic forms is an endless work in progress that has to be constantly reachieved. As Cassirer would say, "It is true that this equilibrium is rather a labile than a static equilibrium; it is not firmly established but liable to all sorts of disturbances (SMC 246). This means that "the ethical world is never given; it is forever in the making" (EM 61). Cassirer's ethical project is not, as Drucilla Cornell said, to "unilaterally condemn" certain cultural forms "as irrational" and purge them so to arrive at a perfected, flawless system; this would fall foul of the very dogmatic metaphysics that he rejects. Instead of an ascetic and unrealistic ban on certain forms of cultural expression, the ethical task of the critical philosopher of culture is instead to walk the tightrope that balances all the different cultural expressions of humankind into a harmonious whole. Cultures, like ecosystems, are healthy when they can support and harmonize diverse forms of cultural expression/life. A culture is "unhealthy" and inhibits human flourishing when it fetishizes and allows certain modes of existence/knowledge/cultural forms to dominate at the expense of others. The ethical task of the philosopher and humankind is to maintain the harmony and health of the space of culture so that diverse kinds of human life can flourish.

Underlying Cassirer's epistemological project (notably in his account of the history of philosophy) is his ethical project. Cassirer's thinking about the relationship between the different symbolic forms is indebted to some of his most admired thinkers: Goethe, Herder, Humboldt, and Leibniz. What is commonly shared between these thinkers, in Cassirer's own assessment, is the new paradigm of the organic that is ultimately traceable to Leibniz. The paradigm of the organic in the thinkers of the *Goethezeit*, it is argued, is the backstory to Cassirer's own thinking about harmony in diversity. The organic *is* the harmony that Cassirer envisaged as existing between the various symbolic forms. Cassirer's ethical project is consistent with his epistemological project. When confronted with the formidable moral challenge of Nazism, Cassirer's answer is still to emphasize harmony, that is, between the different philosophical forms. This paradigm of organic harmony is of ethical relevance for thinking about our contemporary world. To find a coherence that does justice to particulars, as opposed to merely asserting a point of unity—which cannot but redound to dogma—requires us to see world cultures as a whole: a whole that is formed by the resonant relationships that exist between the parts; parts that are constantly changing and thus require the utmost human effort to maintain. Unity is not a given that we discover, but something that must be created through attention to the parts. This does not, however, imply that there is no normative task for humankind. The task now, as it was for Cassirer, is still to find harmony in contrariety, as in the case of the bow and the lyre.

Culture and Harmony

In chapter 1, it was suggested that many of the themes in the classical Confucian philosophy of culture can be seen from the perspective of the organic. This chapter has fleshed out this idea in greater detail. Ultimately, this story comes back to what Cassirer would call a functionalist view as opposed to a substance view. The functionalist or organic view *assumes* the radical particularity of all things and therefore sees order as emergent from the *relationships* that obtain between them. It is for this reason that philosophers who think under this organic paradigm—Leibniz, Goethe, Humboldt, Herder, and Cassirer—embrace holism and pluralism. It is because the organic paradigm dispatches with the idea of an ontologically stable order that the human being becomes so important as the maker of order.

The Confucian concept of harmony resonates with Cassirer's own thinking about reconciling the different symbolic forms into a coherent whole without sacrificing their particularity. The shared point of similarity between Confucian harmony and Cassirer's own ideas on harmony rests on the paradigm of the organic. In the organic world each thing follows its own internal dictates without the whole redounding to chaos, as the whole is the functional law of the parts. Transplanting this model onto the human realm, we can say that the functional law of the whole (harmony) is created through the cooperation of the diverse particular (cultures) and it is also up to us to be able to find the coherence among the particulars with our own creative judgments.

Under a substance view, because the essences of things are determinate for all time, it is conceivable that the law governing the relationship between things is similarly determinate. This view becomes unavailable under an organic paradigm. It is because there is no conception that things can be defined for all times that opens up a space of freedom and possibility. It is up to the actions of the particulars to define the law of the whole. Transplanted onto the human realm, this means that we become wholly responsible for the law of the whole, as it is only ever a product of our own actions. This, then, is the *humanism* of Confucianism and Cassirer.

Conclusion

This project has described the importance of culture for classical Confucianism in dialogue with Ernst Cassirer's philosophy of symbolic forms. In so doing, it has provided an account of how and why culture can and should be a philosophical paradigm that captures the essence of humanity. As we have seen from chapters 1 and 2, culture is integrally related to the use of the (linguistic) sign. The lesson found in language, that it allows the human being to have a more meaningful relationship to the world by creatively consolidating certain meanings already phenomenally present in it, is extended to other cultural forms. This understanding of culture is perhaps most exquisitely exemplified through the Confucian understanding of poetry, which was explored in chapter 3. Poetry brings to a higher order what was nebulously present both in the self and in the world. It is therefore unsurprising, as we saw in chapter 4, that the philosophical rationalization of how the written script is related to the Dao, follows this same humanist paradigm. It is human culture, symbolized by language, that both manifests and creatively extends the Dao. Underlying all of these four chapters is the implicit understanding of the self that was explored in chapter 5: the Confucians self *is* its potential for culture.

It is for this reason that culture *is* so important for this tradition, because culture *can* creatively extend the source. In chapter 2, it was seen how culture, in terms of a sign, could order the phenomenal world. In chapter 3, we saw that culture worked on the raw material of the emotions in terms of Music/poetry and gave it form. In chapter 4, we saw how language manifested and extended the Dao, and in chapter 5, we saw how cultural forms act to shape the human being itself. In all these aspects, the Confucian tradition *assumed* that the "source" necessarily tends toward expression in a humanly created, material form such that the source is consummated by humanly created forms. Humans form a continuum among the myriad things, the common denominator of which is the tendency of all natural things towards self-expression. If everything *needs* to be manifested for its realization/consummation, then the Confucian tradition, by implication, did not assume a dualistic, substance-attribute/reality-appearance paradigm. It is the "thing's" self-expression—its properties, if you will—that, once consolidated into a form, consummates the thing itself—its substance, if you will. This assumption, as we saw in chapters 3, 4, and 5, is also a normative injunction. One *should* make oneself known through the various facta of culture in order to consummate the self, and so to allow for a harmonious society. Under the Confucian view, the self is never an insular one that speaks a private language that none can understand. One necessarily manifests oneself in a socially understandable language.

If the reader casts her mind, Cassirer's conception of *Geist* was explained as that which necessarily needs to be manifested in material culture (one can think of this as a German equivalent of 文以載道—that is, *Wen* can be a vehicle for the Dao). It is this conception of *Geist* as inextricable from its manifestation, and this very manifesting that furthers *Geist*, that is comparable to the Confucian philosophy of culture. Mere expression itself, as we saw in chapter 3, is not a cultural form. This form has to be a socially created one for it to be more than the *mere* expression of affect. It is this particular conception of cultural forms that I had in mind when I wrote in the introduction that the Cassirerian conception of form might have overcome the dualism that paralyzed Hans Castorp in *The Magic Mountain*.

If humans are merely at one extreme on a continuum of all natural things that manifest, and are manifested in their own language—*wen*—then *wen*, or a communicative patterning, is what is commensurable between the myriad things. One gets a picture of a world in which the myriad things are all manifesting their patterns, and so communicating. This is one way in which one can understand *tian ren he yi*. The other, is the fact that it is ultimately the human being who consummates the language of the myriad things.

Harmony, it was argued in chapter 6, overcomes the dichotomy between a homogenizing unity and a mere babel of heterogeneity, while pari passu emphasizing the humanist point that it is the human being who must find this "harmony in contrariety." Whereas the dualism of universal and particular is foundational to Western philosophy, openness to change and diversity is intrinsic to Confucian (and Chinese) philosophy. The Confucian discourse of harmony provides a sophisticated model for thinking about diversity. It is a similar discourse of harmony to which Cassirer turns in his reconciliation between the antithetical extremes of *disjecta membra* and homogenizing universalism among the diverse means of human world-making. Both Confucianism and Cassirer looked optimistically upon a vision whereby we affirm diversity to the benefit of the whole.

Thematically, we can say that there are two key themes in this project. First, a nonsubstance understanding of the world and an attendant stress on the fact that the empirical manifestation—pattern—of the "thing" *is* the "thing." This leads to a "linguistic turn" view of language and attendant stress on the importance of "language"—or "intercommunicative patterning" (*wen*). Secondly, it is this nonsubstance worldview that leads to *tian ren he yi*. The self is no longer a substantial self—it is a functional self. This self, like the sage of *Xici* 1.4, becomes a correlative point that requires the myriad things for its existence. It is this noninsular, nonexclusive, and nonexclusionary view of the self that is capable of embracing pluralism and for whom harmony is important. The functional self *requires* the myriad things for its existence and so has less of a tendency to see things outside the self as a threat to the integrity of the self. As order is not pregiven and has to be found by this self, order is achieved from the bottom up, by giving coherence—harmony—to the existing myriad things.

Throughout this project, and in chapter 6 in particular, it was stressed that the commensurability between Cassirer and Confucianism is not accidental. The historical reasons for their commensurability, it is hoped, will allow us to reconceive the historical narrative of intellectual traditions in a more cosmopolitan manner. The two traditions, like two nonparallel lines, bisect on this point about culture. In (what should be) our cosmopolitan age, perhaps this is one way to tell the story of our philosophical commonalities: where our traditions bisect, and why. This *could* be one of the greater services that philosophy can provide: reflecting on the nature of our intellectual world in a nonprovincial, pluralistic manner, and, in so doing, providing a practical contribution to our lived realities. Philosophy ought always to be—and this is a Confucian-Cassirerian conviction—in the service of humanity. This kind of exercise in philosophical translation, I hope to have demonstrated, can provide insights about our commonalities and differences, and thus contribute to a better understanding of our own tradition as well as those of other peoples. This kind of enlarged mentality is in the spirit of Confucianism, and I hope that in creatively extending Cassirer's thought I have been faithful to his spirit.

Appendix 1

Definitions of *Wen*

There are broadly six different ways in which *wen* is used in the Chinese classics: (1) as a naturally occurring pattern; (2) as the human creation of patterns; (3) as the civil and cultured qualities denotative of a sophisticated civilization; (4) as the outward form to an inner "substance"; (5) in the sense of correct (moral) form or model human conduct; and (6) in the sense of an elegant, correct form in language/sophisticated literary language.

   1. *Wen* as the "natural pattern of lines, including distinctive markings on animals and natural phenomena" (Kroll 2015, 476) occurs in the "Yan Du" chapter of the *Lunheng* (80 CE; 论衡·言毒). For example, we read that the "Pallas pit viper has many *wen*."[1] In the "Horses' Hoofs" chapter of the *Zhaungzi* (庄子·马蹄), we read, "If the five colors had not been confused, how should the ornamental figures [*wen*] have been formed?"[2] In the "Nine Pieces" chapter of the *Chu Ci* (楚辞·九章·橘颂), we read that "when green and yellow mix, *wenzhang* is splendid."[3] In the "Kao Gong Ji" chapter of the *Rites of Zhou* (周礼·考工记), we read that when green is [juxtaposed] with red, it is called *wen*."[4] In the *Yue Ji*, we read that "the five colors, form a complete and elegant whole [*wen*], without any confusion."[5] In *Xici* 2.10 we read, "Since the Dao consists of change and action, we refer to it in terms of the 'moving lines' [*yao*]. Since the moving lines consist of different classes, we refer to them as 'things' [*wu* 物]. Since these things mix in together, we refer to these as 'patterns' [*wen* 文]. When these patterns [*wen* 文] involve discrepancies, fortune is at issue there"[6] (Lynn 1994: 92–93). The *Shuowenjiezi* writes that *wen* "is the crisscrossing of lines, and *xiang* [象] is the crisscrossing of *wen*."[7]

191

This definition of *wen* corresponds with the earliest script for *wen*, which is similar to *yao* [爻]—the hexagram lines of the *Yijing* (Sun 2014, 24).

2. *Wen* as the human creation of patterns appears in the "Royal Regulations" chapter of the *Book of Rites* (礼记·王制): "The east is called *yi* [夷] [and they wear their] hair loose and pattern [their] bodies [*wenshen* 文身]. There are those who do not cook [their] food."[8] In the "Easy and Free Wandering" chapter of the *Zhuangzi* (庄子·逍遥游): "The people of *Yue* cut [their] hair and pattern [*wen* 文] [their] bodies."[9]

3. *Wen* in the sense of "the refined, civil, or cultured qualities, as opp. to (ant.) 武 *wǔ*, martial attainments or prowess" (Kroll 2015, 476) appears in the "Canon of Yao" of the *Shang Shu* (尚书·尧典): Examining into antiquity, [we find that] Di Yao was styled Fangxun. He was attentive, bright, cultured [*Wen*, 文], and thoughtful—naturally and without effort."[10]

4. *Wen* as the outward form to an inner "substance"; as "designed or incised pattern of lines, surface ornament, elaboration, as added to (ant.) 质 *zhì*, basic stuff, plainness" (Kroll 2015, 476), can be found in the "Rites in Formation of Character" chapter of the *Book of Rites* (礼记·礼器), where we read that "the rules as instituted by the ancient kings had their foundational elements [*ben* 本] and their outward and elegant form [*wen* 文]. A true heart and good faith are their foundational elements [*ben* 本]. The correct principles [*yili* 义理] are its outward and elegant form [*wen* 文]: Without the foundational element [*ben* 本], they could not have been established; without the elegant form [*wen* 文], they could not have been put in practice."[11] In the *Analects*, *wenzhang* (文章) is used to describe the teachings of Confucius (5.13)[12] and the former sages (8.19).[13] The same reference to the *wenzhang* of the sages occurs in *Zhongyong*, passage 31.

5. *Wen* in the sense of correct (moral) form is the predominant way it is used in the Confucian classics. This correct moral form is simultaneous with the idea of its being aesthetically pleasing. In the *Yue Ji*, we read that "Music springs from the inward movements [of the heart-mind]; ritual appears in the outward movements [of the body]. Hence it is the rule to make ritual as austere and brief as possible, and to give to music its fullest development. The austerity of ritual leads to the forward exhibition of them, and therein their beauty [*wen* 文] resides; the full exhibition of music leads to the introspective consideration of it, and therein its beauty [*wen* 文] resides."[14]

6. *Wen* in the sense of an elegant, correct form in language, of "consciously devised pattern of words" (Kroll 2015, 476) can be found

in the 23rd year of Duke Xi chapter of the *Zuo Zhuan*: "I am not as cultured [*Wen*] as Zhao Cui."[15] *Wen* in the human realm designates both literature (*Wenxue* 文学) and the written word (*Wenzi* 文字). It is elegance (*Wenti* 文体) and style (*Wenfeng* 文风); it is education in the humanities (*Wenjiao* 文教); it is civilization (*Wenming* 文明) and culture itself (*Wenhua* 文化).

A definition that encompasses all the above senses of *wen* would be "the self-presencing of a material patterning that manifests order." *Wen* is a manifested pattern that conveys (internal) dispositions and is applicable to both the natural and the human realms. This definition communicates the philosophical rationalization of *wen* by Xu Shen, Liu Xie, and Song Lian.

Appendix 2

A Brief History of *Wen*

In Chinese history, the earliest known occurrences of *wen* are found among inscriptions on the oracle bones, as well as on some bronze vessels from the later part of the Shang dynasty (ca. 1600–1046 BCE). The original meaning of the word is not known for certain. The interpretation given in the *Shuowen* (see point 1, in Appendix 1) is corroborated by various ancient texts. In the *Book of Poetry*, for example, there is a "patterned mat" (*wenyin*文茵), glossed as a mat made of tiger skin (James Liu 1975, 7). In the *Shang Shu* (尚书) we already see *wen* used in terms of *Wenjiao* (文教): as civil education as opposed to military prowess. In the "Tribute of Yu" (禹贡) chapter, in the section that lays out the different zones and levels of tributes/taxes people should pay/make, we read that "five hundred *li* from the Tribute Zone is the Zone of Peace [*Suifu*], where within three hundred *li* one should appoint governors to implement education [文教]"[1] (my translation). In fact, *wen* is most prominently used in the *Shang Shu*, with regard to civilizing peoples/other tribes through education as opposed to physically dominating them. In "Counsels of the Great Yu" chapter, we read how Yu, in his struggles with the rebellious Miao tribe, retreated his army and instead instantiated the grace of civilization (*Wende* 文德), and thereupon the Miao tribe submitted to Yu. *Wen* is used in this instance as the civilizing virtues of the *junzi* that, like the polestar analogy of the *Analects*, draws those of lesser virtue to him.

According to Martin Kern, throughout the Eastern Zhou *wen* encompassed a great variety of written forms, among them charts (*tu* 图), inscriptions, and writing itself (Kern 2001, 46). By the Warring States, the Qin, and the Han periods, "*wen* becomes heavily laden with cosmological meaning and related to a great variety of changing and accumulating cultural practices; and beyond denoting specific phenomena, the term may carry the general meaning of something like 'cultural accomplishment,' as is reflected in its ongoing use in posthumous epithets" (44). According to James Liu, in some texts of the fourth century BCE, *wen* was used to signify written words or writing in general. From the second century BCE, however, it started to take on the meaning of "literature" (James Liu 1975, 8). By the Eastern Han, beyond "criss-cross patterns," *wen* comes to stand predominantly for "writing," "writings," "script," and "scriptures," and in particular "the written composition as an emblem of civil achievement" (Kern 2001, 46). Furthermore, *Wen* had by this time been differentiated into a number of compounds, that is, *Wenxue* (文学), *Wencai* (文采), *Wenzhang* (文章), *Wenci* (文辞), and so on. Kern suggests that, of these terms, *Wenzhang* refers most concretely to "writing" and "writings" (2001, 47). *Wenxue*, in Warring States times, however, is "clearly related to textual learning" (48).

Appendix 3

Partial Translation of Song Lian's "The Origins of *Wen*" (*Wenyuan* 文原)

Song Lian (1310–81) believed that *Wen*[1] was not merely belles lettres (非专指辞翰之文); *Wen* are instead the image (象 *xiang*) manifestation of the Dao itself. In his essay "The Origins of *Wen*" (文原), one finds a descriptive encomium on what *Wen* is, and what humans are prescriptively compelled to realize. This part of Song Lian's essay is translated here.

When did the *Wen* [文] of humanity become discernible? Undoubtedly its origins can be traced to the age of Baoxi.[2] In looking up, Baoxi observed comprehensively; in looking down, Baoxi scrutinized meticulously, and depicted odd and even as the *Xiang* [象] of *yin* and *yang*.[3] In changing, it [the Dao] achieves free-flow,[4] and its vitality cannot be exhausted,[5] thereby becoming the spontaneous *Wen* of heaven and earth. It is not solely because the utmost Dao encompasses all and neglects nothing that in fashioning implements it follows the images [*xiang*] as the supreme guide,[6] for without *Wen*, indeed nothing would have been accomplished. For example, governance through the adoption of robes was inspired by the hexagrams of *Qian* and *Kun*.[7] The idea of putting a ridgepole at the top and rafters below was taken from the hexagram *Dazhuang*.[8] The idea for keeping written tallies was taken from the hexagram *Kuai*.[9] The benefit to be gained from boats, paddles, cows, and horses was inspired by the hexagrams *Huan* and *Sui*.[10] The idea for the pestle and mortar as well as the inner and outer coffins were taken from the hexagrams *Xiaoguo* and *Daguo*.[11] The idea for doubling the door and striking the watchman's clapper was taken from the hexagram *Yu*.[12] The idea for the use of the

bow and arrow was taken from the hexagram *Kui*.[13] Which of these are
not the brilliant *Wen* itself? By itself it is both that which initiates and
that which brings things to completion.[14] It [*Wen*] is the expression of
natural order and the common law of the people. The carrying out of
ceremonial form, [ritual] music, punishment, and governance; the normative model of regiments, battalions, and punitive expeditions; the
differentiation of units in the well-field system; the difference between
civilization and barbarism: all conforms to and symbolizes [*xiang* 象] it
[*Wen* of humanity]. Thus, all that which has to do with the victuals of
humankind and the provisions of life are within the bounds of *Wen*.
There is nothing that is not ruled by *Wen*. However, if there were no
means by which to record the deeds after they were done, then [the
deeds] could not be further carried out. [As a result], one began to entrust
literature in illuminating its *Wen*. I will give a few cursory examples. Yu
divided the land and, following the course of the hills, he cut down the
trees. He determined the highest hills and largest rivers [in the several
regions].[15] Once this was completed, he wrote the text [*Wen*] *Tribute of
Yu*. The Zhou dynasty instantiated the various rituals of friendly missions,
having an audience with the King, enjoying offerings of food with the
sovereign, honoring the spirits with cooked food, [as well as] marriage
and mourning rituals. Once the proper conduct for meeting and greeting
people was established was the text [*Wen*] of the *Book of Etiquettes and
Ceremonials* written. When Confucius resided among his fellow villagers,
his expressions and actions were calm and measured. When his disciples
all saw this, they then wrote the text [*Wen*] *Xiang Dang* [乡党]. On no
occasion did the maxims and great lessons from the sages occur in any
other way. There was necessarily the actuality before its accompanying
record [*Wen*]. There was never an instance of the disciples' records
being prior [to the act]. This is analogous to hearing the music between
heaven and earth[16] and then knowing the rise and fall of its sounds,
the contraction and dilation in the positions of a dance;[17] it was only
after [Confucius] practiced archery in the orchard of Jue Xiang that the
spectators appeared, standing around like a wall,[18] and Xu Dian raised
his drinking vessel[19] [for a speech]. Should one exceed these bounds and
be guided by one's own subjective speculations instead, then ultimately
one cannot be on intimate terms [with the actuality or Dao]. Formerly,
Ziyou and Zixia were known for being students of *Wen*. This means
merely observing how things come together without obstruction[20] and
deliberating upon its disposition for detriment and benefit, and it is not

specifically limited to the *Wen* of belles lettres. Ah! The *Wen* of which I speak is born of heaven, conveyed by the earth, and propagated by the sages. Once its roots are established, then its ends are set in their proper channels. Once its form is ascertained, then its use becomes manifest. These are what have control over the great transformation of *yin* and *yang*, regulate the three most important social relationships,[21] and order the six social relations. It is that which traverses the terminus a quo and terminus ad quem of the universe, orders the myriad things, and completes the eight corners of the world. Ah! Those who do not know the *Wen* of the warp of heaven and the weft of the earth, how could they be fit to talk about it?

The effecting of *Wen* is necessarily in virtue of *qi*-cultivation. [Human] *qi* is coeval with heaven and earth. Should it fill [the body], it can be counterpart to the three numina[22] and sovereign of the myriad things. Should this not be the case, then it is because one is but a petty man. Therefore, the exemplary gentleman concerns himself with the internal as opposed to the external, with the great as opposed to the small. Physical might [of extraordinary people] is capable of lifting a cauldron. While the common people struggle with this, Wu Huo was capable of achieving it. That the exemplary gentleman does not esteem this is because he considers it to be limited to the small. Intellectual might [of extraordinary people] is capable of vanquishing a tiger. While the common people struggle with this, Feng Fu was capable of achieving it. That the exemplary gentleman does not esteem this is because he considers it to be striving after the external. Should *qi* be appropriately cultivated, there is nothing that it does not cover, nothing that it does not exhaustively reach. Should one grasp *qi* fully and apply it to *Wen*, then there is nothing that one cannot harmonize with, nothing that one cannot encompass. The borders of the highest heaven[23] cannot be glimpsed. The origins of the arrangement of the world's eight pillars[24] is unfathomable; but the magnitude of our *Wen* is such that it achieves this. The ceaseless circulation of the sun and moon, the firmament's myriad stars do not orbit in disorder on account of the blazing light of our *Wen*. The Yuanpu garden of the ethereal beings atop Mount Kunlun[25] achieves its utmost purity, the nine stories of celestial palace of the Cengcheng [of Mount Kunlun][26] achieves its profundity on account of the loftiness of our *Wen*. The south and north, west and east seas are inexhaustibly magnanimous and nurturing, and so give life to the fishes, the dragons, the waves and the tides, due to the profundity of our *Wen*. The thunder and lightning stimulate it. The wind and cloud contract and extend it, the rain and dew moisten and nourish it, even the ethereal ghosts and numinous spirits were never once able to thoroughly comprehend its terminus a quo and terminus ad quem.[27] All that resides between above and below spontaneously gain their color and shape. Those with wings, fly; those with feet, run; those who are submerged in water, swim; those that are planted, bloom. [It is] so immense and so minute, so lofty and so lowly, that it is impossible to enumerate and formulate. Our *Wen* achieves this because it endows form in conformity with the material's disposition. Ah! This *Wen*, when the sages acquired it, they transmitted to the coming ages as a sacred text. Once the virtuous people acquire it, then it can be unfailingly valid in any application.[28] It supports heaven and earth without trespassing, illuminates the sun and moon without excess, and helps coordinate the four seasons without transgression. Is this not the consummation of *Wen*? The Great Dao weakens and *Wen* declines daily [when] we strive after the external as opposed to the internal and we are limited to the small as opposed to setting our intentions upon the large. There is no other cause for this than that the four flaws, eight obscurities, and nine scourges afflict it [*Wen*]. What is it that we call the four flaws? Not making a distinction between the elegant and the common is dissolution; not bringing the root and branch into accord is incompletion; not tying the sinew and bones [of the text] together is sloppiness; not achieving the objective is mediocrity. These then are the four flaws that despoil *Wen*'s form. What is it that we call the eight obscurities? The dissimulating uses it to despoil the authentic, the elliptical uses it to erode the rounded, the mediocre uses it to sully the extraordinary, the emaciated uses it to triumph over the voluptuous, the crude uses it to disarray the rarefied, the piecemeal use it to harm the integral, the ignoble uses it to extinguish the ecumenical, and the purblind uses it to impair the enlightened. These then are the eight things that harm the very bone and marrow of *Wen*. What is it that we call the nine scourges? It churns up the thoroughly genuine, dissipates the numinous, disorientates *qi*, yields to private interest, extinguishes knowledge, beautifies the obtuse, disregards heaven, obscures omens, and brings ruin to actualities. These then are the nine things that cause *Wen*'s heart to die. Should any one of these be present, then the heart [of *Wen*] will die. When the heart dies then *Wen* will be brought to ruin. The spring blossom competes with the autumn grass for the foot of the mountains. The eagle cries in the forest while the cricket calls by the steps. The water overflows the footprints of a cow and the fire blaze outshines the tail of a firefly. One can put garments on a clay image but it still cannot see or hear. Flies and midges are born and die in earthenware. That they do not know the extent of the four seas [the world] and the vastness of the six directions [the universe] is all because they have no knowledge of *qi*-cultivation. If people can cultivate their *qi*, then their feelings will be deep and their *Wen* will be clear.[29] When their *qi* flourishes, then their spirit will be transformed and [human *Wen*] will carry out tasks of equal worth as heaven and earth. Would it not indeed be tragedy if [such a *Wen*] carries out tasks of equal worth as heaven and earth and yet its wisdom ends up in the hands of a petty man?

Glossary

There are a few key terms that I use in this project. I will explain how I use them.

correlative thinking

Many sinologists, since the 1950s have embraced the term "correlative cosmology" to describe a distinctively Chinese, protoscientific attitude to nature (Nylan 2010, 398). Scholars who have used the term are Émile Durkheim and Marcel Mauss, Marcel Granet, Hellmut Wilhelm, Joseph Needham and Wang Ling, John Henderson, Benjamin Schwartz, A. C. Graham, John Major, David L Hall and Roger T. Ames, and Aihe Wang. I will hazard my own definition: "Correlative thinking describes a world in which the myriad things mutually affect and respond to each other. It describes the fundamental sympathy that exists between all things in the world."

***Geist*/spirit**

Geist is often translated as "mind," "intellect," or "spirit." It is a key term in Hegel's phenomenology. It is one of the terms Hegel had in mind when he said he wished to teach philosophy to speak German and is difficult to translate into English. In the Hegelian sense, it is that which flows through and is manifest in the human world, in the sense of the national spirit, or the spirit of different ages. For Cassirer, "We must not understand the term 'Geist' or spirit as designating a metaphysical entity opposed to another entity called 'matter.' . . . The term 'Geist' is correct; but we must not use it as a name of a substance—a thing 'quod in se est et per se concipitur' [what is in itself and is conceived through itself]. We should use it in a functional sense as a comprehensive

203

name for all those functions which constitute and build up the world of human culture" (Cassirer 1945, 113–14). For Cassirer, *Geist* requires its materialization in what we can call "objective *Geist*"—that is, the facta of culture. As Christian Möckel describes it, Cassirer's view of *Geist* must not be understood as merely the will to master life, but rather as the will to form (*Gestaltung, Formung*) (Möckel 2003, 384). John Michael Krois and Donald Phillip Verene write that for Cassirer, *Geist* involves both senses of its standard translation into "mind" or "spirit"; sometimes, however, it is best rendered by "culture" (*PSF* 4:xn6).

humanism

By "humanism" I mean a secular humanism whereby humans are recognized as the creators of their own values. The best way I can think of to describe Cassirer's humanism is to quote this satire of his famous 1929 encounter with Heidegger at Davos. A young Emmanuel Lévinas, who was present at the occasion, parodied him as intoning, "Humboldt, culture, Humboldt, culture" (Lévinas 1994, 210; quoted in Skidelsky 2008, 1). Humboldt referred to Wilhelm von Humboldt, philosopher, statesman, and pioneer of the modern university. Culture referred to the ideal, shared by educated nineteenth-century Germans, that self-realization is the goal of life and that we realize ourselves by embracing the world as opposed to sinking into introspection, as in German pietism.

The German humanism that Cassirer embodies can be most easily understood through the tradition that he is a legacy of: the *Goethezeit*. The Humboldtian idea of education as *Bildung* is most famously elaborated upon and upheld by Hans-Georg Gadamer. Gadamer premised his magnum opus, *Truth and Method*, on the fact that objectivity in the humanities does not rely on the same methods as in the exact sciences. The point of the humanities lies in the Herderian idea of "rising up to humanity through culture" (Emporbildung zur Humanität; Gadamer 2004, 9). It is through humanistic learning that we overcome our provincialism and raise ourselves up to a certain universalism and become free, to uphold our own human dignity. For Gadamer, we can never hope to obtain a bird's-eye view that would enable us to transcend our own limited perspectives. Unlike the sciences, which seek to discover verifiable laws, the humanities should teach us that there is no ultimate foundation for understanding the truth about human beings; what truth there is lies in embracing a pluralism of different perspectives with which we elevate ourselves to a relatively higher universalism. This universalism is thus a task, a terminus ad quem (as opposed to a terminus a quo) that we never reach, toward which our efforts must constantly be aimed.

With respect to the Chinese tradition, I am referring to the cluster of words associated with the word *Wen*: *renwen* (人文), *Wenming* (文明), *Wenhua* (文化), *Wenzi* (文字), *Wenxue* (文学), *Wenjiao* (文教). My claim is that the Chinese tradition, from the formative period that I cover in this project, had a comparable understanding of humanism to the German period of which Cassirer is a legacy. In its most general sense, *wen* is "pattern"; *wen* is also "literature," "writing" itself. *Wen* is to be "cultivated," to have the civility (*Wenming* 文明), grace and sensibility (*Wenhua* 文化) that results from education (*wenjiao* 文教). *Wen* is the civil aspect of society, as opposed to the military (*wu* 武). A person of *Wen* unites the semantic multivalence of the word: becoming *accomplished* (*Wen*) through education, he can serve the government in a *civil* (*wen*) post, his competence for the role having been examined by a test of his *writing* (*Wenzhang* 文章). Such a person of *wen* (*Wenren* 文人) will then be drawn by *literature* itself (*Wenxue* 文学) or by the *humanities* (*renwen* 人文).

tian ren he yi (天人合一)

This phrase literally means heaven/cosmos/sky and man's union into one. By *tian ren he yi*, I mean "a mutually participatory relationship between man and the cosmos." Liu Xiaogan writes that "in the twentieth century, '*tian ren he yi*' has become a mature proverbial expression of traditional Chinese characteristics. Some call it the most foundational statement of Chinese philosophy, or way of thinking/orientation" (Liu 2011, 68). Perhaps the most famous representative of this sentiment is Qian Mu (钱穆; 1895–1990), who wrote in his article "The Contributions of Chinese Culture towards the Future of Humankind" that, although he had often spoken about *tian ren he yi*, it was only in his later years that he realized that "this concept was the natural point of belonging for traditional Chinese culture." He proposes that *tian ren he yi* is Chinese culture's biggest contribution to humankind (Qian 1991, 93). In this project, I make the point that the post-Kantian tradition to which Cassirer is indebted, aimed for a similar *tian ren he yi*. For the Confucian tradition this *tian ren he yi* is an *assumption*—it is a terminus a quo; whereas for the German tradition I refer to, this *tian ren he yi* is a terminus ad quem.

Notes

Introduction

1. See appendix 1 for all the classical Chinese uses of *wen*.

2. See Anghie (2004, 13–31).

3. The source of the principles behind Vitoria's proto–international law were "all Western and thoroughly Christo-Eurocentric in their normative orientation," i.e., Roman law, Holy scripture, classical writers, St. Augustine and St. Thomas (Williams 1990, 101). Likewise, Alberico Gentili, as the first writer to develop Vitoria's arguments on the issue of the justification for universal empire, saw Roman law as the civil expression of the law of nature. Roman law was thus not simply the accumulated customs of all the peoples of the entire world but was the ontological structure of reality itself: Roman law was natural law per se (Pagden 2015, 83–84).

4. For an introduction to natural science and philosophy's implication in racial theorization during colonialism, see chapters 1–9 in Bernasconi and Lott (2000, 1–83).

5. My use of the term "form" is thus strictly qualified. Although the most immediate association with the term is perhaps the misleading Platonic conception of form as the substantial, eternal essences of things behind their appearances, "form" is still the most appropriate term, all things considered, for describing the conception of a "cultural organization of experience" that is shared between Cassirer and the Confucians. In his famous encounter with Heidegger at the Davos debate of 1929, Cassirer stressed again and again how his, and the Marburg neo-Kantians', understanding of Kant was functional: "Being in the new metaphysics is, in my language, no longer the Being of a substance, but rather the Being that starts from a variety of functional determinations and meanings" (nicht mehr das Sein einer Substanz, sondern das Sein, das von einer Manigfaltigkeit von funktionellen Bestimmungen und Bedeutung ausgeht; cited in Gordon 2010, 208).

In the Confucian context, underlying the various concepts foundational to a Confucian conception of culture—*xiang* (象), *shi* (诗), *wen* (文), *li* (礼)—is the idea that one has to give "form" (*xing* 形) to experience. *Xici* 1.12 expresses this: "Therefore what is above physical form [*xing* 形] pertains to the Dao, and what is below physical form pertains to concrete objects [*qi* 器]" (Lynn 1994, 67; modified).

6. Although ritual is a key aspect of the Confucian conception of culture, I have not concentrated on it in this project. This is because I do not have any substantial insight to add to the many great works that already exist on the subject.

7. Other claimants to this title could conceivably be Giambattista Vico and especially the American pragmatist John Dewey. Vico is, in my opinion, more suitably understood as the *father* of the philosophy of culture, but not the "greatest." Part of the reason I have chosen to focus on Ernst Cassirer's philosophy is that, as a historical thinker, he makes his intellectual lineage very clear. This intellectual genealogy becomes very useful in this comparative thesis for explaining how and why Cassirer came to have a conception of culture comparable with the Confucian tradition. Key figures in this story are, as we will see, Leibniz and the thinkers of the *Goethezeit*.

8. By "classical" I refer to texts written before and during the Han Dynasty. An exception will be the *Literary Mind and Carving of Dragons*, as, despite its post-Han composition date, it is the first comprehensive work of literary criticism.

9. As Oswald Schwemmer has written, Cassirer has become a symbolic leader for those who see him as a pioneer of a "modern" way of doing philosophy. Cassirer's revival is rooted, for Schwemmer, in his cultural definition of *Geist* (Schwemmer 1997, 9).

10. Most of the influential postwar thinkers were influenced by Heidegger—Alexander Kojève, Hans Jonas, Rudolf Bultmann, Lévinas, Sartre, Arendt, Jaspers, Gadamer, Marcuse, and Strauss.

11. By which I mean the Weberian and Foucauldian analysis of the bureaucratic state. Modernity as distinguished by the complex interplay of various institutions seems to require that an ethics adequate to it is a system of distributive justice (the correct social allocation of goods in a society). The kind of ethical system based on the cultivation of personal morality is seen as inadequate for the realities of the modern world. In *The Trouble with Confucianism*, William Theodore de Bary describes this malaise that modern writers tend to see in Confucianism: "Still others who find Neo-Confucians to blame do so . . . , citing their impractical idealism, naive optimism, and simple moralistic approach to politics that was altogether incapable of coping with the economic complications and Byzantine complexities of imperial politics" (de Bary 1991, 54).

12. For an account of how the West invented Confucianism as a religion, see Sun (2013).

13. That is, no purely (causal) neurological explanation of depression is enough to "solve" the question of emotional suffering and therefore tell us

how to deal with it. It is this scientific-deterministic mindset that leads to the pathologization of human emotions today and causes more problems than it solves. Human beings are ultimately more than chemistry. My position is very similar to Mary Midgley when she writes, "And for our real problems in the world, which are essentially social and moral, biochemical solutions (as proposed in genetic engineering) are usually irrelevant. . . . These schemes still seem to me to be just displacement activities proposed in order to avoid facing our real difficulties" (2002, x).

14. In July 1917, one of the most influential writers in Central Europe, Hermann Bahr (1863–1934) published an essay on the current situation in Germany and Austria-Hungary, searching for a "contemporary Goethe" who could harness the dangerous forces in modernity. Bahr's candidate for this con-temporary Goethe was Cassirer (Bahr 1917, 1484).

15. Jesinghausen-Lauster has argued that Cassirer's philosophy is chiefly (*hauptsächlich*) influenced by Goethe. He writes that "my thesis is that Cassirer sought to overcome Kant through recourse to Goethe" (Jesighausen-Lauster 1985, 68). As early as 1951, in a review of the fourth volume of *The Problem of Knowledge*, Isabel Stearns writes that "one feels that Cassirer's references to Goethe suggest a certain completion to his thought which he could not as a *critical* [Kantian] thinker, allow himself explicitly to formulate in a conclusive manner (119). Donald Phillip Verene writes that "there is a separate study to be written of Goethe's influence on Cassirer" (2011, xiii). Sebastian Luft writes, "Goethe's influence on Cassirer is vast, and a full appreciation of Goethe's influence on Cassirer would demand a full-scale study of Goethe's thought itself" (2015b, 143). A special volume edited by Barbara Naumann and Birgit Recki, *Cassirer und Goethe: Neue Aspekte einer philosophisch-literarischen Wahlverwandtschaft*, contains several essays exploring the relationship between Goethe and Cassirer. I have especially drawn on John Michael Krois's (2002) "Die Goethischen Elemente in Cassirers Philosophie" and Massimo Ferrari's (2002) "Was wären wir ohne Goethe? Motive der frühen Goethe-Rezeption bei Ernst Cassirer."

16. In the manuscript of a course Cassirer offered on Goethe in Sweden, he explains his own lifelong interest in Goethe thus: "[One does not feel] such a universal sense of spiritual [*geistige*] liberation from any other poet in world literature as from him." Goethe was a liberator in every field to which he directed his attention: "Goethe wanted to act as the liberator from the nets of philistines, from intellectual pressure, intellectual narrowness, and timidity, from simple-mindedness, and prejudice—and this he regarded as the meaning of his life-work" (2003b, 241).

17. Throughout this book, unidentified translations are my own, but they will be identified in certain circumstances.

18. Leo Strauss similarly summarizes Cassirer's project as a reconciliation of dualisms in his review of *The Myth of the State*: "Possibly Cassirer believed

that while the enlightenment was right in rejecting myth, it laid itself open to legitimate criticism by failing to give an adequate account of myth, and that, with his analysis of myth filling that lacuna, the fundamental moral-political thesis of the enlightenment no longer encounters serious difficulties" (1947, 127).

19. Mann's novels represent the mood that Peter Gay describes when he writes about Heidegger's philosophy: "Their general purport seemed plain enough: man is thrown into the world, lost and afraid; he must learn to face nothingness and death." Heidegger gave a philosophical respectability to the love affair with "unreason and death that dominated so many Germans in this hard time" (Gay 2001, 82). The abiding theme in Mann's oeuvre is similarly the fragility of the human will in the face of life. "The three names," Mann famously wrote in *Reflections of a Nonpolitical Man*, "I must acknowledge when I search for the basis of my intellectual-artistic development—Schopenhauer, Nietzsche and Wagner—are like triple stars of eternally united spirits that shines powerfully in the German sky" (1983, 49). Mann was a novelist of the *Lebensphilosophie* esprit.

20. In his book A *Philosophy of Culture: The Scope of Holistic Pragmatism*, for example, Morton White examines the development of a "philosophy of culture" in the American tradition. For White, philosophy of culture emerged with William James and John Dewey, Nelson Goodman's works on art, W. V. O. Quine's works on the philosophy of science, Oliver Wendell Homes's work on legal philosophy, and John Rawls's work on political philosophy (White 2002, 1). Under this interpretation of the philosophy of culture, then, it began to take shape in the late nineteenth and the twentieth centuries. The fact that White had to define and defend such a "philosophy of culture" indicates that it is still far from established. The only other philosopher who has arguably taken culture serious as relevant to the philosophical enterprise is John Dewey, especially in his late works.

21. By "positivism," I refer to the way that the term was deployed by Auguste Comte, in which only positive facts and observable phenomena, and the objective relations of these and the laws that determine them, are recognized. Comtean positivism formatively influenced sociology. Émile Durkheim, for example, wrote in *The Rules of Sociological Method* that the main goal for sociologists is "to extend the scope of scientific rationalism to cover human behavior by demonstrating that . . . it is capable of being reduced to relationships of cause and effect. . . . What has been called our positivism is but a consequence of this rationalism" (1982, 33).

22. As one Cassirer commentator puts it, "the philosophy of symbolic forms is the philosophy that one needs when one has recognized that the physicalistic naturalization of *Geist* is doomed to failure" (Kreis 2010, 11). "The simple basic idea [*Grundgedanke*] of the philosophy of objective spirit is that our nature is the world in which we live and not the world of which the natural sciences speak" (14).

23. I develop these points in my article "Orientalism and Enlightenment Positivism: A Critique of Anglophone Sinology, Comparative Literature, and Philosophy" (Xiang 2018).

24. The above is taken from my article "Orientalism and Enlightenment Positivism" (Xiang 2018, 27–28).

25. This inability to concede "freedom" to China, and the non-"West" in general has, historically, been a defining feature of Western racism. In the appendix to the introduction of his lectures on the *Philosophy of World History*, for example, Hegel talks of the oriental realm as one still immersed in external nature and so being unable to "attain the inward conditions of subjective freedom" (1975, 202). See my article "The Racism of Philosophy's Fear of Cultural Relativism" (Xiang 2020) with regard to this issue.

26. The section covering the literature review is taken from my article "Orientalism and Enlightenment Positivism" (Xiang 2018, 40).

27. I think Brook Ziporyn makes the same criticism of this historicizing tendency in sinology when he writes that "the same consideration applies to the problem of 'essentialism' when talking about 'the Chinese tradition.' In my view, the historicist attack on essentialism, which is almost the primary dogma of intellectual history in our day, is well-intentioned but misguided. It may seem like progress when, instead of saying, 'The Chinese think like this,' as the first few generations of unabashed orientalists were prone to do, we say, 'Members of this school of thought in the mid-Tang period in the Zhejiang region thought like this,' or better, 'This guy, at this time and place, in this text, meant this'" (2012, 13). My criticism of this historicizing is that it leaves us with *meaningless disjecta membra*.

Chapter 1

1. This understanding of "culture" must be distinguished from the Kantian idea that culture is a bridge between our determinacy as natural objects and the transcendent world of freedom. Culture is not a bridge to an *existing* world of freedom, as it is for Kant; it *creates* an immanent space of possibility in which we can freely exercise our specifically human capacities, in infinitely indeterminate ways.

2. In this qualified sense, this use of "freedom" also serves as a corrective against the prevalent notion of Confucianism as merely a set of pragmatic norms for governing behavior, and not about personal realization.

3. I am taking this definition from Michael Forster's work on Herder (Forster 2010, 1). As we will see later in this chapter, Charles Taylor takes this view of language to be a typically "Romantic" understanding of growth, and he terms this particular paradigm "expressivism." For Taylor, this expressivist paradigm

is ultimately modeled on biological notions of growth. Materialization in a concrete form is to realize something that was only previously a nebulous potential.

4. It is important to stress that for Cassirer language is only one symbolic form among many others and does not necessarily take precedence over the others. I use the term "linguistic turn" to emphasize the idea that spirit (meaning) is dependent on and bounded to a concrete, sensory sign (such as language), *not* that all the symbolic forms are reducible to language.

5. The *Yijing* is traditionally regarded as the collected work of four of the Chinese tradition's greatest sages: the legendary Fu Xi (伏羲), who created the trigrams and with it a whole swathe of cultural institutions; the historical Wen Wang (文王) (ca. 1100–1050 BCE), the founder of the Zhou dynasty (1046–256); Zhou Gong (周公) (ca. 1090–1032 BCE), a son of Wen Wang who consolidated the founding of the Zhou dynasty; and Confucius (551–479 BCE), born five hundred years after the death of Wen Wang. Evolving from a mantic tradition dating back more than 3000 years, the *Yijing* found its present form around 1800 years ago (Nielsen 2003, xv). After 136 BCE—the year that Confucianism was adopted as the state orthodoxy—the *Yijing* became the preeminent book of the Confucian classics.

6. Which are traditionally attributed to Confucius and are "almost certainly Warring States [475–221 BCE] compositions" (Lewis 1999, 242)

7. There are many passages in the *Zuo Zhuan* and *Guoyu* that show the literati trying to intellectually appropriate the *Yijing* from the professional diviners (Lewis 1999, 243–52).

8. For Mark Edward Lewis, there are two levels of evidence for this claim. The first is internal to the *Xici* itself; the second is found externally in the wider tradition. In terms of the internal evidence, the fact that writing is the final invention in *Xici* 2.2 and that it is the only invention that supplants an earlier one—the knotted cords—"marks writing as the culmination of Fu Xi's invention of the trigrams" (Lewis 1999, 199). The structure of the text itself, as moving from hexagrams to written characters, recapitulates the historical invention. In terms of the external evidence, in the apocryphal literature, the trigrams were described as "old scripts" (*gu wen* 古文)—as the origins of written characters. In the Xu Shen's postface to the *Shuowen Jiezi*, for example, we are given an account of the origins of writing that is modelled on the *Xici* 2.2, so that "the invention of writing is traced directly to the trigrams" (Lewis 1999, 199). The most detailed account of Cang Jie's invention of graphs, in *Chun qiu yuan ming bao* (春秋元命包) is an expanded version of the account of Fu Xi's discovery of the trigrams. The early Jin dynasty *Di wang shi ji* (帝王世纪) attributes the invention of writing directly to Fu Xi, as does the fourth century *Shi yi ji* (拾遗记) (Lewis 1999, 199). I might add to Lewis's authoritative guide that, in the later imperial tradition, Song Lian's (1310–81) "The Origins of Wen" (*Wen yuan* 文原) follows the same paradigm of attributing the origins of language to Fu Xi.

For another account of the early history of the identification between the genesis of *wen* in the *Shuowen* with the *Xici*, see William G. Boltz's *The Origin and Early Development of the Chinese Writing System* (1994, esp. ch. 4 and pp. 129–38). Boltz deems the Cang Jie and Fu Xi legends to be from no earlier than ca. 300 BCE (130). According to him, after the Han dynasty, Fu Xi was directly associated with the invention of writing and often explicitly designated as its creator (136).

9. The hexagrams were not simply seen as "one technology among others, but rather the ultimate form of those capacities that made possible all the sagely inventions and institutions" (Lewis 1999, 197).

10. Fu Xi, also known as Paoxi. Culture hero in Chinese legend and mythology, credited with the invention of hunting, fishing, and cooking as well as the Cangjie system of writing Chinese characters. Fu Xi was counted as the first of the Three Sovereigns at the beginning of the Chinese dynastic period.

11. Xu Shen's postface to the *Shuowen Jiezi* (说文解字) and the opening chapter of Liu Xie's *The Literary Mind and the Carving of Dragons* (文心雕龙), for example, closely mirror the sage's invention of the trigrams in *Xici* 2.2.

12. I am well aware that throughout history there have been those who have been skeptical about the "Confucian" heritage of the *Xici*—notably Ouyang Xiu. In modern times, the Confucian orientation of the text has been questioned by Feng Youlan, Gu Jiegang, Qian Mu, and Hou Wailu. Chen Guying has famously argued that the *Xici* was written by Daoists. In an article entitled "The Writing of the Xici Zhuan and the Making of the Yijing," Edward Shaughnessy argues that there are different strata to the text based on their grammatical constructions (2001, 199). I refer to this text as Confucian because the key passage that I refer to, *Xici* 2.2, is evidently defending the importance of social institutions. This "stratum" of the text, at least, is clearly a Confucian orientation. In fact, in its defense of social institutions such as funerary rites, *Xici* 2.2 sounds much like Han Yu's (韩愈) argument in favor of Confucianism against Daoism and Buddhism in "Origins of the Way" (原道).

13. For reasons that will become obvious, my interpretation of the *Xici* is thus diametrically opposed to Puett's, who writes, "The authors of the *Xici zhuan* argue strongly for the efficacy of divination . . . not because it is *wen* but because it is *shen* [神]" (2002, 189).

14. "To enter into Ernst Cassirer's philosophy" is thus "to become immersed in the history of philosophy and the general historical development of culture" (Krois 1987, ix). His own philosophical works are saturated with historical discussions, while his historical works are interwoven with his own philosophical theses. Hans Morgenthau once described this feature of Cassirer's work thus: "In truth, he was not a historian of philosophy, but a philosopher who used history as a vehicle for philosophic thought" (1947, 142).

15. In almost all of Cassirer's works, even the strictly epistemological works such as *Das Erkenntnisproblem* and *Substance and Function*, there is the stress on the new humanism for man's intellectual and ethical liberation. In his more directly humanistic works such as *Freiheit und Form* and *The Individual and the Cosmos in Renaissance Philosophy*, Cassirer's emphasis is on the humanism won through Europe's overcoming of medieval ontology.

16. This second epicenter is derived from the first, in the sense that the figures of the *Goethezeit* had the same conception of humanism as the Renaissance: "All of these authors followed the Renaissance in viewing man as a being whose constant task consists in perfecting his own self, in fulfilling his latent possibilities, again against any heteronomous tutelage of reason" (Grondin 1995, 112).

17. I have avoided using the term Romantic, as it is a still rather ill-defined international movement crossing many disciplines, so I would have to define it before using it, and this is outside the scope of this project.

18. I am grateful to Guido Kreis for suggesting to me that I could frame my project in terms of "symbolic idealism."

19. For Puett is referencing passages 1.11 and 2.2 in particular and adds, "By claiming that the sage, in creating the trigrams, has simply replicated the patterns he has observed in the natural world, the author denies the connotations of artifice . . ." (2001, 87).

20. For Lewis, the "fullness of meaning offered by the *Yi* is possible because it is directly rooted in the patterns of the cosmos" (1999, 254–55).

21. For Peterson, "*hsiang* [*xiang*] are independent of any human observer; they are 'out there,' whether or not we look" (1982, 80). Puett summarizes Peterson's position: "As Willard Peterson has convincingly argued, the basic claim of the *Xici zhuan* is that the *Yi* is itself in accord with the processes of nature" (2002, 190).

22. Similarly, Rorty takes "representationalism" to be antithetical to "humanism." The humanist claim that "human beings have responsibilities only to one another entails giving up both representationalism and realism" (2007, 134). For Rorty, one needs to "get beyond representationalism, and thus into an intellectual world in which human beings are responsible only to each other" (2004, 4).

23. In the sense that, if reality is always already given, I will always long after a state where I have *immediate* access to this reality. Even if a naive realist allows that words can theoretically fully capture states of affairs, *because* language is always secondary upon that reality, the suspicion will be ever present that language has not fully captured a given reality.

24. I follow Hans-Johann Glock in holding that the "linguistic turn" of twentieth century analytic philosophy was anticipated by figures such as Hamann and Herder of eighteenth-century Germany (2015, 374). Michael Forster similarly writes that the definition of the linguistic turn as "thought is essentially dependent on and bounded by language" and that "meaning consists in the use

of words" must be traced to a series of German thinkers of the eighteenth and nineteenth centuries: "including Herder, Hamann, Schleiermacher, Friedrich Schlegel, Wilhelm von Humboldt, and Hegel" (Forster 2010, 1).

25. Under this view, "the concept does not appear as something foreign to sensuous reality, but forms a *part* of this reality; it is a selection from what is immediately contained in it" (SF 5).

26. For Cassirer, objectivity in science is thus understood in terms of the "unity" and "permanence" of physical theory (SF 322).

27. Which is to be found in *Substance and Function, Freiheit und Form, The Individual and the Cosmos in Renaissance Philosophy, The Philosophy of the Enlightenment, Das Erkenntnisproblem,* and "The Phenomenology of the Linguistic Form" (the latter is in PSF 1:115–76).

28. Cf. Cassirer's discussion of Parmenides's monism in "Mythic, Aesthetic and Theoretical Space": "Absolute identity, unity, and uniformity alone constitute the basic logical character of being. Being cannot transform its nature without denying and losing it in this transformation, without falling victim to its opposite—non-being" (1969, 7–8).

29. Nicolas of Cusa was also a crucial figure in this story for Cassirer: "Time and again, he [Cusa] seeks to connect the general and the universal to the particular, to the immediate sensible" (1963, 31).

30. "In the foundation for the general characteristic laid down by Leibniz, we admittedly find the point of view not only that language serves for the expression and presentation of a finished world of concepts and ideas [*Vorstellungen*] but also that language contains a particular power and gift of 'inventing'; it not only dismantles and puts together in an analytic fashion the content of consciousness but also expands it in a synthetic way" (KEH 110).

31. See the letter to Cohn from 1903: "I claim . . . that the entire metaphysical theory of *representation* [*Abbildtheorie*] is definitely overcome with Leibniz: there are no absolute objects that have an effect on consciousness and thereby create in it the representation as after-image [*Nachbild*]" (Cassirer 2009, 9; my translation).

32. "It is one of the essential advantages of the sign—as Leibniz pointed out in his *Characteristica generalis*, that it serves not only to represent, but above all to *discover* certain logical relations—that it not only offers a symbolic abbreviation for what is already known, but opens up new roads into the unknown" (PSF 1:109). Michael Forster, who traces the linguistic turn—"thinking is essentially dependent on language-possession and bounded in its scope by the thinker's capacity for linguistic articulation *simpliciter*" (2010, 59)—to Herder in particular, remarks that Herder had a "single ulterior source: the Leibniz-Wolff tradition" (61).

33. "The object cannot be regarded as a naked thing in itself, independent of the essential categories of natural science: for only within these categories which are required to constitute its form can it be described at all" (PSF 1:76).

34. "A system of physical concepts must reflect the relations between objective things as well as the nature of their mutual dependency, but this is only possible in so far as these concepts pertain from the outset to a definite, homogeneous intellectual orientation" (*PSF* 1:76).

35. 人能弘道, 非道弘人。

36. I take Cassirer to be referring to Johann Georg Hamann's *Metakritik über den Purismus der Vernuft* and Johann Gottfried Herder's *Metakritik zur Kritik der reinen Vernunft*.

37. Cassirer talked of his own work as "structural." In *An Essay on Man*, he writes, "In our study of language, art, and myth the problem of meaning takes precedence over the problem of historical development. . . . This structural view of culture must precede the merely historical view" (*EM* 69). For Krois, "Cassirer uses the term *structural* here in its contemporary sense—for a methodology developed primarily in linguistics by Ferdinand de Saussure, N. S. Trubetzkoy, Roman Jakobson, and others, but with clear parallels in fields such as biology (in the evolutionary theory of Goethe, Cuvier, and Geoffry de Sainte-Hilaire)" (1987, 74).

Cassirer's lecture "Structuralism in Modern Linguistics," read to the Linguistic Circle of New York on February 10, 1945, is seen as the first pronouncement of structuralism as an interdisciplinary methodology. See David Robey (1972, 2) and Peter Caws (1972, 64). There are many studies on the points of agreement between Cassirer's methodology and contemporary structuralism. See Roger Silverstone (1976), Reto Luzius Fetz (1981), and Edward Seltzer, "The Problem of Objectivity: A Study of Objectivity Reflected in a Comparison of the Philosophies of E. Cassirer, J. Piaget, and E. Husserl" (1969). Krois singles out the shared concept of "transformation" for special discussion: " 'Transformations' in language, in perception, and in biological processes, Cassirer claims, are radically different from mechanical processes so that the concept of causality is inapplicable to them" (1987, 74).

In her memoirs, Toni Cassirer recalls how Cassirer met and conversed with Roman Jakobson (a pioneer of the structural analysis of language) on the same freighter emigrating to the United States from Göterborg between May 20 and June 4, 1941: "The conversation lasted . . . nearly the whole fortnight of the passage and was extremely exciting and rewarding for both scholars. Whether it was stormy or not, whether the mines were dancing before us or not, whether the war news were positive or not—the two scholars discussed their linguistic problems with the greatest enthusiasm" (T. Cassirer 1981, 282; my translation).

38. Note that Zhang Dongsun is the current pinyin romanization of 张东荪. The bibliographic citation cites Zhang Dongsun as Chang Tung-sun, as this was how his name was rendered under the standard Wade-Giles system of romanization when he wrote the article.

39. This article originally appeared under the title "Thought, Language, and Culture" in the *Yenching Journal of Social Studies* in 1939 Vol. 1 (2), 155–191. This was a translation by Li Anzhai (李安宅) of the original Chinese article of 1938,《思想语言与文化》in the journal《社会学界》.

40. "The rules of 'contradiction' and 'excluded middle' are simply corollaries of the law of identity" (Chang 1952, 213n10).

41. "It is characteristic of Western philosophy to penetrate into the background of a thing, while the characteristic of Chinese thought lies in exclusive attention to the correlational implications between different signs, such as *yin* and *yang*. . . . It is also because of this fact that there is no trace of the idea of substance in Chinese thought. . . . Chinese thought takes cognizance only of the signs and the relations between them" (Chang 1952, 216).

42. For example, in *Substance and Function*, Cassirer talks of how assigning a real number to a temperature by measuring a volume of mercury presupposes the laws of geometry as well as the law relating temperature to the expansion of mercury (SF 142–43).

43. For Kasulis, the jigsaw (holographic) paradigm attained its fullest philosophical expression in the Chinese Huayan school of Buddhism (2015, 35).

44. "Instead of complaining that we cannot penetrate to the 'inside of nature,' we have to realize that for us there is no other 'inside' than that which is revealed through observation and analysis of phenomena" (*DI* 135).

45. "The reality of the physicist stands over against the reality of immediate perception as something through and through mediated; as a system, not of existing things or properties, but of abstract intellectual symbols, which serve to express certain relations of magnitude and measure, certain functional coordinations and dependencies of phenomena" (SF 357).

46. As Cassirer writes in *Determinism and Indeterminism in Modern Physics*: "Heinrich Hertz is the first modern scientist to have effected a decisive turn from the *copy theory of physical knowledge to a purely symbolic theory*. The basic concepts of natural science no longer appear as mere copies and reproductions of immediate material data; rather, they are represented as *constructive projects* of physical thinking—and the only condition of their theoretical validity and significance is that their logical consequences must always accord with the observable data. In this sense, the whole world of physical concepts may now be defined as a world of *pure signs*, as was done by Helmholtz in his theory of knowledge" (*PSF* 3:20; my emphases). In his article "Philosophy, Thought and Language," Hans-Johann Glock similarly points to how (the "neo-Kantian philosopher scientist") Heinrich Hertz's idea that scientific explanation is determined by formal constraints parallels the eighteenth-century linguistic turn toward language as the parameters of thought (Glock 1997, 156).

47. In the sense that human creations, like objects and ruins in the stories of German Romanticism (e.g., E. T. A. Hoffmann), become alienated, uncanny, and fearsome (*ungeheuer*). Toward the end of the paper (Cassirer 2012), Cassirer repeatedly confronts cultural pessimists such as Georg Simmel, Ludwig Klages, and Walter Rathenau.

48. I am referring to a story in the Heaven and Earth (天地) chapter of the Outer Chapters of the *Zhuangzi* where Zigong and Confucius happened upon an old farmer and suggested to him that using a piece of technology to water his fields would be more convenient than his more primitive practice. The farmer responded contemptuously that technology leads to a utilitarian, means-ends frame of mind, and thus takes one away from the Dao. I think *the* Daoist position with regard to technology would be much more sophisticated than that presented in the story here. I personally think that the Daoists' position is always an ironizing one in relation to a dominant narrative. It would thus be counter to the Daoist project to dogmatically assert that such and such is "bad." The Daoist position wouldn't necessarily be anti-culture as such; the key moment for the Daoists would be that we *recognize* how provisional cultural forms are. This story from the Outer Chapters might be pushing the Daoist message too far.

49. Cassirer's account of the scientific understanding as it relates to the philosophical issues of Kant's third Critique is paralleled by his 1936 publication *Determinism and Indeterminism in Modern Science*. In *Determinism and Indeterminism*, Cassirer formulated three stages in the acquisition of scientific knowledge: statements of the results of measurements, statements of laws, and statements of principles. Measurements deal with the gathering of data; statements of law join the particular measurements together into a united whole. Cassirer cites as examples of statements of law, the time and distances of fall with Galileo; distances and velocities with Kepler; and lengths and periods of the pendulum with Huyghens. Statements of principles are condensations of statements of laws; the laws themselves can be understood as special cases of these principles. "Principles are not themselves laws, but rules for seeking and finding laws. . . . They refer not directly to phenomena but to the form of the laws according to which we order these phenomena. . . . It is . . . the birthplace of natural laws" (*DI* 52–53). These categories are mutually defining; neither is ontologically prior to the other—the possibility of each category implies and presupposes the existence of the other. Related to this point is that, even in the lowest category, the statement of the results of measurement, there is no immediate access to "reality" through sense data. It is this very *symbolic* transformation from perceptual phenomena to "physical description" through the "physical concepts of measure and law," however, that allows for the possibility of scientific knowledge.

50. In this interpretation of Kant, we can see Cassirer's debt to Hermann Cohen and the Marburg neo-Kantians.

51. "We can never adequately understand organized beings and their inner possibilities, and indeed we cannot even apprehend thereby that they exist and how they exist merely through the mechanical principles of nature" (PK 122).

52. The reader might be struck by the similarities between Cassirer's ideas about scientific systems being heuristics for understanding nature and Thomas Kuhn's concept of paradigms. Michael Friedman (2008) has traced the links between Thomas Kuhn and the neo-Kantian tradition. I will pick up on the point between the flexibility of a prioris.

53. For Cassirer, "the purpose of the *Critique of Pure Reason* was not to ground philosophical knowledge once and for all in a fixed dogmatic system of concepts, but to open for it the 'continuous development of a science' in which there can be only relative, not absolute, stopping points" (SF 355). This means that Cassirer regarded Kant's system of the three Critiques not as a finished system but rather a working through of a continuous idea, where the third Critique is a culmination and resolution of the problems posed by the first two (see KLT).

54. For another account of Cassirer's overcoming of the Kantian antinomy, see Kreis (2010, 343–51, in the section "Tranzendentale Freiheit und Natur").

55. Cassirer similarly remarks upon the centrality of the organic paradigm in German Romanticism:

> Herder's prize essay marks the transition from the older rationalistic concept of "reflective form," which dominated the philosophy of the Enlightenment, to the Romantic concept of "organic form." . . . It would be unjust to suppose that the designation of language as an organism was a mere image or poetic metaphor. . . . For them [the Romantics], the "organism" signified not a particular class of phenomena, but a universal speculative principle, a principle which indeed constitutes the ultimate goal and systematic focus of Romantic speculation. The problem of the organism was a center to which the Romantics repeatedly found themselves drawn back from the most diverse fields. (PSF 1:153–54)

Chapter 2

1. The vocabulary of "concrete universal" is borrowed from Cassirer's work on the philosophy of language. I am therefore borrowing this term in order to make a comparative point. The Chinese tradition itself obviously has no such vocabulary.

2. In 1.1 of the *Xici*, we see *xiang* being used in its first sense—as a spontaneously generated, communicative, sensuous image:

As heaven is high and noble and earth is low and humble, so it is
that *Qian* and *Kun* are defined. . . . In heaven this [process] creates
images [*xiang* 象], and on earth it creates physical forms [*xing* 形];
this is how change and transformation manifest themselves. (Lynn
1994, 47; modified; 天尊地卑, 乾坤定矣。. . . 在天成像, 在地成形,
变化见矣。)

As far as I can see, the use of *xiang* as the spontaneous pattern of the
world's processes can also be found in: *Xici* 1.2, 1.3, 1.5, 1.10, 1.11, and 2.1.

3. The use of *xiang* in the sense of a semblance can be found in 2.1,
"The lines reproduce how particular things act, and the images [象] provide like-
nesses [像] of particular things" (Lynn 1994, 76; 爻也者, 效此者也。象也者, 像此
者也); and 2.3, "This is why the *Changes* [*yi* 易] as such consist of images [*xiang*
象]. The term *image* means 'the making of semblances'" (Lynn 1994, 80; 是故
《易》者, 象也; 象也者, 像也。). This usage can further be found in 1.9 and 1.12.

4. We find *xiang* used in its third sense of the trigrams/hexagrams in
1.8: "The sages had the means to perceive the mysteries [赜] of the world and,
drawing comparison [拟] to them with analogous things, made images [像] out of
those things that seemed appropriate [宜]. This is why these are called 'images'
[象]'" (Lynn 1994, 56–57; 圣人有以见天下之赜, 而拟诸其形容, 像其物宜, 是故谓
之象。).

5. Mou Zongsan writes, for example, that there are three meanings to
xiang in the *Xici*: (1) in terms of phenomena (*xian xiang* 现象), (2) in terms of
deriving a symbol or analogical image from phenomena (*qu xiang* 取象), and
(3) in terms of deriving a law from phenomena (Mou 2003, 9). For Richard J.
Smith, the *xiang* of the *Xici*, refers to "both representations and concepts, that
is, not only symbols for things that appear in nature (physical objects such as
mountains, bodies of water, the sun, the moon, and the stars), but also ideas
that can be grasped, positions that can be determined, situations that can be
identified, and processes that can be discerned" (2008, 39). In other contexts,
xiang can refer to "the actual graphic representations of things, including the
lines, doubled lines, trigrams, and hexagrams of the *Changes*" (274 footnote 38).

6. The commentary "Explaining the Trigrams" (说卦传) provides an
explanation of the *xiang* of each trigram, whereas the "Commentary on the
Images" (象传) provides an explanation of the *xiang* in each hexagram.

7. As Pauline Yu writes, "Implicit throughout the Great Commentary
[*Xici*], . . . is the assumption of a seamless connection, if not virtual identity, between
an object, its perception, and its representation, aided by the semantic multivalence of the term *xiang*. Such a conception never developed in the West, which
preferred to stress the distinction between representation and world" (1987, 40).

8. Likewise, in the introduction to *Focusing the Familiar*, Ames and Hall
write, "There is in classical Confucianism an unwillingness to separate description

and prescription, reality and its interpretation. Everything is always experienced from one perspective or another, where both experiencer and experienced context are implicated in the event. There is no design beyond how the non-additive sum of these particular perspectives construe their worlds" (2001, 36).

9. Zhang Dongsun has the same idea as I do when he writes that, "According to ancient Chinese thought, first came the signs then the development of things. [. . .] Although platonic ideas have a superficial resemblance, it must be remembered that Plato's 'ideas' are self-existent, which is not true in the case of the eight diagrams." (Chang 1952, 216) I think Zhang would have agreed with me that the *Xici* is operating under a "symbolic idealism" which overcomes the dualism of idealism and realism in Western philosophy.

10. In the chapter "The Interplay of Image and Concept" of *Heaven, Earth, and Man in the Book of Changes*, Hellmut Wilhelm gives a similarly "Kantian" reading of the *Xici*: "It is thus not simple recognition but the process of contemplation through which the contact between the self and the images is consummated" (Wilhelm 1977, 198–99). Wilhelm's interpretation of the *Xici* thus evokes Kant's togetherness principle, according to which, "thoughts without content are empty, intuitions without concepts are blind" (A51/B75; Kant 1996, 107). The mere data of impressions (images) are meaningless without human processing.

11. 圣人有以见天下之赜, 而拟诸其形容, 像其物宜, 是故谓之象。

12. 赜, 杂乱也。象, 卦之象, 如说卦所列者。

Note that Zhu Xi has commonly been regarded as the greatest Confucian since Confucius and Mencius. His commentaries on the Four Books—the *Analects, Mencius, Great Learning,* and *Doctrine of the Mean*—became the basis of the civil service examination for entry into the bureaucracy between 1313 and 1905.

13. Lynn, following Kong Yingda, takes *ze* to mean "mysteries" (幽深难见) (Wang and Kong 1999, 274).

14. 赜, 杂也。拟, 比拟也。诸犹乎也。万物之性各有其宜, 故曰「物宜」, 此言圣人有以见到天下事物之复杂, 从而用易卦拟其形态, 象征其物宜, 所以谓卦体曰象。

15. A variation of *Xici* 1.8 appears in *Xici* 1.12, where we read, "Therefore, as for the images [*xiang* 象], the sages had the means to perceive the confusion [*ze* 赜] of the world and, drawing comparisons [*xiang* 像] to them with analogous things, made images [*xiang* 象] out of those things that seemed appropriate" (Lynn 1994, 68; modified). The stress on the essential role of human creativity is even more unambiguously put in this passage.

16. 夫《易》, 圣人之所以极深而研几也。

17. 极未形之理则曰深, 适动微之会则曰几。

18. 古者包牺氏之王天下也, 仰则观象于天, 俯则观法于地, 观鸟兽之文与地之宜, 近取诸身, 远取诸物, 于是始作八卦, 以通神明之德, 以类万物之情。

19. Note that the Ralph Manheim translation of *PSF* 1 has translated "Zeichengebung" as "symbolic action" (*PSF* 1: 107).

20. "If perception did not embrace an originally symbolic element, it would offer no support and no starting point for the symbolism of language" (*PSF* 3:232).

21. The English translation of *Prägnanz* perhaps does not capture its full meaning in German. *Prägnanz* derives from the German *prägen* (to mint, emboss, impress, shape, mould, and coin) and the Latin *praegnens* (laden or ready to give birth). It embodies at once the ideas of giving form and fecundity. The English "pregnancy" only has the idea of fecundity.

22. To prove that perception itself is meaningful, Cassirer offers a thought experiment. In his 1927 essay "Das Symbolproblem und seine Stellung im System der Philosophie" (The Problem of the Symbol and Its Place in the System of Philosophy), Cassirer gives a phenomenological proof on how our perceptions are impregnated with meaning. He repeats this proof in the third volume of *PSF* (*PSF* 3:200–202), which appeared in the same year. In his proof, Cassirer asks us to consider the *Linienzug*, or graph-like line drawing. He asks us first to consider its sensory qualities, its shape, and physical qualities. A cultist might regard the line as a mark with magical qualities, an art historian might see it as an aesthetic object, whereas a mathematician might see it as a geometrical figure. The line thus always appears in some framework of meaning, and is what Cassirer meant when he said that symbolic pregnancy is "*the* way in which a perception as a sensory experience contains at the same time a certain nonintuitive meaning which it immediately and concretely represents."

23. Citing Husserl (*SF* 25n15), Cassirer claims that abstraction entails "directed 'intentions,' . . . the intelligent accomplishment of the most diversified and mutual independent acts of thought, each of which involves a particular sort of *meaning* of the content, a special direction of objective reference" (*SF* 25).

24. "The fluid impression assumes form and duration for us only when we *mould* it by symbolic action in one direction or another" (*PSF* 1:107).

25. One *could* interpret this genesis story to be a temporal one (i.e., there was a moment in history when the sages invented the trigrams/hexagrams), if we take what the sages invented to be a *more* sophisticated symbolic system than they previously had. I have interpreted what the sages invented to be an arch-symbol that represents symbolism/symbolic consciousness per se. This is because, as we see in *Xici* 2.2, the trigrams/hexagrams were understood to be the ur-symbolic system from which all the other institutions of culture are derived.

26. Again, my interpretation of the *Xici* is at odds with Puett's, who argues that "the *Xici zhuan*'s account of the creation of the *Yi* by the sages is a historical narrative" (2002, 193).

27. Again, I stress that, for Cassirer, Baoxi would not have been able to see "patterns" without an already sophisticated "symbolic consciousness" that Bao Xi *invents*. If we were to strictly follow Cassirer's line of interpretation, this story is anachronistic in that Baoxi already has this "symbolic consciousness" prior

to the invention of the trigrams. As I say, however, we can see the writers of the *Xici* as, *ex post facto*, explaining *how* we came to have symbols and symbolic consciousness by *positing* a fictional, "state of nature" narrative. In any case, I think the general point must be conceded that it is the invention of the trigrams that allowed for higher levels of human consciousness, and this is the key point that Cassirer similarly wants to stress. I want to emphasize the importance of *language* in the formation of civilization for both Confucianism and Cassirer.

28. 是故形而上者谓之道, 形而下者谓之器。

29. 与天地相似, 故不违; 知周乎万物, 而道济天下, 故不过; 旁行而不流, 乐天知命, 故不忧; 安土敦乎仁, 故能爱。范围天地之化而不过, 曲成万物而不遗, 通乎昼夜之道而知, 故神无方而《易》无体。

30. The evidence for identifying the *yi* (易) of this passage with the sage is this: "Looking up, we use it [*Yi*] to observe the configurations of heaven, and, looking down, we use it to examine the patterns of earth" (仰以观于天文, 俯以察于地理) is structurally very similar to *Xici* 2.2, when Baoxi "looked upward and observed the images in heaven and looked downward and observed the models that the earth provided" (仰则观象于天, 俯则观法于地) (Lynn 2004, 51, 77; modified).

31. As Krois notes, "Symbolic pregnance seems to be little more than a broadly formulated restatement of what Cassirer termed a symbolic form, but now he refers to the 'sensory' in general instead of to a 'sensory sign'" (Krois 1987, 54).

32. My interpretation of the Cassirerian self as function is echoed by Simon Truwant's article, "Cassirer's Functional Conception of the Human Being" (2015). Guido Kreis, in his *Cassirer und die Formen des Geistes*, writes that Cassirer's concept of the function leads naturally to a functional understanding of subjectivity. The subject is not a "substantial" one but a "functional connection point of orders [*funktionaler Ordungszusammenhang*]" (2010, 93). "Subjectivity is the nonobjective, regulated, total order of all objective experience" (93). My own interpretation of the mutual dependency between the sage/hermeneutic sign and the welter of phenomena is indebted to Kreis's discussion of Cassirer's functional subject (28).

33. Related to the idea that we must first separate before we harmonize what was separated is the idea found in the "Discourse on Music" (乐论) of the *Xunzi* that "music unites what is similar, whereas ritual differentiates" (乐合同, 礼别异). Although the Confucians here were making a social as opposed to epistemological point, there is a similar operative logic. Although, prior to human mediation, there is a holistic unity, it is only once humans have ordered the world and then unite it again that there is a meaningful integration. The whole that was prior to separation was an amorphous, chaotic whole. The whole that reunites the parts that have been divided is different in nature from the whole prior to division.

34. The *Zhongyong* is attributed to Kong Ji (孔伋; 483–402 BCE), the grandson of Confucius. The *Zhongyong* achieved canonical status when Zhu Xi made it one of the Four Books. The Four Books became the standard resource for the imperial examination system. I have chosen to use Ames and Hall's translation, as I agree with their interpretation of the Chinese cosmology as a processual one.

35. 唯天下至诚, 为能尽其性; 能尽其性, 则能尽人之性; 能尽人之性, 则能尽物之性; 能尽物之性, 则可以赞天地之化育; 可以赞天地之化育, 则可以与天地参矣。

36. 诚者自成也, 而道自道也。诚者物之终始, 不诚无物。是故君子诚之为贵。诚者非自成己而已也, 所以成物也。成己, 仁也; 成物, 知也。性之德也, 合外内之道也, 故时措之宜也。

37. 诚者, 天之道也; 诚之者, 人之道也。诚者不勉而中, 不思而得, 从容中道, 圣人也。诚之者, 择善而固执之者也。

38. Compare this to Cassirer's point about the relationship between symbolic pregnancy and the symbol: "This act of recognition is necessarily bound up with the function of representation and presupposes it. Only where we succeed, as it were, in compressing a total phenomenon into one of its factors, in concentrating it symbolically, in 'having' it in a state of 'pregnance' in the particular factor—only then do we raise it out of the stream of temporal change" (*PSF* 3:114).

39. My thoughts on the relationship between Cassirer, Goethe, and the organic are indebted to Christian Möckel's discussion in the chapter "Lebensform und Lehrform (1916–1921)" of his monograph *Das Urphänomen des Lebens: Ernst Cassirers Lebensbegriff* (2003, 73–140).

40. In *Freiheit und Form*, Cassirer emphasizes the unique way that the German tradition inherited the Renaissance. While the Italian Renaissance is characterized by a new form of political thought and the French Renaissance—in the figure of Montaigne—embodied a new kind of individualism, the German Renaissance is characterized by a new conception of the religious relationship between the particular and the universal (*FF* 1–7). Goethe, for Cassirer, represented the high point of this new relationship.

41. Cassirer's view of Goethe's science as a kind of phenomenology is not so controversial today. Cf. *Goethe's Way of Science: A Phenomenology of Nature*, edited by David Seamon and Arthur Zajonc (1998) on this matter.

42. In the preface to his *Theory of Color*, Goethe likens this description to describing someone's personality: "In reality, any attempt to express the inner nature of a thing is fruitless. What we perceive are effects, and a complete record of these effects ought to encompass this inner nature. We labor in vain to describe a person's character, but when we draw together his actions, his deeds, a picture of his character will emerge" (1988, 158).

43. In "Der Versuch als Vermittler zwischen Objekt und Subjekt" (The Experiment as Mediator between Object and Subject). (Goethe 1988, 11–17)

44. The previous two quotations were from the introduction to *PSF* 1 written by Charles Hendel.

45. "This schematism of our understanding . . . is an art concealed in the depths of the human soul, whose real modes of activity is hardly likely ever to allow us to uncover" (A-141/B180–81; Kant 1996, 214).

46. Cassirer's idea of the symbolic form, then, "was not Aristotelian but rather borrowed from Goethe" (Krois 2002, 167).

47. In his description of the linguistic turn, Shaughnessy is referring explicitly to the passage I cited (the dialogue between the Daoist and Confucius). I think his claim about the linguistic turn encompasses the *Xici* 1.12 passage I cited in the section "Symbols and Reality" (which occurs before the dialogue between the Daoist and Confucius), however, because its content is repeated in the passage that he cited. In both the passage that I cited and the one that Shaughnessy cited (although the idea is more ambiguous in his), there is the suggestion that the sages' symbolic system affects reality.

48. I have used Shaughnessy's translation, as Lynn took the hexagrams to be expressing the sages' meaning—which is disputable. I have amended the Shaughnessy translation at one point: the original read, "This being so, then how can the thoughts of the sages not be seen?" I thought the "not" was perhaps a typo.

子曰: "书不尽言, 言不尽意。然则圣人之意, 其不可见乎？" 子曰: "圣人立像以尽意, 设卦以尽情伪, 系辞焉以尽其言。变而通之以尽利, 鼓之舞之以尽神。"

49. For Lewis, "Here the system of visual signs and natural referents formed by the images, hexagrams, and appended phrases figures as an alternative to conventional speech. This fullness of meaning offered by the *Yi* is possible because it is directly rooted in the patterns of the cosmos, and hence is not translatable into ordinary language. It remains the province of the sages and those who imitate them" (Lewis 1999, 254–55).

50. For Peterson, "the 'Commentary' anticipates the objection that words surely are an inadequate means of conveying the sages' understanding of the complexities of change" by arguing that "the *Change* is a text with words, but it includes much that is not susceptible of verbalization; it cannot be dismissed as mere verbiage" (Peterson 1982, 98–99).

51. 阴阳不测之谓神。

52. The *Gu Hanyu Changyongzi Zidian* (古汉语常用字字典) (Wang 2011) agrees with my argument here. It gives *shen* four definitions: (1) "that which is especially elevated and mysterious [特别高超, 神奇]," and cites *Xici* 1.5 (which I have already used) as an example; (2) natural laws (自然规律), as in *Xunzi* chapter 17: "That which is accomplished without anyone's doing it and which is obtained without anyone's seeking it is called the work of *shen*" (Hutton 2014, 175; modified); (3) Spiritedness (精神); (4) spirit/soul (神灵). The *Gu Hanyu Changyongzi Zidian* thus takes *Shen* in *Xici* 1.5 not to refer to natural laws, but that which lies beyond natural laws: the ultimate au-delà.

53. Han Kangbo comments on the use of "numinous" in *Xici* 1.5: "'The numinous' refers to the ultimate extent of change and transformation, the expression used to address the myriad things in terms of their subtlety, and is something for which it is impossible to formulate questions" (Lynn 1994, 54–55).

54. "In contending that the great innovations were inspired by trigrams and hexagrams, the 'Commentary' [*Xici*] effectively subordinates to the *Change* the sages who were venerated by the society as culture heroes" (Peterson 1982, 112). Puett cites this passage approvingly: "As Willard Peterson correctly points out" (Puett 2002, 193), and titles his section on the *Xici*, "Submitting to the Trigrams: The *Xici zhuan*" (188).

55. Which is precisely what Puett argues: "The vision of history set forth in the *Xici zhuan* is one of gradual loss. . . . Our only means of attaining an understanding of the universe is through the *Yi*, the text authored by the sages of antiquity so that we may act properly in this world" (Puett 2002, 194). "It [*Xici*] was presenting the *Yi* as the proper textual authority for cosmological speculations" (195). The authors of the *Xici*, according to Puett, is thus arguing for the textual authority of the *Xici* (195).

56. And, I speculate, it is for the reasons I outlined that Mou Zongsan stresses that understanding *xiang* as just phenomena, is superficial (Mou 2003, 9).

57. In my article "The Symbolic Construction of Reality: The *Xici* and Ernst Cassirer's *Philosophy of Symbolic Forms*" (2019a), I expound more upon the intellectual-historical context of the *Xici*. From the perspective of intellectual history, there was pervasive concern with the agency of the human being at the time of the *Xici*'s composition—a "humanistic" milieu. With regard to this context, therefore, it is also incongruous to see the *Xici* as subscribing to a view of the human as passively copying from the universe. For reasons of length, I will not deal with this intellectual-historical background in this project.

58. 夫象者, 出意者也。言者, 明象者也。尽意莫若象, 尽象莫若言。言生于象, 故可寻言以观象; 象生于意, 故可寻象以观意。意以象尽, 象以言着。故言者所以明象, 得象而忘言; 象者, 所以存意, 得意而忘象。

Chapter 3

1. 文以载道

2. The *Book of Odes* was in existence by the sixth century BCE, and so predates the Great Preface by several centuries. Traditionally, the preface was attributed to one of Confucius's disciples, Zixia (子夏), but modern scholarship has generally accepted the Han historian Fan Ye's (范晔; 389–445) assignment, in his *History of the Later Han* (*Hou Han Shu* 后汉书), of authorship to Wei Hong (卫宏; 25–57). Certainly, however, its basic premises have a long heritage and can be seen in *The Book of Documents* (*Shang Shu* 尚书).

3. 志之所之也，在心为志，发言为诗。

4. 因此，大家公认最早说明诗之来源的"诗言志"（《尚书·舜典》）的"志"，乃是以情感为基底的志，而非普通所说的意志的志。

5. In reference to this passage, Xu Fuguan writes that *zhi* means the spirit of the piece of music ("志"是形成一个文章的精神) (Xu 2013c, 21). I follow this interpretation in that I do not think Confucius's idea of *zhi* entailed anything about political ambitions.

6. Traditionally, music and poetry shared an identity, as the *Odes* were sung—poetry was a song—and, therefore, the same logic of emotions underlies Confucian discourse on music and poetry.

7. "敢问夫子恶乎长?" 曰: "我知言, 我善养吾浩然之气。"

8. 曰: 诐辞知其所蔽, 淫辞知其所陷, 邪辞知其所离, 遁辞知其所穷。

9. 子曰: 视其所以。观其所由。察其所安。人焉廋哉。人焉廋哉。

10. I am using the word "expressive" here in the way that Charles Taylor and subsequently Michael Forster used the term to refer to Herder's philosophy of language.

11. The assumption that emotions are provoked by contact and interaction with the world is expressed in the GP and made explicit in many later texts. Lu Ji's (陆机; 261–303) *Exposition on Literature* (*Wen fu* 文赋), for example, begins with the assertion that the writer "stands at the center of the universe":

He moves with the four seasons, to sigh at transience,
And looks at the myriad objects, contemplating their complexity.
He laments the falling leaves during autumn's vigor,
And delights in the tender branches of fragrant spring. (quoted in
    Yu 1987, 33; 遵四时以叹逝, 瞻万物而思纷; 悲落叶于劲秋, 喜柔条
    于芳春。)

These ideas are also expressed frequently throughout Liu Xie's *The Literary Mind and the Carving of Dragons*. Chapter six, "An Exegesis of Poetry" (明诗) says "Man is endowed with seven emotions. When stimulated by external objects, these emotions rise in response. In responding to objects one sings to express his sentiments. All this is perfectly spontaneous" (Hsieh 2015, 40; 人禀七情, 应物斯感, 感物吟志, 莫非自然。). In Chapter 46, "The Physical World," Liu Xie writes, "When phenomena in the physical world change, our heart-minds are also affected" (物色之动, 心亦摇焉。) (my translation). "All Things exert influence on one another/are mutually resonant. Who is there that can rest unmoved?" (Hsieh 2015, 323; 物色相召, 人谁获安?).

12. 志有之, 言以足志, 文以足言。不言谁知其志? 言而无文, 行而不远。This saying is attributed to Confucius and also appears in the Kongzi Jiayu (孔子家语).

13. In the GP we read that "emotions [*qing* 情] move in one's essential being [*Zhong* 中] and take form in words. When speaking them does not suffice,

then one sighs or chants them. If sighing and chanting do not suffice, then one sings out. If singing out does not suffice, then unconsciously one taps them out with the hand, dances to them, treads to their measures and stomps them. Emotions come forth in sounds, and when the sounds create patterns [wen 文], they are called music" (Levy 2001, 919–20).

14. While I agree with So Jeong Park that "the hierarchical relationship among shēng, yīn, and yuè only represents one position in the Confucian tradition of musical discourse" (Park 2013, 335), I think it is *this* hierarchical discourse, premised on the fact that yue is morally superior to sheng and yin, which is related to the discourse on zhi (志).

15. While Erica Fox Brindley (Brindley 2012, 89–110) and James Harold have explained the morally beneficial effects of music in terms of a psychological, physiological emotional response, I think that it is separate from the other idea in the *Yue Ji* mentioned by Cook, that music communicates the zhi (志) of its creator. Harold writes, for example, "Notice that the emphasis in these ancient writers tends to be on what we would now call automatic causal processes" 2016, 346). They are "pre-reflective and automatic" (346) worked through "activity and habit, not through the conscious leaning of moral principles and beliefs" (347). I wish to emphasize that zhi is, in fact, reflective and thus music's moral component isn't purely due to its merely causal, prereflective aspects. Again, I feel that Harold's understanding, like the sinologists' interpretation of the genesis of xiang in the Xici, is too dualistic. The Chinese conception of music, as I will discuss, is not *either* purely affective and prereflective *or* reflective; it marries both.

16. 情发于声，声成文谓之音。

17. Cassirer specifically talks about his metaphysics in relation to Goethe's *Urphänomen* in "Basis Phenomena," in *PSF* 4 (127–90).

18. "All 'culture,' the entire development of 'geist,' leads away in fact from mere 'life'—into a realm of symbolic, hence merely significative and not immediate, 'living' forms. . . . All culture takes place in and proves itself in the creative process, in the activity of the symbolic forms, and through these forms life awakens to self-conscious life, and becomes mind" (*PSF* 4:230–31).

19. Cook notes that "several of the mainland Chinese writers of the *Yue Ji* have noted that it exhibits at times a sort of 'dialectical' thinking" (1995, 13).

20. 夫声乐之入人也深，其化人也速，故先王谨为之文。

21. 先王以是经夫妇，成孝敬，厚人伦，美教化，移风俗。

22. In a passage much reminiscent of Cassirer's view of art as catharsis, Xu Fuguan (who often cites Cassirer's EM) writes, "The original nature of emotions [qing 情] is like smoke and mist: it is ethereal and nebulous. In its original state, it is shapeless and invisible and thus cannot be objectively captured. Through language and external things, the poet . . . allows what was amorphously hidden in the subject to be projected outward and objectified" (Xu 2013a, 90). Li Zehou similarly writes that "the form of inner emotions is invisible; what can be seen

are the artistic forms corresponding to these emotions" (Z. Li 2010, 21). He goes on to quote Cassirer's student, Susanne Langer (1895–1985), who defined art as "feeling in form" (Z. Li 2010, 21).

23. I can discern three categories in the various descriptions of poetic technique: (1) "meaningful environment" (*yijing* 意境), "meaningful image" (*yixiang* 意象), "the mutual mixing of feelings and scenery" (*qing jing jiao rong* 情景交融), "dissolving feelings into the scenery" (*rong qing ru jing* 融情入景), "housing emotions within the scenery" (*yu qing yu jing*, 寓情于景), "moving feelings into the scenery" (*yi jing ru jing* 移情入景); (2) "feelings being aroused from the encounter with environment" (*chu jing sheng qing* 触景生情), "encountering an environment that gives rise to sorrowful feelings" (*chu jing shang qing* 触景伤情); (3) "borrowing the scenery to express emotions" (*jie jing shuqing fa* 借景抒情), "describing objects to house feelings" (*yong wu yu qing* 咏物寓情), "describing objects to give voice to intention" (*yong wu yan zhi* 咏物言志), "expressing intent through objects" (*tuo wu yan zhi* 托物言志). All of these fall under the three categories described in the GP: *fu* (赋), *bi* (比), *xing* (兴). As I see it, the first two categories fall under *xing*, while the last category falls under *bi*.

24. For a summary of this debate please see Saussy (1993, 24–27). Saussy disagrees with the view that allegory does not exist in Chinese poetics. Obviously, I think he is wrong and grossly misunderstands Chinese aesthetics.

25. Gu Xiong (顾敻; fl. 916)《诉衷情·永夜抛人何处去》换我心为你心, 使之相忆深。

26. For the contemporary philosopher Ye Lang (叶朗), the poetic techniques of *fu*, *bi*, and *xing* mentioned in the GP of the *Book of Odes*—which I think are all encompassed by the idea of *yijing* (意境)—can be traced to the idea of *xiang* in the *Xici* (Ye 2015, 64).

27. In seeing art as a replacement for religion, Cassirer echoes the Romantics' idea of replacing religion with art, and the aesthetic education of man (*Bildung*).

28. 发乎情, 民之性也; 止乎礼义, 先王之泽也。

29. 故人不能不乐, 乐则不能无形, 形而不为道, 则不能无乱。

Chapter 4

1. In this chapter I use the capitalized *Wen* to indicate the specifically human *Wen* such as words, literature, and human culture. When I have used *wen* in its uncapitalized form, I am referring to natural patterning in general.

2. 人之有文也, 犹禽之有毛也。毛有五色, 皆生于体。苟有文无实, 是则五色之禽, 毛安生也。

3. 圣人虎别, 其文炳也。君子豹别, 其文蔚也。辩人狸别, 其文萃也。

4. In this project, I will not go into the matter of what *wen* meant in the early Chinese ancestral cult, i.e., in posthumous designations (*shi* 谥) of deceased

ancestors. Claudius C. Müller takes it for granted that the earliest usages of *wen* were in its later sense of refined culture. "Knowledge and use of Scripture is a social privilege, and it is not surprising that the ancestors of ancient China were often given the honorific name *wen*: ancestor worship as an integral part of Chinese civilization was the ritual privilege of the aristocracy, who celebrated in their forefathers the 'perfection' (as *wen* is to be understood here) of their culture" (Müller 1980, 48; my translation). Lothar von Falkenhausen, following Arthur Waley, sees little continuity between the earliest uses of *wen* in post-humous designations and all the later meanings of *wen* that I have explored in this project (Falkenhausen 1996).

5. As an indication of the potency this word has, let us take three examples from the classics. Sima Qian writes in *Records of the Grand Historian* (*Shi Ji* 史记), for example, "To arrive at the disposition of the obscure and man-ifest, to illuminate the bounds of heaven and man lies in *wen*" (《史记·文苑列传》达幽显之情, 明天人之际, 其在文乎。). *Wen* is used here as if it has magical powers, capable of unlocking the mysterious powers of the world. In the *Huangdi Sijing* (黄帝四经), we read that "the activities that form a triad with heaven and earth are called *wen*" (动静参天地谓之文)—suggesting that *wen* is commensurate with the formative powers of the world. In the "Methodology of Reading Posthumous Titles" of the *Yi Zhou Shu Zhuan* (逸周书·谥法解) we read that "comprehensively embracing heaven and earth is called *wen; Dao De* being broad and deep is called *wen*; industrious in study and being curious is called *wen*; extending benevolence to the people is called *wen*; caring for the people and endowing them with ritual forms is called *wen*; bestowing titles to the people is called *wen*" (经纬天地曰文。道德博厚曰文。勤学好问曰文。慈惠爱民曰文。愍民惠礼曰文。锡民爵位曰文。). Here, *wen* is that which is on a par with the utmost mysteries of the world, and simultaneously that which is model human conduct. Such a loaded term seems to defy explanation, but its simultaneous ill-definedness and yet prevalence shows how deeply embedded it is in classical Chinese culture.

6. 理者, 成物之文也 。

7. 治玉也。从玉里声。

8. Historically, *wen* and *li* were terms that were closely associated with each other: *Wenli* (文理) is a term often used in the late Zhou period (Chow 1979, 13).

9. For a summary of the historical development of this concept see Chow (1979, 3–4).

10. 道沿圣以垂文, 圣因文而明道。

11. 文者贯道之器也, 不深于斯道有至焉者不也。

12. 文所以载道也。

13. 我所谓文, 必与道具 。

14. 文便是道

15. Similar iterations to Liu Xie's rationalization of *Wen* can be found in Zhi Yu's (挚虞; d. 312) *Collection of Literature Arranged by Genre* (文章流别集), Lu Ji's (陸機陆机; 261–303) *Poetic Exposition on Literature* (文赋) (James Liu

1975, 20–21), Xiao Tong's (萧统; 501–31) *Selections of Refined Literature* (文选; James Liu 1975, 25–26).

16. See also 傍及万品, 动植皆文: 龙凤以藻绘呈瑞, 虎豹以炳蔚凝姿 (1.2).

17. Gold, wood, water, fire, and earth.

18. 辅相天地而不过, 昭明日月而不忒, 调燮四时而无愆, 此岂非文之至者乎?

19. 呜呼! 吾之所谓文者, 天生之, 地载之, 圣人宣之, 本建则其末治, 体着则其用章, 斯所谓秉阴阳之大化, 正三纲而齐六纪者也。亘宇宙之始终, 类万物而周八极者也。

20. "Human *Wen* originated in the Great Ultimate [*taiji* 太极]. 'Mysteriously assisting the gods,' the images [*xiang* 象] of the *Changes* are the earliest expressions of this pattern. Baoxi began [the *Book of Changes*] by drawing [the eight trigrams], and Confucius completed it by writing the 'Wings.' [One of the Wings], the 'Wen-yan' [文言] or 'Words with Patterns,' was written especially to explain the *Qian* and *Kun* hexagrams. The pattern [*wen*] of words indeed express the heart-mind of the universe! From the Yellow River Map, were born the eight trigrams, and from the Writing from the River Luo, came the nine categories. For these and for the fruits contained in the jade and gold decorated tablets and the flowers blooming in red words and green strips was any one responsible? No. They are natural, organic expressions of the *li* [理] of the numinous [*shen* 神]" (Hsieh 2015, 9; modified).

21. 人文之显, 始于何时? 实肇于庖牺之世。庖牺仰观俯察, 画奇偶以象阴阳。

22. 非惟至道含括无遗, 而其制器尚象, 亦非文不能成。

23. 如垂衣裳以治, 取诸乾坤, 上栋下宇而取诸大壮 [. . .] 何莫非灿然之文! 自是推而存之, 天理民彝之叔, 礼乐刑政之施, 师旅征伐之法, 井牧州里之辨, 华夷内外之别, 复皆则而象之, 故有关民用及一切孺纶范围之具, 悉囿乎文。

24. 辞之所以能鼓天下者, 乃道之文也。

25. Herder's grand project was summarized by Zammito thus: "to find how man as a creature of nature figured in man as an artifice of culture, to read these two dimensions of man in continuity" (2001, 136). As Charles Taylor writes, "Herder offered a picture of nature as a great current of sympathy, running through all things. 'Siehe die ganze Natur, betrachte die grosse Analogie der Schöpfung. Alles fühlt sich und seines Gleichen, Leben wallet ze Leben' ('See the whole of nature, behold the great analogy of creation. Everything feels itself and its like, life reverberates to life'). Man is the creature who can become aware of this and bring it to expression. His calling as 'an epitome and steward of creation' is 'dass er Sensorium seines Gottes in allem Lebenden der Schöpfung, nach dem Masse es ihm verwandt ist, werde' ('That he becomes the organ of sense of his God in all the living things of creation, according to the measure of their relation to him'). [*Vom Erkennen und Empfinden der menschlichen Seele*]" (Taylor 1989, 369).

Chapter 5

1. This understanding of "human nature" thus contrasts with the "essentialist" conception of human nature that Michael Sandel speaks of in *Liberalism*

and the Limits of Justice: "To speak of human nature, . . . is often to suggest a classical teleological conception, associated with the notion of a universal human essence, invariant in all times and places" (1998, 50).

2. In more "Daoist" terms, the self would be an empty self.

3. Sandel's characterization of the Rawlsian individual is the kind of skeptical attitude that I have in mind here: "The Rawlsian self is not only a subject of possession, but an antecedently individuated subject, standing always at a certain distance from the interests it has. One consequence of this distance is to put the self beyond the reach of experience, to make it invulnerable, to fix its identity once and for all. No commitment could grip me so deeply that I could not understand myself without it. No transformation of life purposes and plans could be so unsettling as to disrupt the contours of my identity. No project could be so essential that turning away from it would call into question the person I am. Given my independence from the values I have, I can always stand apart from them; my public identity as a moral person 'is not affected by changes over time' in my conception of the good (Rawls 1980, 544–5)" (1998, 62). While Sandel is more narrowly focused on Rawlsian skepticism about the need for society in the constitution of the moral self, I am making the metaphysical point that we need society and the cultural forms of society to have meaning per se.

4. King Wen is the father of King Wu, who overthrew the Shang Dynasty and founded the Zhou Dynasty. Confucius believed that the Golden Age of humankind had been realized with by the cultural heroes King Wen (d. ca. 1050 BCE), his son King Wu (r. 1045–1043) and the virtuous regent, the Duke of Zhou (r. ca. 1043–1036 BCE).

5. 道之显者谓之文, 盖礼乐制度之谓。

6. In *Analects* 14.12, we read the following:

> Zilu asked about the complete person.
> The Master said, "Take a person as wise as Zang Wuzhong, as free of desire as Gongchuo, as courageous as Zhuangzi of Bian, and as accomplished in the arts as Ran Qiu, and then acculturate [*wen* 文] them by means of ritual and music [*li yue* 礼乐]—such a man might be called a complete person." (Slingerland 2003, 158)

7. In his introduction to the "Discourse on Ritual" chapter of the *Xunzi*, Knoblock writes, "*Wen* is intrinsically rewarding, producing pleasure and beauty of itself (19.2c). Form allows for a sense of completion and fulfilment, emphasizes the appropriateness of the action, and assures that beginning and end shall be one. Without form, life would be coarse and crude. Ritual forms provide for ornamentation, refinement, and order" (1994, 54).

8. We find many passages in the *Analects* that speak to the nonutilitarian value with which Confucius regarded learning. In *Analects* 8.12, we read that "the Master said, 'It is not easy to find someone who is able to learn for even

the space of three years without a thought given to official salary'" (Slingerland 2003, 82). In *Analects* 14.24, we read that "the Master said, 'In ancient times scholars learned for their own sake; these days they learn for the sake of others'" (Slingerland 2003, 164). Similarly, in *Xunzi* chapter 21, "Undoing Fixation," we read that "Mozi was fixated on the useful and did not understand the value of good form [*Wen* 文]" (Hutton 2014, 226). The value of *Wen* cannot be measured in utilitarian terms.

9. A. C. Graham emphasizes the nonteleological nature of the Mencian understanding of the self and its cultivation. He writes that "*xing* is conceived in terms of spontaneous development in a certain direction rather than of its origin or goal" (quoted in Ames 2002, 74).

10. Lee Yearley eloquently summarizes this as follows: "In a discovery [i.e., substance] model, however, human nature exists as a permanent set of dispositions that are obscured but that can be contacted or discovered. People do not cultivate inchoate capacities. Rather they discover a hidden ontological reality that defines them. . . . An ontological reality, the true self, always is present no matter what specific humans, particular instances of it, are or do" (1990, 60).

11. Relatedly, this is why the Confucian tradition does not have a conception of the unconscious—the *true* self *is* manifested in culture.

12. 圣人, 文质者也。

13. Cf. Roger Ames (2002) and Irene Bloom's (2002) discussion of this issue in *Mencius: Contexts and Interpretation*. Ames advocates a more processual, social, "anti-essentialistic" understanding of Mencian *renxing*, whereas Bloom advocates a more "biological" interpretation.

14. 天命之谓性, 率性之谓道, 修道之谓教。

15. 三年之丧, 何也? 曰: 称情而立文

16. In his translation of the *Xunzi*, John Knoblock translates *Wen* as "good form." Masayuki Sato translates *Wen* as refinement/elegance, whereas Kurtis Hagen (2007) translates it as "cultural patterns." The Hutton translation which I have used, translates *Wen* as "proper form."

17. Chung-ying Cheng provides a helpful summary:

> For both Confucianists and Taoists, the *tao* as the concrete universal and ultimate ontological source of creativity is in the nature of all things that relates everything together in the organic network of all things, on the one hand, and individuates each thing of each type on each level, on the other. However, . . . whereas the Taoists would consider going (back) to the *tao* and imitate and embody the *tao* as the general and ultimate way of fulfilling the life of human beings, the Confucianists would consider developing and cultivating one's nature as the correct way of consummating and illuminating the *tao*. Hence, the immanentization principle prescribes not only that all truth and value of being are innate and inherent in the nature of things and human beings, but that nature has the cultivatable

power to reveal, fulfil, and substantiate the *tao*. This is considered meaningful not only for the individual persons or things themselves but for the *tao* itself. (Cheng 1991, 17)

18. Again, we are reminded of *Xici* 1.12, which says, "Therefore what is above physical form [*xing* 形] pertains to the Dao, and what is below physical form pertains to concrete objects [*qi* 器]."

19. *Analects* 8.19: "The Master said, 'How great was Yao as a ruler! So majestic! It is heaven that is great, and it was Yao who modelled himself upon it. So vast! Among the common people there were none who were able to find words to describe him. How majestic in his accomplishments, and glorious in cultural splendour [*wenzhang* 文章]'" (Slingerland 2003, 84).

20. Bronze Seal:

Oracle Bone:

http://humanum.arts.cuhk.edu.hk/Lexis/lexi-mf/search.php?word=%E6%96%87

21. I am aware that the description I am giving here sounds rather Hegelian. Guido Kreis, I think, gives a rather Hegelian reading of Cassirer, of which my interpretation here might be reminiscent. See Kreis, in the sections of his book that are titled "Die Theorie des sozialen Handlungraums," "Die Theorie der Anerkennung," and "Das Problem der Entfremdung" (2010, 314–28).

22. 仲子生而有文在其手。

23. For example, when Ji was born, he had a *mark* (*wen* 文) on his hand that said *you* (友). He was accordingly given this name. 及生有文在其手曰友遂以名之。

24. For a similar treatment of the relationship between *Bildung*, Confucian cultivation and "aesthetic" education, see Sigurðsson (2015, 81–94).

25. Ames's summary of the Confucian understanding of human nature echoes this nonteleological development of one's talents: "Our 'nature' or perhaps better, our 'natural propensities' as humans do not reference a given source or

design, but rather point to a shared, as yet undefined capacity to grow and to 'design' ourselves in unique and distinctive ways" (2017, 14).

26. Similarly, Gadamer has written that "the concept of *Bildung* most clearly indicates the profound intellectual change that still causes us to experience the century of Goethe as contemporary" (Gadamer 2004, 8–9).

27. It is worth noting that the first figure that Gadamer evokes—in *Truth and Method*—in his defense of "humanism" and the associated project of *Bildung*, is also Herder (Gadamer 2002, 9).

28. Footnote provided by Michael Forster.

29. "When the sage governs the world, they would first use the virtue of *Wen* [*Wende* 文德] and latterly the prowess of the martial. Generally, the use of the martial is not enough to make [the populace] acquiesce. The education through *Wen* [*Wenhua* 文化] being not enough, then you can use punishment" (my translation; 圣人之治天下也, 先文德而后武力。凡武之兴为不服也。文化不改, 然后加诛。).

30. Leo Strauss, for example, criticizes Cassirer's aestheticism and so his limp defense of Kantian moral principles. Strauss, in fact, suggested that Cassirer should have rewritten his *PSF* with a focus on morality (Strauss 1947, 128).

31. Relatedly, I think it is this perceived impossibility of having an absolute standard that Cassirer, famously, never wrote an "ethics." There is much debate within Cassirer scholarship as to whether Cassirer had an ethical philosophy or not. For Birgit Recki, although Cassirer's "overall thinking is ethically impregnated" and the "impulse towards practical self-determination" in his cultural anthropology can be seen from the beginning, "the moment of its normative orientation remains conceptually vague" (1997, 72). For Peter Eli Gordon, "Vigorous attention to political or social thought remains noticeably underdeveloped in Cassirer's scholarship" (2005, 132). Habermas thought that the "the normative foundations [of the *PSF*] remained entirely unclear" due to Cassirer's "perspectivism" (2001, 23). For a summary of this issue, see Recki (2004, 129–209). I think it is clear that Cassirer is a deeply moral person, but his sensitivity to diversity and holism suggests that he is highly sensitive to the validity of different perspectives.

32. I am making the Nietzschean point that philosophy's obsession with certainty is just a replacement for the loss of God.

33. *Veri criterium est id ipsum fecisse* (cf. SMC, 104n12). In "Descartes, Leibniz, and Vico" (SMC 102–7), Cassirer refers to Vico's *De antiquissima Italorum sapientia*, in which he writes, "The criterion of the truth is to have made it." For Vico, man demonstrates his freedom more in the understanding of history, as history was made by human beings. Nature, because it is made by God and not man, is "always external to man and beyond the power of human knowledge" (SMC 104). According to Tom Rockmore, Hobbes and Vico introduced "constructivism" to modern philosophy (2011, 58).

34. 三人行, 必有我师焉; 择其善者而从之, 其不善者而改之。

Chapter 6

1. My use of the "organic" in relation to Cassirer needs to be qualified. Cassirer uses organic paradigms in relation to the cultural world *analogically*. Cassirer rejects the "organological" view of life, seen, for example, in Oswald Spengler, in which the cultural realm is subordinated to the biological and has no independent stability.

2. What I have called the "organic paradigm" and the related concepts of harmony and correlative thinking has also been termed *ars contextualis* by Hall and Ames (1998a).

3. The harmony in the bow and the lyre is a reference to a Heraclitus fragment (Diels 51): "Men do not understand how that which is torn in different directions comes into accord with itself—harmony in contrariety, as in the case of the bow and the lyre" (Heraclitus 1907, 31). Chenyang Li also points to this idea of harmony as similar to the Confucian project of harmony in his *The Confucian Philosophy of Harmony* (Li 2014, 28).

4. 万物并育而不相害, 道并行而不相悖。

5. Many scholars have described Chinese cosmology as "organismic": Tu Wei-ming (1985, 38–40), Needham (1956, 281), and Frederick Mote. Mote writes that, "The genuine Chinese cosmogony is that of an organismic process, meaning that all parts of the entire cosmos belong to one organic whole and that all interact as participants in one spontaneously self-generating life process" (1971, 20).

6. It is a historical fact that thinkers from this period were influenced by the harmony found in the organic world. As Masayuki Sato notes, "Indisputably Jixia and Daoist thinkers of the mid-to-late Warring States period were fascinated by the orderly state of the human body, as every component of each system maintained the perfect balance of the whole. . . . Another analogy that attracted Jixia and Daoist thinkers was the constant motion of Heaven and the inexhaustible procreation of the myriad things on Earth, which they assumed to be a manifestation of the Way" (Sato 2003, 317). Sato, following many mainland Chinese scholars, argues that Xunzi was influenced by the Jixia school; Sato also contends that their influence can be seen in the *Guanzi* and *Yanzi Chunqiu* (68).

7. Cassirer's philosophy has been likened to the process metaphysics of Alfred North Whitehead—which is seen by Hall and Ames as one of the closest parallels in the Western tradition with Chinese metaphysics. Whitehead himself characterizes his own process philosophy as "the philosophy of the organism," which approximates more to "some strains of Indian, or Chinese, thought, than to western Asiatic, or European thought" (1978, 7). Cassirer's work "constituted one of the earliest and most developed forms of process philosophy in the twentieth century, different but analogous to the project of Whitehead" (Moynahan

2014, xxix). Verene writes that "Cassirer can rightly be described as a process philosopher in metaphysics" and compares Cassirer to Whitehead (2008, 100).

8. As Tu Wei-ming writes, the organismic process is an open, as opposed to a closed, system: "As there is no temporal beginning to specify, no closure is ever contemplated. The cosmos is forever expanding; the great transformation is unceasing" (Tu 1985, 39).

9. Drucilla Cornell has been inspired by Cassirer's *PSF* to theorize a *Symbolic Forms for a New Humanity*. Cornell similarly emphasizes Cassirer's interpretation of the third Critique as breaking down the distinction between the actual and the possible (Cornell and Panfilio 2010, 25).

10. He cites as examples Nussbaum's *The Fragility of Goodness* and *Love's Knowledge* as well as Karl Popper's critique of Plato's conception of harmony in the *Republic* (Li 2014, 7–8).

11. In a 1920 essay, " 'Spirit' [*Geist*] and 'Life' in Contemporary Philosophy," Cassirer writes that "the metaphysical concept of 'being' [*Sein*]" is marked by this peculiarity, that "it possesses a strongly absolutist character. Within it there is basically no room for 'being' of a different stamp and different *type of meaning*. Rather we are led sooner or later to a simple 'either-or'—to that 'crisis' between being and non-being by which the first great thinker of Western metaphysics, Parmenides, already found himself confronted" (1949, 872).

12. "As soon as the point of gravity in thought shifts from the pole of being to the pole of order in the total theoretical view of reality . . . , then a victory of pluralism over abstract monism, of a multiplicity of forms over a single form, is established. The most diverse intellectual structures and the most manifold principles of formation under the dominance of the concept of order can exist together freely and easily which in actuality, in the harsh space in which objects encounter each other, seem to be at odds with each other and exclude each other" (Cassirer 1969, 8). The reason "order" can be so tolerant, as opposed to being, is because "the pure function of the concept of order is one and the same regardless of what special matter and within what special area of spirit (*Geist*) it takes effect." (8).

13. The six characteristics I have listed here echo the five characteristics that Li Chenyang takes to be characteristic of Confucian harmony, heterogeneity, tension, coordination and cooperation, transformation and growth, and renewal (Li 2014, 9). These characteristics, as I argue, are characteristics of an organicist philosophy (of harmony). In a metaphysics based on the *functional* correlation between the part and the whole, a change in one part of the whole has the potential to change the meaning of the whole. Similarly, a new definition of the whole will have a bearing on the meaning of any part. Preceding Li, Tu Wei-ming lists similar characteristics for the organismic process: "The organismic process as a spontaneously self-generating life process exhibits three basic motifs:

continuity, wholeness, and dynamism" (Tu 1989b, 69; Tu 1985, 38). I think Li's work echoes the concept of "aesthetic order" (i.e., Confucian cosmology as *ars contextualis*) as described by Hall and Ames (1987, 246–49). This "aesthetic order" that Hall and Ames believe characterizes classical Chinese metaphysics, as we will see, also characterizes Cassirer's description of a functional metaphysics.

14. Frederick Beiser and Joseph Needham similarly take Leibniz to be the father of the organic. Cf. Beiser (2003, 84) and Needham (1956, 499).

15. In the mechanical-physical, conception, the part composes the whole in association with other parts, but the part itself can further be dissected into individual parts, and so on into infinite regress. Similarly, the paradox of Newtonian space was not resolved until Leibniz replaced the "metaphysical category of substance" or "the concept of being" with "the concept of order" (Cassirer 1969, 6). Only when science gave up the idea that space was a "thing" in favor of relation were the contradictions that had resulted from Newton's concept of absolute space and time resolved.

16. Cassirer writes that Linnaeus was "an indefatigable and inexorable logician" who was possessed by "a veritable mania for classification" (*PK* 127).

17. See also "The Purpose Set Forth (from *On Morphology*)" (Goethe 1988, 64); "The Experiment as Mediator between Object and Subject" (Goethe 1988, 15–16); and "Observation on Morphology in General" (Goethe 1988, 58).

18. Cassirer's view that Goethe's *phenomenological* methodology was able to overcome the antinomies of science is not controversial. See the works of Seamon and Zajonc (1989), Dennis L. Sepper (1988), Henri Bortoft (2010), and Olaf Müller (2015).

19. Cassirer's view of this connection is preceded by the works of Wilhelm Windelband, Rudolf Eucken, Georg Simmel, Karl Vorländer, Dietrich Mahnke, and Bruno Bauch.

20. In this, J. W. von Troll is in agreement with Cassirer (Goethe 1946, 68).

21. Uexküll's theory that each animal is both confined to and experiences the world through its own *Umwelt* was one of the sources for Cassirer's own philosophy of symbolic forms.

22. In *Politics*, chapter 8, Aristotle writes, "Now if nature makes nothing incomplete, and nothing in vain, the inference must be that she has made all animals for the sake of man." (*Politics*, 1256b12; Aristotle 1905, 40).

23. "The assessment of the extent to which Neo-Confucian philosophy directly influenced Leibniz will involve detailed bibliographical references" (Needham 1956, 504, footnote g)—implying that it is unnecessary to ask if Leibniz was influenced by Chinese philosophy or not.

24. Eric S. Nelson also notes the "holistic naturalism" and "correlative thinking" shared between Leibniz's *Monadology* and the metaphysics of harmony found in the *Yijing*: "The harmony Leibniz identifies, like that of the *Yijing* itself, does not proceed by subsuming a particular under a universal or mediating it

within a totality." "The whole is not totalitarian but a harmony among multiple individual singularities that addresses and allows each to respond according to its own natural propensity" (Nelson 2011, 389).

25.《易》之为书也! 不可远, 为道也屡迁, 变动不居, 周流六虚, 上下无常, 刚柔相易, 不可为典要, 唯变所适。

26. This, I take it, was Goethe's point about how "life" cannot be grasped because life *is* change.

27. 天地之道, 可壹言而尽也。其为物不贰, 则其生物不测。

28. 子在川上, 曰: "逝者如斯夫! 不舍昼夜。"

29. *Analects* 7.21: "The Master did not talk about: extraordinary things, feats of strength, disorder, and spiritual beings" (子不语怪, 力, 乱, 神). In *Analects* 5.13, it is said of Confucius that "we do not hear him discourse on subjects such as *xing* and *tiandao*."

30. 子曰: "君子博学于文, 约之以礼, 亦可以弗畔矣夫!"

A similar appeal to broadness can be found in *Zhongyong* 20: "Study the way broadly, ask about it in detail, reflect on it carefully, analyze it clearly, and advance on it with earnestness. Where there is something that one has yet to study or that, having studied it, has yet to master, do not stop; where there is something that one has yet to ask about or that, having asked about it, has yet to understand, do not stop; where there is something that one has yet to reflect upon or that, having reflected on it, has yet to grasp, do not stop; where there is something that one has yet to analyze or that, having analyzed it, is still not clear about, do not stop; where there is the proper way that one has not yet advanced on or that, having advanced on it, has yet to do so with earnestness, do not stop" (Ames and Hall 2001, 104). 博学之, 审问之, 慎思之, 明辨之, 笃行之。有弗学, 学之弗能, 弗措也; 有弗问, 问之弗知, 弗措也; 有弗思, 思之弗得, 弗措也; 有弗辨, 辨之弗明, 弗措也, 有弗行, 行之弗笃, 弗措也。

31. 君子学欲其博, 故於文无不考

32. 子曰: "吾有知乎哉? 无知也。有鄙夫问于我, 空空如也, 我叩其两端而竭焉。"

33. 子曰: "舜其大知也与! 舜好问而好察迩言, 隐恶而扬善, 执其两端, 用其中于民, 其斯以为舜乎!"

34. 子曰: "加我数年, 五十以学易, 可以无大过矣。"

35. Similar records about Confucius's love of the *Changes* in old age can be found in the *Book of Han*.

36. 孔子晚而喜易, 序彖、系、象、说卦、文言。读易, 韦编三绝。曰: "假我数年, 若是, 我于易则彬彬矣。"

37. One can see an expression of Confucius's distaste for the *Changes* in *Analects* 13.22:

The Master said, "The Southerners have a saying, 'The fate of a person who lacks constancy cannot be diagnosed by the shaman-healers [*wuyi* 巫医].' How well put!"

[It is also said,] "One inconstant in virtue will probably incur disgrace." The Master commented, "It simply cannot be foretold through divination."

(Slingerland 2003, 149) 子曰: "南人有言曰: '人而无恒, 不可以作巫医。'善夫!" "不恒其德, 或承之羞。"子曰: "不占而已矣。"

38. 子曰: "《易》, 我后其卜祝矣, 我观其德义耳也。幽赞而达乎数, 明数而达乎德, 又仁守者而义行之耳。赞而不达于数, 则其为之巫; 数而不达于德, 则其为之史。史巫之筮, 乡之而未也, 好之而非也。后世之疑丘者, 或以《易》乎? 吾求其德而已, 吾与史巫同途而殊归者也。

39.

≡ *Qian* (乾): Heaven/Sky (*tian* 天)

≡≡ *Kun* (坤): Earth (*di* 地)

Yang trigrams (sons)

≡≡ *Zhen* (震): Thunder (*lei* 雷) (eldest son)

≡≡ *Kan* (坎): Water (*shui* 水) (middle son)

≡≡ *Gen* (艮): Mountain (*shan* 山) (youngest son)

Yin trigrams (daughters)

≡ *Xun* (巽): Wind (*feng* 风) (eldest daughter)

≡ *Li* (离): Fire (*huo* 火) (middle daughter)

≡ *Dui* (兑): Lake/Marsh (*ze* 泽) (youngest daughter)

40. We can also see this "arbitrariness" in the four basic images. The four basic images are:

少陽 ≡≡ 太陽 ≡ 少陰 ≡≡ 太陰 ≡≡

These situational symbols are taken to represent the four seasons: spring (young *yang*), summer (old *yang*), autumn (young *yin*), and winter (old *yin*). The lines are read from bottom to top, so that in spring, from a background of *yin*, *yang* starts to break through.

41. For example, it is hard to see how there is just one logic that unites the different phenomena under the trigram *Xun*. "Xun [Compliance] is wood, is the wind, is the Eldest Daughter, is the straightness of a marking cord, is the carpenter [or 'carpenter's square'], is the spotless and pure, is the lengthy, is the high, is the now-advancing and now-receding, is the unresolved, and is odor. In respect to men, it is the balding, the broad in forehead, the ones with much

white in their eyes, the ones who keep close to what is profitable and who market things for threefold gain. At the end point of its development it is the trigram of impetuosity [i.e., it turns into Zhen (Quake)]" (Lynn 1994, 124; modified).

42. 乾为马。

43. 为良马、为瘠马、为驳马

44. 其于马也，为善鸣、为馵足，为的颡。

45. 其于马也，为美脊、为亟心、为下首、为薄蹄、为曳。

46. The six lines of the hexagram can be read as (1) two trigrams, (2) but they can also be read as three pairs (*sanji* 三极), representing, from bottom to top, earth, man, and heaven. The lines from bottom to top can be read as (3) the temporal development of a situation, from incipience to full manifestation, or (4) bureaucratic hierarchy. (5) Sometimes they are interpreted as four stacked interlocking trigrams. (6) Each trigram has a symbolic association that might influence the interpretation of each line within a hexagram. (7) But each individual line can also be read without reference to the symbolism of the whole. (8) The odd positions (1, 3, and 5) are regarded as yang, and the even positions are regarded as *yin*. If a *yin* line is in a *yin* position, or vice versa, then it is called "correct" (*zheng* 正). (9) The second and fifth positions are called "central" and are auspicious positions because they are the center of the inner and outer trigrams. (10) Opposite valences (*yin-yang*) in positions 1 and 3, 2 and 4, or 3 and 6 "correspond" (*xiangying* 相应), which is also auspicious. (11) Opposite valences next to each other "support" each other, which can also be auspicious (Ziporyn 2012, 240).

47. 万物为道一偏，一物为万物一偏。愚者为一物一偏，而自以为知道，无知也。

48. For a summary of the different types of relationships encompassed by *yin yang*, see Wang (2012, 7–12).

49. 生生之谓易。

50. 一阴一阳之谓道。继之者善也，成之者性也。

51. In the first chapter of *Determinism and Indeterminism*, Cassirer writes about "the Laplacean spirit," which Cassirer uses to describe Pierre-Simone de Laplace's vision of an all-embracing spirit possessing complete knowledge of the universe at a given moment. This god-like, fully deterministic knowledge, is, Cassirer believes, capable of both metaphysical and epistemological interpretation.

52. For a helpful summary of the relationship between the dialectical change between *yin* and *yang*, harmony, and life in the *Yijing*, see Cheng (1977, 212–13).

53. *Zhongyong* 23: "Next one cultivates these processes and events with discretion [*qu* 曲] so that each aspect of them [*qu* 曲] is able to realize its own creativity [*cheng* 诚]. Where there is creativity there is something determinate [*xing* 形]; when there is something determinate, it is manifest [*zhe* 著]; when it is manifest, there is understanding [*ming* 明]; when there is understanding, others are affected [*dong* 动]; when others are affected, they change; when they

change, they are transformed [*hua* 化]. And only those of utmost creativity (*zhicheng* 至诚) in the world are able to effect transformation" (Ames and Hall 2001, 105). 其次致曲。曲能有诚, 诚则形, 形则著, 著则明, 明则动, 动则变, 变则化。唯天下至诚为能化。

54. *Zhongyong* 30: "Zhongni (Confucius) revered Yao and Shun as his ancestors and carried on their ways; he emulated and made illustrious the ways of Kings Wen and Wu. He modeled himself above on the rhythm of the turning of the seasons, and below he was attuned to the patterns of water and earth. He is comparable to the heavens and the earth, sheltering and supporting everything that is. He is comparable to the progress of the four seasons, and the alternating brightness of the sun and moon. All things nurtured together and do not cause injury to one another; the various ways [*dao* 道] traveled together and are not conflicted [*xiangbei* 相悖]. Their lesser excellences [*de* 德] are to be seen as flowing streams; their greater excellences are to be seen as massive transformations [*hua* 化]. This is why the heavens and the earth are so great" (Ames and Hall 2001, 111–12; modified). 仲尼祖述尧、舜, 宪章文、武; 上律天时, 下袭水土。辟如天地之无不持载, 无不覆帱, 辟如四时之错行, 如日月之代明。万物并育而不相害, 道并行而不相悖, 小德川流, 大德敦化, 此天地之所以为大也。

55. *Zhongyong* 26: "Thus, the utmost creativity (*zhicheng* 至诚) is ceaseless. Unceasing, it is enduring; enduring, it is effective; effective, it reaches far into the distance; reaching far into the distance, it is broad and thick; being broad and thick, it is high and brilliant. Its breadth and thickness enable it to bear up everything; its height and brilliance enable it to envelope everything; reaching far into the distance enables it to realize all events. Broad and thick, it is companion to the earth; high and brilliant, it is companion to the heavens; far-reaching and enduring, it is without limit" (Ames and Hall 2001, 107). 故至诚无息。不息则久, 久则徵, 徵则悠远, 悠远则博厚, 博厚则高明。博厚, 所以载物也; 高明, 所以覆物也; 悠久, 所以成物也。博厚配地, 高明配天, 悠久无疆。

56. This connection is not arbitrary, as Nietzsche once talked of how his project is modeled on Buddhism: "I could become the Buddha of Europe," he wrote in 1883 (Panaïoti 2013, 2). For more on the Connection between Buddhism and Nietzsche, cf. Panaïoti, *Nietzsche and Buddhist Philosophy* (2013) and Graham Parkes, *Nietzsche and Asian Thought* (1996).

57. 和, 相应也。

58. The 20th year of Duke Zhao chapter of the *Zuo Zhuan* contains a discussion about harmony in terms of flavors: "Harmony is like soup, it requires water, fire, vinegar, sauce, salt, and plum in order to cook fish and meat. It is cooked with firewood. The cook has to harmonize and balance them to get the flavor. He has to compensate for what is deficient and take away from what is excessive" (my Translation). 和如羹焉, 水火醯醢盐梅以烹鱼肉, 燀之以薪, 宰夫和之, 齐之以味, 济其不及, 以洩其过。

59. 物得其常曰乐极, 极之所集曰声, 声应相保曰和, 细大不逾曰平。

60. Goethe's ideal of world literature is embodied by the idea that one can conceptualize all the literatures of the world as a symphonic whole while maintaining the individuality of each work without losing sight of the whole (Said 2003, xviii, in the preface to the 25th anniv. ed.).

61. 夫和实生物，同则不继。以他平他谓之和，故能丰长而物归之。若以同裨同，尽乃弃矣。

62. 声一无听，物一无文，味一无果，物一不讲。

63. Perhaps Cassirer would have found interesting A. C. Graham's general conclusion about "Chinese philosophy": "The final tendency of the schools was towards syncretism; philosophers settle for 'I see the whole thing, you are one-sided' rather than 'I am right, you are wrong'" (1989, 398).

64. Cf. also Gordon (2005, 132).

65. Fitting, therefore, that Kant never traveled more than 145 km from Königsberg. For Foucault, Kant's *Anthropology* revealed the untenability of the universality and necessity of the a priori categories (Allen 2003, 186). The empirical fact of difference makes an illusion of the universality and necessity of the Kantian a prioris.

66. As Karyn Lai writes, "Apprehending many perspectives broadens and enriches one's understanding of the world. This in turn engenders an attitude of openness in negotiation" rather than an instinct for domination (2006, 366, 371). To know that one's perspective is not universal is to realize that the universal is not a given; it must be reached through the broadening of one's perspectives. It is only through *dialogue* with others that we establish any common ground that could reasonably be called a "universal."

67. The latter parts of this lecture corresponds to the last chapter of *The Myth of the State*. I have focused on this lecture, as Cassirer's argument is clearer in this work.

68. "To banish myth, to eradicate it root and branch, would mean an impoverishment. . . . there is no danger that mankind ever will forget or renounce the language of myth. For this language is not restricted to a special field; it pervades the whole of man's life and existence" (SMC 245).

69. As Cassirer put it in his unpublished conclusion to *The Myth of the State*, "Mythical thought is emotional thought" (quoted in Krois 2012, 101). In this same conclusion, he quotes Hume, "A passion can only be overcome with a stronger passion" (quoted in Krois 2012, 102). See also Krois 2005.

70. He is the father of modern British anthropology, intellectually indebted to Herder through *Völkerpsychologie* (see Forster 2010, 204), and his thought bears many compelling parallels (see Forster 2010, 204–20).

71. Cassirer quotes Boas favorably in the *Myth of the State* as advancing the view that "primitive" consciousness is *not*, contra Lévy-Bruhl (MS 13), an evolutionary stage of mankind, but a sophisticated worldview in its own right (MS 14).

72. As we have already seen, Cassirer's solution to the sometimes volcanic power of the emotions is to express them through art. It is the function of art to give form to our emotions so that we are no longer their slaves (see EM 149).

73. See Donald Philip Verene's note on this (SMC 104n12; SMC 102–7).

74. It is for this reason that, against the dominant cultural pessimism around technology of his time, Cassirer embraced technology as a symbolic form (Cassirer 2012).

75. Under this category Cassirer sees Nietzsche, Schopenhauer, Ludwig Klages, Max Scheler, Bergson, and Heidegger. For Cassirer's criticism of Ludwig Klages, see Cassirer PSF 4 (23–32). For Cassirer's criticism of Max Scheler, see Cassirer (1949).

76. Which he criticizes in The Logic of the Cultural Sciences (LCS 34–55). Cassirer's criticism of logical positivism is related to his criticism of empiricism, which he characterized in Substance and Function as a "passive surrender to the object" (SF 113). For an account of the Marburg school's opposition to Machian positivism, see Skidelsky (2008, 9–21).

77. Cassirer is a child of the Enlightenment in that he sometimes errs toward giving a privileged status to science among the symbolic forms. As Verene writes, however, this should not be taken "to violate his principle that a philosophy of symbolic forms assigns each its proper place in human culture as a whole" (2011, 101).

78. The same can be applied on the level of the individual self. Each self is, as William James had it, a plurality of selves (James 1890, 334–35). The self can only maintain its critical powers if there is a robust ecosystem of many different roles/identities that one plays, i.e., doctor, wife, friend, etc.

79. Racism or racial discourse subordinates a human being's becoming to her being (i.e., her race). In this sense, racism operates according to a substance ontology (Xiang 2019b, 2–3). Further, racism fallaciously takes much that is merely cultural difference to be ontological and hierarchizes this difference. Racism is anathema to Cassirer's definition of human beings as a symbolic animal in that, under racism, one is not defined according to one's acculturation or cultural achievements, but one's "race" (see Xiang 2019c). Racism is an inherently totalizing ideology, and when this ideology comes to predominate in social discourses (such as in white supremacism), it is perilous. Cassirer, I would argue, would follow Herder in seeing human difference in terms of culture as opposed to race, and, further, would not hierarchize this difference. "Herder rejected the differentiation of humanity into races. . . . [His] rejection of the concept of race is directed against Kant" (Bernasconi and Lott 2000, 23).

Appendix 1

1. 蝮蛇多文 。

2. 五色不乱, 孰为文采。

3. 青黄杂糅, 文章烂兮。

4. 青与赤谓之文

5. 五色成文而不乱。

6. 道有变动, 故曰爻; 爻有等, 故曰物; 物相杂, 故曰文; 文不当, 故吉凶生焉。

7. 文: 错画也。象交文。

8. 东方曰夷, 被发文身, 有不火食者也。

9. 越人断发文身。

10. 曰若稽古帝尧, 曰放勋, 钦、明、文、思、安安

11. 先王之立礼也, 有本有文。忠信, 礼之本也; 义理, 礼之文也。无本不立, 无文不行。

12. 子贡曰: "夫子之文章, 可得而闻也; 夫子之言性与天道, 不可得而闻也。"

13. 子曰: "大哉, 尧之为君也! 巍巍乎! 唯天为大, 唯尧则之。荡荡乎! 民无能名焉。巍巍乎! 其有成功也; 焕乎, 其有文章!"

14. 乐也者, 动于内者也; 礼也者, 动于外者也。故礼主其减, 乐主其盈。礼减而进, 以进为文: 乐盈而反, 以反为文。

15. 吾不如衰之文也。

Appendix 2

1. 五百里绥服: 三百里揆文教

Appendix 3

1. I have capitalized *Wen* here to indicate that Song Lian is referring to human *Wen* and not just patterning (*wen*) in general. Sometimes, for emphasis, I have also prefixed *Wen* with "human."

2. Also known as Paoxi and Fuxi. Culture hero in Chinese legend and mythology, credited with the invention of hunting, fishing, and cooking, as well as the Cangjie system of writing Chinese characters, ca. 12,000 BCE. Fu Xi was counted as the first of the Three Sovereigns at the beginning of the Chinese dynastic period.

3. This passage is modelled on *Great Commentary*, part 2, section 2: "When in ancient times Lord Baoxi ruled the world as sovereign, he looked upward and observed the images [*xiang*] in heaven and looked downward and observed the models [*fa*] that the earth provided. He observed the patterns [*wen*] on birds and beasts and what things were suitable [*yi*] for the land. Nearby, adopting them from his own person, and afar adopting them from other things, he thereupon made the eight trigrams in order to become thoroughly conversant with the virtues [*de*] inherent in the numinous and the bright and to classify the myriad things in terms of their inherent dispositions [*qing*]" (Richard J. Lynn translation, 77; modified).

"古者包牺氏之王天下也，仰则观象於天，俯则观法於地，观鸟兽之文，与地之宜，近取诸身，远取诸物，於是始作八卦，以通神明之德，以类万物之情。"

4. This passage is modeled on *Great Commentary*, part 2, section 2: "As for [the Dao of] change, when one process of it reaches its limit, a change from one state to another occurs. As such, change achieves free flow, and with this free flow, it lasts forever" (Lynn 1994, 78).

"《易》穷则变，变则通，通则久。"

5. This passage is modeled on *Great Commentary*, part 1, section 5: "In its capacity to produce and reproduce we call it 'change.'" (Lynn 1994, 54).

"生生之谓易。"

6. This passage is modeled on *Great Commentary*, part 1, section 10: "In fashioning implements, we regard its images [*xiang*] as the supreme guide" (Lynn 1994, 62).

"以制器者尚其象"

7. This passage is referring to *Great Commentary*, part 2, section 2: "The Yellow Emperor, Yao and Shun let their robes hang loosely down, and the world was thereby governed." They probably got the idea for this from the hexagrams *Qian* and *Kun*. (Lynn 1994, 78; modified).

"黄帝、尧、舜垂衣裳而天下治，盖取诸《乾》、《坤》。"

Yang Tiancai and Zhang Shanwen write that the long robes were an emblem of civilization, as in remote antiquity people wore animals skins that were short and small. The long robes, as a contrast to this, is a sign of civilization (*Zhouyi* 2015, 611).

8. This is a reference to *Great Commentary*, part 2, section 2: "In remote antiquity, caves were dwellings and the open country was a place to stay. The sage of later ages had these exchanged for proper houses, putting a ridgepole at the top and rafters below in order to protect against the wind and the rain. They probably got the idea for this from the hexagram *Dazhuang*" (Lynn 1994, 79).

"上古穴居而野处，后世圣人易之以宫室，上栋下宇，以待风雨，盖取诸《大壮》。"

9. This is a reference to *Great Commentary*, part 2, section 2: "In remote antiquity, people knotted cords to keep things in order. The sages of later ages had these exchanged for written tallies, and by means of these all the various officials were kept in order, and the myriad folk were supervised. The probably got the idea for this from the hexagram *Kuai*" (Lynn 1994, 80).

"上古结绳而治，后世圣人易之以书契，百官以治，万民以察，盖取诸《夬》。"

10. These are two references to *Great Commentary*, part 2, section 2. The first reference to the *Huan* hexagram is as follows: "They hollowed out some tree trunks to make boats and whittled down others to make paddles. The benefit of boats and paddles was such that one could cross over to where it had been impossible to go. This allowed faraway places to be reached and so benefited

the entire world. They probably got the idea for this from the hexagram *Huan*" (Lynn 1994, 78–79).

"刳木为舟, 剡木为楫, 舟楫之利, 以济不通, 致远以利天下, 盖取诸《涣》。"

The second reference to the *Sui* hexagram is as follows: "They domesticated the ox and harnessed the horse to conveyances. This allowed heavy loads to be pulled and faraway places to be reached and so benefited the entire world. They probably got the idea for this from the hexagram *Sui*" (Lynn 1994, 79).

"服牛乘马, 引重致远, 以利天下, 盖取诸《随》。"

11. These are two references to *Great Commentary*, part 2, section 2. The first reference to the *Xiaoguo* hexagram is as follows: "They cut tree trunks to make pestles and hollowed out the ground to make mortars. The benefit of pestles and mortars was such that the myriad folk used them to get relief from want. They probably got the idea for this from the hexagram *Xiaoguo*" (Lynn 1994, 79).

"断木为杵, 掘地为臼, 臼杵之利, 万民以济, 盖取诸《小过》。"

The second reference to the *Daguo* hexagram is as follows: "In antiquity, for burying the dead, people wrapped them thickly with firewood and buried them out in the wilds, where they neither made grave mounds not planted trees. For the period of mourning there was no definite amount of time. The sages of later ages had this exchanged for inner and outer coffins. They probably got the idea for this from the hexagram *Daguo*" (Lynn 1994, 79–80).

"古之葬者, 厚衣之以薪, 葬之中野, 不封不树, 丧期无数, 后世圣人易之以棺椁, 盖取诸《大过》。"

12. This is a reference to *Great Commentary*, part 2, section 2: "They had gates doubled and had watchmen's clappers struck and so made provision against robbers. They probably got the idea from the hexagram *Yu*" (Lynn 1994, 79).

"重门击柝, 以待暴客, 盖取诸《豫》。"

13. This is a reference to *Great Commentary*, part 2, section 2: "They strung pieces of wood to make bows and whittled others to make arrows. The benefit of bows and arrows was such that they dominated the world. They probably got the idea for this from the hexagram *Kui*" (Lynn 1994, 79).

"弦木为弧, 剡木为矢, 弧矢之利, 以威天下, 盖取诸《睽》。"

14. This is a reference to *Great Commentary*, part 1, section 12: "To plumb the mysteries of the world to the utmost is dependent on the hexagrams; to drum the people into action all over the world is dependent on the appended phrases; to transform things and regulate them is dependent on change; *to initiate things and carry them out is dependent on the unobstructed flow of change*; to be aware of the numinous and bring it to light is dependent on the men involved; to accomplish things while remaining silent and to be trusted without speaking is something intrinsic to virtuous conduct" (Lynn 1994, 68; modified).

"极天下之赜者, 存乎卦; 鼓天下之动者, 存乎辞; 化而裁之存乎变; 推而行之存乎通; 神而明之存乎其人; 默而成之不言而信, 存乎德行。"

15.《尚书·禹贡》

16.《庄子·天运》"帝张咸池之乐于洞庭之野。" According to Cheng Xuanying's commentaries "洞庭之野" means between heaven and earth.

17. This is a reference to the "Yueji" chapter of the *Book of Rites*: "Diminishing and extending, looking up and looking down, the contraction and dilation in the positions of a dance are the *wen* of music."

《礼记·乐记》: "屈伸俯仰, 缀兆舒疾, 乐之文也。"

18. This is a reference to the "Sheji" chapter of the *Book of Rites*: "[Once], when Confucius was conducting an archery meeting in a vegetable garden of Jue Xiang, the spectators surrounded it like a wall."

《礼记·射义》"孔子射于矍相之圃, 盖观者如堵墙。"

19. This is a reference to the "Sheji" chapter of the *Book of Rites*: "And then [Confucius] asked Gongwang Qiu and Xu Dian to raise their drinking vessels and make a speech."

《礼记·射义》"又使公罔之裘、序点, 扬觯而语。"

20. This is a reference to *Great Commentary*, part 1, section 8: "The sages had the means to perceive the activities taking place in the world, and, observing how things come together and without obstruction, they thus enacted statutes and rituals accordingly" (Lynn 1994, 57; modified).

圣人有以见天下之动, 而观其会通, 以行其典礼

21. Ruler/subject, father/son, husband/wife.

22. Heaven, earth, and man.

23.《楚辞·天问》"九天之际, 安放安属?"

24.《楚辞·天问》"八柱何当?"

25.《楚辞·天问》"昆仑县圃, 其尻安在?"

26.《楚辞·天问》"增城九重, 其高几里?"

27. This passage bears great resemblance to *Xici* 1.1: "In heaven this [process] creates images, and on earth it creates physical forms; this is how change and transformation manifest themselves. . . . *It* [the Dao] *arouses things with claps of thunder, moistens them with wind and rain.* Sun and moon go through their cycles, so now it is cold, now it is hot. The Dao of *Qian* forms the male; the Dao of *Kun* forms the female. *Qian* has mastery over the great *beginning of things*, and *Kun* acts to bring things to completion. *Qian* through ease provides mastery over things, and *Kun* through simplicity provides capability" (Lynn 1994, 47–48; my emphases).

"在天成象, 在地成形, 变化见矣。是故, . . . 鼓之以雷霆, 润之以风雨, 日月运行, 一寒一暑, 乾道成男, 坤道成女。乾知大始, 坤作成物。乾以易知, 坤以简能。"

28. This passage bears great resemblance to《礼记·祭义》"推而放诸东海而准, 推而放诸西海而准, 推而放诸南海而准, 推而放诸北海而准。"

29. This passage bears great resemblance to《礼记·乐记》"是故情深而文名, 气盛而化神。"

Glossary

1. I believe this is taken from Spinoza's *Ethics* 1d3.

Works Cited

Abram, David. 2017. *The Spell of the Sensuous: Perception and Language in a More-Than-Human World.* 20th anniv. ed. New York: Vintage.

Allen, Amy. 2003. "Foucault and Enlightenment: A Critical Reappraisal." *Constellations* 10 (2): 180–98.

Ames, Roger T. 1991. "Meaning as Imaging: Prolegomena to a Confucian Epistemology." In *Culture and Modernity: East-West Philosophic Perspectives,* edited by Eliot Deutsch, 227–44. Honolulu: University of Hawaii Press.

———. 2002. "Mencius and a Process Notion of Human Nature." In *Mencius: Contexts and Interpretations,* edited by Alan K. L. Chan, 72–90. Honolulu: University of Hawaii Press.

———. 2017. "Recovering a Confucian Conception of Human Nature: A Challenge to the Ideology of Individualism." *Acta Koreana* 20, no. 1 (June): 1–19.

Ames, Roger T., and Hall, David L. 2001. *Focusing the Familiar: A Translation and Philosophical Interpretation of the Zhongyong.* Honolulu: University of Hawaii Press.

Amrine, Frederick. 1998. "The Metamorphosis of the Scientist." In *Goethe's Way of Science: A Phenomenology of Nature,* edited by David Seamon and Arthur Zajonc, 33–54. Albany: State University of New York Press.

Anghie, Antony. 2004. *Imperialism, Sovereignty and the Making of International Law.* Cambridge: Cambridge University Press.

Appiah, Anthony. 2007. *Cosmopolitanism: Ethics in a World of Strangers.* London: Penguin.

Aristotle. 1905. *Politics.* Translated by Benjamin Jowett. New York: Cosimo.

———. 1984. *The Complete Works of Aristotle.* Vol. 2, edited by Jonathan Barnes. Princeton, NJ: Princeton University Press.

———. 2018. *Physics.* Translated by Charles David Chanel Reeve. Indianapolis: Hackett.

Bachner, Andrea. 2014. *Beyond Sinology: Chinese Writing and the Scripts of Culture.* New York: Columbia University Press.

Bahr, Hermann. 1917. "Über Ernst Cassirer." *Die neue Rundschau* 28:1483–1515.

Bayer, Thora Ilin. 2001. *Cassirer's Metaphysics of Symbolic Forms: A Philosophical Commentary*. New Haven, CT: Yale University Press.

Beiser, Frederick C. 1987. *The Fate of Reason: German Philosophy from Kant to Fichte*. Cambridge, MA: Harvard University Press.

———. 2003. *The Romantic Imperative: The Concept of Early German Romanticism*. Cambridge, MA: Harvard University Press.

Bernasconi, Robert, and Tommy L. Lott, eds. 2000. *The Idea of Race*. Indianapolis: Hackett.

Bloom, Irene. 2002. "Biology and Culture in the Mencian View of Human Nature." In *Mencius: Contexts and Interpretations*, edited by Alan K. L. Chan, 91–102. Honolulu: University of Hawaii Press.

Bol, Peter. 1992. *"This Culture of Ours": Intellectual Transitions in T'ang and Sung China*. Stanford, CA: Stanford University Press.

Boltz, William G. 1994. *The Origin and Early Development of the Chinese Writing System*. New Haven, CT: American Oriental Society.

Bortoft, Henri. 2010. *The Wholeness of Nature: Goethe's Way toward a Science of Conscious Participation in Nature*. Edinburgh: Floris.

Brindley, Erica Fox. 2012. *Music, Cosmology, and the Politics of Harmony in Early China*. Albany: State University of New York Press.

Bruya, Brian. 2003. "Qing 情 and Emotion in Early Chinese Thought." In *Chinese Philosophy and the Trends of the 21st Century Civilization*, edited by Fang Keli and Zhu Bian, 151–76. Hong Kong: Commercial Press.

Cassirer, Ernst. 1923. *Substance and Function, and Einstein's Theory of Relativity*. New York: Dover.

———. 1944. *An Essay on Man*. New Haven, CT: Yale University Press.

———. 1945. "Structuralism in Modern Linguistics." *Word* 1 (2): 99–120.

———. 1946a. *Language and Myth*. Translated by Susanne K. Langer. New York: Harper.

———. 1946b. *The Myth of the State*. New Haven, CT: Yale University Press.

———. 1949. " 'Spirit' and 'Life' in Contemporary Philosophy." Translated by Robert Walter Bretall and Paul Arthur Schilpp. In *The Philosophy of Ernst Cassirer*, edited by Paul Arthur Schilpp, 857–80. La Salle, IL: Open Court.

———. 1950. *The Problem of Knowledge: Philosophy, Science, and History since Hegel*. Translated by William H. Woglom and Charles W. Hendel. New Haven, CT: Yale University Press.

———. 1951. *The Philosophy of the Enlightenment*. Princeton, NJ: Princeton University Press.

———. 1955a. *The Philosophy of Symbolic Forms*. Vol. 1, *Language*, translated by Ralph Manheim. New Haven, CT: Yale University Press.

———. 1955b. *The Philosophy of Symbolic Forms*. Vol. 2, *Mythical Thought*, translated by Ralph Manheim. New Haven, CT: Yale University Press.

———. 1956. *Determinism and Indeterminism in Modern Physics: Historical and Systematic Studies of the Problem of Causality*. Translated by Otto Theodor Benfey. New Haven, CT: Yale University Press.

———. 1957. *The Philosophy of Symbolic Forms*. Vol. 3, *The Phenomenology of Knowledge*, translated by Ralph Manheim. New Haven, CT: Yale University Press.

———. 1961. "Naturalistic and Humanistic Philosophies of Culture." In *The Logic of the Humanities*, translated by Clarence Smith Howe, 3–38. New Haven, CT: Yale University Press.

———. 1963. *The Individual and the Cosmos in Renaissance Philosophy*. Translated by Mario Domandi. Chicago: University of Chicago Press.

———. 1969. "Mythic, Aesthetic and Theoretical Space." Translated by Donald Phillip Verene and Lerke Holzwarth Foster. *Man and World* 2 (1): 3–17.

———. 1979. *Symbol, Myth, and Culture: Essays and Lectures of Ernst Cassirer, 1935–1945*. Edited by Donald Phillip Verene. New Haven, CT: Yale University Press.

———. 1981. *Kant's Life and Thought*. Translated by James Haden. New Haven, CT: Yale University Press.

———. 1996. *The Philosophy of Symbolic Forms*. Vol. 4, *The Metaphysics of Symbolic Forms*, edited by John Michael Krois and Donald Phillip Verene. Translated by John Michael Krois. New Haven, CT: Yale University Press.

———. 2000. *The Logic of the Cultural Sciences*. Translated by S. G. Lofts. New Haven, CT: Yale University Press.

———. 2001a. *Freiheit und Form*. In *Gesammelte Werke: Hamburger Ausgabe*, Bd. 7, edited by Birgit Recki. Hamburg: Meiner.

———. 2001b. "Kant und die moderne Mathematik." In *Gesammelte Werke: Hamburger Ausgabe*, Bd. 9, *Aufsätze und kleine Schriften 1902–1921*, edited by Birgit Recki, 37–82. Hamburg: Meiner.

———. 2003a. "Der Begriff der symbolischen Form im Aufbau der Geisteswissenschaften." In *Gesammelte Werke: Hamburger Ausgabe* Bd. 16, *Aufsätze und kleine Schrifte (1922–1926)*, edited by Birgit Recki, 75–104. Hamburg: Meiner.

———. 2003b. "Der Junge Goethe." In *Nachgelassene Manuskripte und Texte*, Bd. 11, *Goethe Vorlesungen (1940–1941)*, edited by John Michael Krois, 5–231. Hamburg: Meiner.

———. 2004. "Goethes Idee der Bildung und Erziehung." In *Gesammelte Werke: Hamburger Ausgabe*, Bd. 18, *Aufsätze und kleine Schriften (1932–1935)*, edited by Birgit Recki, 410–34. Hamburg: Meiner.

———. 2007a. "Goethe and the Kantian Philosophy." In *Gesammelte Werke: Hamburger Ausgabe*, Bd. 24, *Aufsätze und kleine Schriften (1941–1946)*, edited by Birgit Recki, 542–78. Hamburg: Meiner.

———. 2007b. "Kant and Rousseau." In *Gesammelte Werke: Hamburger Ausgabe*, Bd. 24, *Aufsätze und kleine Schriften (1941–1946)*, edited by Birgit Recki, 491–541. Hamburg: Meiner.

————. 2009. *Nachgelassene Manuskripte und Texte*, Bd. 18, *Briefe: Ausgewählter-wissenschaftlicher Briefwechsel*, edited by John Michael Krois, 8–9 Hamburg: Meiner.

————. 2010. *Philosophie der symbolischen Formen*. Erster Teil, *Die Sprache*. Edited by Claus Rosenkranz. Hamburg: Meiner.

————. 2012. "Form and Technology." In *Ernst Cassirer on Form and Technology: Contemporary Readings*, edited by Aud Sissel Hoel and Ingvild Folkvord. New York: Palgrave Macmillan.

————. 2013a. "Language and the Construction of the World of Objects (1932)." In *The Warburg Years (1919–1933): Essays on Language, Art, Myth, and Technology*, 334–62. New Haven, CT: Yale University Press.

————. 2013b. "The Concept of Symbolic Form in the Construction of the Human Sciences (1923)." In *The Warburg Years (1919–1933): Essays on Language, Art, Myth, and Technology*, 72–100. New Haven, CT: Yale University Press.

————. 2013c. "The Kantian Element in Wilhelm von Humboldt's Philosophy of Language (1923)." In *The Warburg Years (1919–1933): Essays on Language, Art, Myth, and Technology*, 101–29. New Haven, CT: Yale University Press.

Cassirer, Toni. 1981. *Mein Leben mit Ernst Cassirer*. Hildesheim: Gerstenberg.

Caws, Peter. 1972. "The Recent Literature of Structuralism." *Philosophische Rundschau* 18 (1/2): 63–78.

Césaire, Aimé. 2010. "Letter to Maurice Thorez." *Social Text* 28, no. 2 (Summer): 145–52.

Chan, Wing-tsit. 1963. *A Sourcebook in Chinese Philosophy*. Princeton, NJ: Princeton University Press.

Chang, Tung-sun. 1952. "A Chinese Philosopher's Theory of Knowledge." *ETC: A Review of General Semantics* 9, no. 3 (Spring): 203–26.

Cheng, Chung-ying. 1977. "Toward Constructing a Dialectics of Harmonization: Harmony and Conflict in Chinese Philosophy." *Journal of Chinese Philosophy* 4, no. 3 (October): 209–45.

————. 1991. *New Dimensions of Confucian and Neo-Confucian Philosophy*. Albany: State University of New York Press.

Chow, Tse-tung. 1979. "Chinese Views on Literature, the Tao, and Their Relationship." *Chinese Literature: Essays, Articles, Reviews* 1, no. 38 (January): 3–29.

Connolly, Cyril. 1951. *The Unquiet Grave: A World Cycle by Palinurus*. Rev. ed. London: Hamish Hamilton.

Cook, Scott. 1995. "Yue Ji 樂記—Record of Music: Introduction, Translation, Notes, and Commentary." *Asian Music* 26, no. 2 (Spring–Summer): 1–96.

Cornell, Drucilla, and Kenneth Michael Panfilio. 2010. *Symbolic Forms for a New Humanity: Cultural and Racial Reconfigurations of Critical Theory*. New York: Fordham University Press.

Dai Lianzhang 戴璉璋. 1988. *Yizhuan zhi Xingcheng jiqi Sixiang* 易传之形成及其四象. Taibei: Wenjin Chubanshe 文津出版社.

de Bary, William Theodore. 1991. *The Trouble with Confucianism.* Cambridge, MA: Harvard University Press.

Dewey, John. 1969. *1882–88.* Vol. 1 of *Early Works, 1882–1898,* edited by Jo Ann Boydston. Carbondale: Southern Illinois University Press.

Durkheim, Émile. 1982. *The Rules of Sociological Method.* Translated by W. D. Halls. New York: Free Press.

Falkenhausen, Lothar von. 1996. "The Concept of Wen in the Ancient Chinese Ancestral Cult." *Chinese Literature: Essays, Articles, Reviews* 18 (December): 1–22.

Ferrari, Massimo. 2002. "Was wären wir ohne Goethe? Motive der frühen Goethe-Rezeption bei Ernst Cassirer." In *Cassirer und Goethe: Neue Aspekte einer philosophischen-literarischen Wahlverwandtschaft,* edited by Barbara Naumann and Birgit Recki, 173–94. Berlin: Akademie Verlag.

———. 2003. *Ernst Cassirer: Stationen einer philosophischen Biographie: Von der Marburger Schule zur Kulturphilosophie.* Translated (from Italian) by Marion Lauschke. Hamburg: Meiner.

Fetz, Reto Luzius. 1981. "Genetische Semiologie? Symboltheorie im Ausgang von Ernst Cassirer und Jean Piaget." *Freiburger Zeitschrift für Philosophie und Theologie* 28 (3): 434–70.

Forster, Michael N. 2010. *After Herder: Philosophy of Language in the German Tradition.* Oxford: Oxford University Press.

Foucault, Michel. 2008. "Introduction à l'Anthropologie de Kant." In *Anthropologie du point de vue pragmatique et Introduction à l'Anthropologie.* Paris: Vrin.

Friedman, Michael. 2005. "Ernst Cassirer and the Philosophy of Science." In *Continental Philosophy of Science,* edited by Gary Gutting, 71–83. Oxford: Blackwell.

———. 2008. "Ernst Cassirer and Thomas Kuhn: The Neo-Kantian Tradition in History and Philosophy of Science." *Philosophical Forum* 39, no. 2 (Summer): 239–52.

Gadamer, Hans-Georg. 2004. *Truth and Method.* 2nd rev. ed. Translated by Joel Weinsheimer and Donald G. Marshall. London: Continuum, 2004.

Gao Heng 高亨. 1979. *Zhouyi Dazhuan Jinzhu* 周易大传今注. Shandong: Qilu Shushe 齐鲁书社.

Gay, Peter. 2001. *Weimar Culture: The Outsider as Insider.* New York: W. W. Norton, 2001.

Glock, Hans-Johann. 1997. "Philosophy, Thought and Language." *Royal Institute of Philosophy Supplement* 42 (March): 151–69.

———. 2015. "Philosophy of Language." *The Oxford Handbook of German Philosophy in the Nineteenth Century,* edited by Michael N. Forster and Kristin Gjesdal, 371–97. Oxford: Oxford University Press.

Goethe, Johann Wolfgang von. 1946. *Goethe's Botany: The Metamorphosis of Plants (1790) and Tabler's Ode to Nature (1782)*. Translated by Agnes Arber. Waltham, MA: Chronica Botanica.

———. 1949. *Wisdom and Experience*. Edited by Ludwig Curtis and Hermann Weigand. Translated by Hermann Weigand. New York: Pantheon.

———. 1981. *Schriften zur Kunst; Schriften zur Literatur; Maximen und Reflexionen*. Bd. 12 of *Goethes Werke*, edited by Erich Trunz and Hans Joachim Schrimpf. Munich: C. H. Beck.

———. 1988. *Scientific Studies*. Edited and translated by Douglas Miller. New York: Suhrkamp.

———. 2003. *Autobiographische Schriften II*. Bd. 10 of *Hamburger Ausgabe*. Munich: Beck.

Goethe, Johann Wolfgang von, and Johann Peter Eckermann. 2009. "Conversations on World Literature (1827)." In *The Princeton Sourcebook in Comparative Literature: From the European Enlightenment to the Global Present*, edited by David Damrosch, Natalie Melas, and Mbongiseni Buthelezi, 17–25. Princeton, NJ: Princeton University Press.

Gordon, Peter E. 2005. "Myth and Modernity: Cassirer's Critique of Heidegger." *New German Critique* 94 (Winter): 127–68.

———. 2010. *Continental Divide: Heidegger, Cassirer, Davos*. Cambridge, MA: Harvard University Press.

Graham, A. C. 1989. *Disputers of the Tao: Philosophical Argument in Ancient China*. La Salle, IL: Open Court.

Grondin, Jean. 1995. *Sources of Hermeneutics*. New York: State University of New York Press.

Habermas, Jürgen. 2001. "The Liberating Power of Symbols: Ernst Cassirer's Humanistic Legacy and the Warburg Library." In *The Liberating Power of Symbols: Philosophical Essays*, translated by Peter Dews, 1–29. Cambridge, UK: Polity.

Hagen, Kurtis. 2007. *The Philosophy of the Xunzi: A Reconstruction*. Chicago: Open Court.

Hall, David L., and Ames, Roger T. 1987. *Thinking Through Confucius*. Albany: State University of New York Press.

———. 1995. *Anticipating China*. Albany: State University of New York Press.

———. 1998a. "Chinese Thinking as *Ars Contextualis*." Section 1 of "Chinese Philosophy," in *Routledge Encyclopedia of Philosophy Online*. Taylor and Francis. https://www.rep.routledge.com/articles/overview/chinese-philosophy/v-1/sections/chinese-thinking-as-ars-contextualis.

———. 1998b. *Thinking from the Han: Self, Truth, and Transcendence in Chinese and Western Culture*. Albany: State University of New York Press.

Hansen, Chad. 1992. *A Daoist Theory of Chinese Thought: A Philosophical Interpretation*. Oxford: Oxford University Press.

Harold, James. 2016. "On the Ancient Idea that Music Shapes Character." *Dao* 15, no. 3 (September): 341–54.

Hegel, Georg Wilhelm Friedrich. 1975. *Lectures on the Philosophy of World History*. Cambridge: Cambridge University Press.

Heitler, Walter. 1998. "Goethean Science." In *Goethe's Way of Science: A Phenomenology of Nature*, edited by David Seamon and Arthur Zajonc, 55–70. Albany: State University of New York Press.

Heraclitus. "Heraclitus." 1907. In *Source Book in Ancient Philosophy*, translated by Charles M. Bakewell, 28–35. New York: Scribner's.

Herder, Johann Gottfried von. 2002. "This Too a Philosophy of History for the Formation of Humanity (1774)." In *Philosophical Writings*, translated and edited by Michael N. Forster, 272–358. Cambridge: Cambridge University Press.

Hsieh, Liu. 2015. *The Literary Mind and the Carving of Dragons*. Translated by Vincent Yu-chung Shih. Hong Kong: Chinese University of Hong Kong.

Hu Shi 胡适. 1997. *Zhongguo Zhexueshi Dagang* 中国哲学史大纲. Shanghai: Shanghai Guji Chubanshe 上海古籍出版社.

Humboldt, Wilhelm von. 1968. *Wilhelm von Humboldts Gesammelte Schriften*. Edited by A. Leitzmann. 15 vols. Berlin: de Gruyter.

———. 1999. *On Language: On the Diversity of Human Language Construction and Its Influence on the Mental Development of the Human Species*. Edited by Michael Losonsky. Translated by Peter Heath. Cambridge: Cambridge University Press.

Hutton, Eric L. 2014. *Xunzi: The Complete Text*. Princeton, NJ: Princeton University Press.

James, William. 1890. *The Principles of Psychology*. Vol. 1. New York: Henry Holt.

Jesinghausen-Lauster, Martin. 1985. *Die Suche nach der symbolischen Form: Der Kreis um die Kulturwissenschaftliche Bibliotek Warburg*. Baden-Baden: Koerner.

Kant, Immanuel. 1996. *Critique of Pure Reason*. Translated by Werner S. Pluhar. Indianapolis: Hackett.

Kasulis, Thomas P. 2015. "The Mosaic and the Jigsaw Puzzle: How It All Fits Together." In *Value and Values: Economics and Justice in an Era of Global Interdependence*, edited by Roger T. Ames and Peter D. Hershock, 27–48. Honolulu: University of Hawaii Press.

Kern, Martin. 2001. "Ritual, Text, and the Formation of the Canon: Historical Transitions of *Wen* in Early China." *T'oung Pao* 87 (1): 43–91.

Knoblock, John. 1994. *Xunzi: A Translation and Study of the Complete Works*. Vol. 3, bks. 17–32. Stanford, CA: Stanford University Press.

Kreis, Guido. 2010. *Cassirer und die Formen des Geistes*. Berlin: Suhrkamp.

Krois, John Michael. 1987. *Cassirer: Symbolic Forms and History*. New Haven, CT: Yale University Press.

———. 2002. "Die Goethischen Elemente in Cassirers Philosophie." In *Cassirer und Goethe: Neue Aspekte einer philosophischen-literarischen Wahlverwandt-*

schaft, edited by Barbara Naumann and Birgit Recki. 157–72. Berlin: Akademie Verlag.

———. 2005. "'A Passion Can Only Be Overcome by a Stronger Passion': Philosophical Anthropology before and after Ernst Cassirer." *European Review* 13, no. 4: 557–75.

———. 2012. "Cassirer's Revision of the Enlightenment Project." In *Philosophie der Kultur—Kultur des Philosophierens: Ernst Cassirer im 20. und 21. Jahrhundert*, edited by Birgit Recki, 89–105. Hamburg: Meiner.

Kroll, Paul W. 2015. *A Student's Dictionary of Classical and Medieval Chinese*. Leiden: Brill.

Lai, Karyn L. 2006. "Philosophy and Philosophical Reasoning in the Zhuangzi: Dealing with Plurality." *Journal of Chinese Philosophy* 33, no. 3 (September): 365–74.

Leibniz, Gottfried Wilhelm. 1994. *Writings on China*. Translated by Daniel J. Cook and Henry Rosemont, Jr. Chicago: Open Court.

Lévinas, Emmanuel. 1994. *Les imprévus de l'histoire*. Saint-Clément-la-Rivière: Fata Morgana.

Levy, Dore J. 2001. "Literary Theory and Criticism." In *The Columbia History of Chinese Literature*, edited by Victor H. Mair, 916–39. New York: Columbia University Press.

Lewis, Mark Edward. 1999. *Writing and Authority in Early China*. Albany: State University of New York Press.

Li, Chenyang. 2014. *The Confucian Philosophy of Harmony*. New York: Routledge.

Li, Feng. 2013. *Early China: A Social and Cultural History*. Cambridge: Cambridge University Press.

Li, Zehou. 2010. *The Chinese Aesthetic Tradition*. Translated by Maija Bell Samei. Honolulu: University of Hawaii Press.

Liu Baonan 刘宝楠. 1990. *Lunyu Zhenyi* 论语正义. Beijing: Zhonghua Shuju 中华书局.

Liu, James J. Y. 1975. *Chinese Theories of Literature*. Chicago: University of Chicago Press.

Liu Xiaogan 刘笑敢. 2011. "On the Identity and Positioning of Chinese Philosophical Studies: A Case Study of *Tian-ren-he-yi* (Union of Heaven and Man) in Ancient and Modern Times 天人合一: 学术、学说和信仰 —— 再论中国哲学之身份及研究取向的不同." *Journal of Nanjing University (Philosophy, Humanities and Social Sciences)* 南京大学学报 (哲学人文科学社会科学) 6:67–156.

Losonsky, Michael. 2006. *Linguistic Turns in Modern Philosophy*. Cambridge: Cambridge University Press.

Luft, Sebastian. 2015a. "The A Priori of Culture: Philosophy of Culture between Rationalism and Relativism—the Example of Lévi-Strauss' Structural Anthropology." *The Philosophy of Ernst Cassirer: A Novel Assessment*. Edited by J. Tyler Friedman and Sebastian Luft, 381–400. Berlin: Walter de Gruyter.

———. 2015b. *The Space of Culture: Towards a Neo-Kantian Philosophy of Culture (Cohen, Natorp, and Cassirer)*. Oxford: Oxford University Press.

Lynn, Richard John, trans. 1994. *The Classic of Changes: A New Translation of the I Ching as Interpreted by Wang Bi*. New York: Columbia University Press.

Mann, Thomas. 1955. *The Magic Mountain*. Translated by H. T. Lowe-Porter. New York: Vintage.

———. 1983. *Reflections of a Nonpolitical Man*. New York: Ungar.

Marks, Jonathan M. 1995. *Human Biodiversity: Genes, Race, and History*. New York: Walter de Gruyter.

Meng, Ke, and Bryan William Van Norden. 2008. *Mengzi: With Selections from Traditional Commentaries*. Indianapolis: Hackett.

Midgley, Mary. 2002. *Evolution as a Religion: Strange Hopes and Strange Fears*. Rev. ed. London: Routledge.

Möckel, Christian. 2003. *Das Urphänomen des Lebens: Ernst Cassirers Lebensbegriff*. Hamburg: Meiner.

Morgenthau, Hans J. 1947. Review of *The Myth of the State*, by Ernst Cassirer. *Ethics* 57:141–42.

Mote, Frederick W. 1971. *Intellectual Foundations of China*. New York: Knopf.

Mou, Zongsan. 2003. *Mou Zongsan xiansheng quanji 1: Zhouyi de Ziran Zhexue yu Daode Hanyi* 牟宗三先生全集 1: 周易的自然哲学与道德含义. Taibei: Taibei Lianjing Chubanshiyegongsi 台北联经出版事业公司.

Moynahan, Gregory B. 2014. *Ernst Cassirer and the Critical Science of Germany, 1899–1919*. London: Anthem.

Müller, Claudius C. 1980. "Die Herausbildung der Gegensätze: Chinesen und Barbaren in der frühen Zeit (I. Jahrtausend v. Chr. bis 200 n. Chr)." In *China und die Fremden: 3000 Jahre Auseinandersetzung in Krieg und Frieden*, edited by Wolfgang Bauer, 43–76. Munich: C. H. Beck.

Müller, Olaf L. 2015. *Mehr Licht: Goethe mit Newton im Streit um die Farben*. Frankfurt am Main: S. Fischer Verlag.

Needham, Joseph. 1956. *Science and Civilization in China*. Cambridge: Cambridge University Press.

Nelson, Eric S. 2011. "The *Yijing* and Philosophy: From Leibniz to Derrida." *Journal of Chinese Philosophy* 38, no. 3 (September): 377–96.

Nielsen, Bent. 2003. *Companion to "Yi Jing" Numerology and Cosmology: Chinese Studies of Images and Numbers from Han* 漢 *(202 BCE–220 CE) to Song* 宋 *(960–1279 CE)*. London: RoutledgeCurzon.

Nietzsche, Friedrich. 2001. *The Gay Science*. Edited by Bernard Williams. Translated by Josefine Nauckhoff and Adrian Del Caro. Cambridge: Cambridge University Press.

———. 2006. *Thus Spoke Zarathustra: A Book for All and None*. Edited by Adrian Del Caro and Robert B. Pippin. Translated by Adrian Del Caro. Cambridge: Cambridge University Press.

Nylan. Michael. 2010. "*Yin-Yang*, Five Phases, and *Qi*." In *China's Early Empires: A Re-appraisal*, edited by Michael Nylan and Michael Loewe. Cambridge: Cambridge University Press.

Owen, Stephen. 1992. *Readings in Chinese Literary Thought*. Cambridge, MA: Harvard University Press.

Pagden, Anthony. 2015. *The Burdens of Empire: 1539 to the Present*. Cambridge: Cambridge University Press.

Panaïoti, Antoine. 2013. *Nietzsche and Buddhist Philosophy*. Cambridge: Cambridge University Press.

Park, So Jeong. 2013. "Musical Thought in the *Zhuangzi*: A Criticism of the Confucian Discourse on Ritual and Music." *Dao* 12, no. 3 (September): 331–50.

Parkes, Graham. 1996. *Nietzsche and Asian Thought*. Chicago: University of Chicago Press.

Peterson, Willard J. 1982. "Making Connections: 'Commentary on the Attached Verbalizations' of the Book of Change." *Harvard Journal of Asiatic Studies* 42, no. 1 (June): 67–116.

Plümacher, Martina. 2008. "Der ethische Impuls in Ernst Cassirers Philosophie der symbolischen Formen." In *Lebendige Form: Zur Metaphysik des Symbolischen in Ernst Cassirers "Nachgelassenen Manuskripten und Texten*," edited by Reto Luzius Fetz and Sebastian Ullrich, 93–116. Hamburg: Meiner 2008.

Puett, Michael. 2001. *The Ambivalence of Creation: Debates Concerning Innovation and Artifice in Early China*. Stanford, CA: Stanford University Press.

———. 2002. *To Become a God: Cosmology, Sacrifice, and Self-Divinization in Early China*. Cambridge, MA: Harvard University Asia Center.

Qian Mu 钱穆. 1991. "Zhongguo Wenhua dui Renlei Weilai keyoude Gongxian 中国文化对人类未来可有的贡献." 中国文化 4:93–96.

Rawls, John. 1980. "Kantian Constructivism in Moral Theory." *Journal of Philosophy* 77, no. 9 (September 9): 515–72.

Recki, Birgit. 1997. "Kultur ohne Moral? Warum Ernst Cassirer trotz der Einsicht in den Primat der praktischen Vernunft keine Ethik schreiben konnte." In *Kultur und Philosophie: Ernst Cassirers Werk und Wirkung*, edited by Dorothea Frede und Reinold Schmücker, 58–78. Darmstadt: Wissenschaftliche Buchgesellschaft.

———. 2004. "Persönliches Ethos, Moral und Politik: Eine Philosophie der symbolischen Normen?" In *Kultur als Praxis: Eine Einführung in Ernst Cassirers Philosophie der symbolischen Formen*, 129–209. Berlin: Akademie Verlag.

Reed, T. J. 1984. *Goethe*. Oxford: Oxford University Press.

Robey, David. 1972. Introduction to *Structuralism: An Introduction*, edited by David Robey, 1–19. Oxford: Clarendon Press.

Rockmore, Tom. 2011. *Kant and Phenomenology*. Chicago: University of Chicago Press.

Rorty, Richard. 1979. *Philosophy and the Mirror of Nature*. Princeton, NJ: Princeton University Press.

———. 1999. *Philosophy and Social Hope*. London: Penguin.

———. 2004. "Philosophy as a Transitional Genre." In *Pragmatism, Critique, Judgement: Essays for Richard Bernstein*, edited by Seyla Benhabib and Nancy Fraser, 3–28. Cambridge, MA: MIT Press.

———. 2007. *Philosophy as Cultural Politics*. Philosophical Papers 4. Cambridge: Cambridge University Press.

Ruskin, John. 1998. *The Genius of John Ruskin: Selections from His Writings*. Edited by John D. Rosenberg. Charlottesville: University Press of Virginia.

Said, Edward. 2003. *Orientalism*. 25th anniv. ed. London: Penguin.

Sandel, Michael J. 1998. *Liberalism and the Limits of Justice*. 2nd ed. Cambridge: Cambridge University Press.

Sato, Masayuki. 2003. *The Confucian Quest for Order: The Origin and Formation of the Political Thought of Xun Zi*. Leiden: Brill.

Saussy, Haun. 1993. *The Problem of a Chinese Aesthetic*. Stanford, CA: Stanford University Press.

Schwemmer, Oswald. 1997. *Ernst Cassirer: Ein Philosoph der europäischen Moderne*. Berlin: Akademie Verlag.

Seamon, David, and Arthur Zajonc, eds. 1998. *Goethe's Way of Science: A Phenomenology of Nature*. Albany: State University of New York Press.

Seltzer, Edward. 1969. "The Problem of Objectivity: A Study of Objectivity Reflected in a Comparison of the Philosophies of E. Cassirer, J. Piaget, and E. Husserl." PhD diss., New School for Social Research.

Sepper, Dennis L. 1988. *Goethe contra Newton: Polemics and the Project for a New Science of Color*. Cambridge: Cambridge University Press.

Shaughnessy, Edward L., trans. 1996. *I Ching: The Classic of Changes*. New York: Ballantine.

———. 2001. "The Writing of the Xici Zhuan and the Making of the Yijing." In *Measuring Historical Heat: Event, Performance and Impact in China and the West*, 197–221. http://www.sino.uni-heidelberg.de/conf/symposium2.pdf.

Shchutskii, Iulian K. 1979. *Researches on the I Ching*. Translated by William L. MacDonald and Tsuyoshi Hasegawa, with Hellmut Wilhelm. Bollingen Series 62.2. Princeton, NJ: Princeton University Press.

Shen, Vincent. 2014. "Wisdom and Hermeneutics of Poetry in Classical Confucianism." In *Dao Companion to Classical Confucian Philosophy*, edited by Vincent Shen, 245–62. London: Springer.

Sigurðsson, Geir. 2015. *Confucian Propriety and Ritual Learning: A Philosophical Interpretation*. Albany: State University of New York Press.

Sikka, Sonia. 2011. *Herder on Humanity and Cultural Difference: Enlightened Relativism*. Cambridge: Cambridge University Press.

Silverstone, Roger. 1976. "Ernst Cassirer and Claude Lévi-Strauss: Two Approaches to the Study of Myth." *Archives de sciences sociales des religions* 21, no. 41 (January–June): 25–36.

Skidelsky, Edward. 2008. *Ernst Cassirer: The Last Philosopher of Culture*. Princeton, NJ: Princeton University Press.

Slingerland, Edward, trans. 2003. *Confucius Analects: With Selections from Traditional Commentaries*. Indianapolis: Hackett.

Smith, Richard J. 2008. *Fathoming the Cosmos and Ordering the World: The Yijing (I Ching, or Classic of Changes) and Its Evolution in China*. Charlottesville: University of Virginia Press.

Stearns, Isabel. 1951. Review of *The Problem of Knowledge*, by Ernst Cassirer. *Review of Metaphysics* 5, no. 1 (September): 109–24.

Strauss, Leo. 1947. Review of *The Myth of the State*, by Ernst Cassirer. *Social Research* 14 (1): 125–28.

Sun, Anna Xiao Dong. 2013. *Confucianism as a World Religion: Contested Histories and Contemporary Realities*. Princeton, NJ: Princeton University Press.

Sun Tao 孙涛. 2014. *Zhongguo Meixueshi: Diyi Juan, Xianqin Juan*. 中国美学史: 第一卷, 先秦卷. Nanjing: Jiangsu Renmin Chubanshe 江苏人民出版社.

Taylor, Charles. 1989. *Sources of the Self: The Making of the Modern Identity*. Cambridge, MA: Harvard University Press.

Truwant, Simon. 2015. "Cassirer's Functional Conception of the Human Being." *Idealistic Studies* 45, no. 2 (Summer): 169–90.

Tu, Wei-ming. 1985. *Confucian Thought: Selfhood as Creative Transformation*. Albany: State University of New York Press.

———. 1989a. *Centrality and Commonality: An Essay on Confucian Religiousness*. Rev. and enl. ed. Albany: State University of New York Press.

———. 1989b. "The Continuity of Being: Chinese Visions of Nature." In *Nature in Asian Traditions of Thought: Essays in Environmental Philosophy*, edited by J. Baird Callicott and Roger T. Ames, 67–78. Albany: State University of New York.

Verene, Donald Phillip. 2008. "Cassirer's Metaphysics." In *The Symbolic Construction of Reality: The Legacy of Ernst Cassirer*, edited by Jeffrey Andrew Barash, 93–103. Chicago: University of Chicago Press.

———. 2011. *The Origins of the Philosophy of Symbolic Forms: Kant, Hegel, and Cassirer*. Evanston, IL: Northwestern University Press.

Wang, Li 王力. 2011. *Gu Hanyu Changyongzi Zidian* (4th ed.) 古汉语常用字字典 (第四版). Beijing: Shangwu Yinshuguan 商务印书馆.

Wang, Robin R. 2012. *Yinyang: The Way of Heaven and Earth in Chinese Thought and Culture*. Cambridge: Cambridge University Press.

Wang, Shuren. 2009. "The Roots of Chinese Philosophy and Culture: An Introduction to 'Xiang' and 'Xiang Thinking.'" *Frontiers of Philosophy in China* 4 (1): 1–12.

White, Morton. 2002. *A Philosophy of Culture: The Scope of Holistic Pragmatism.* Princeton, NJ: Princeton University Press.

Whitehead, Alfred North. 1948. *Science and the Modern World.* New York: Pelican Mentor Books.

———. 1978. *Process and Reality.* New York: Free Press.

Wilhelm, Hellmut. 1977. *Heaven, Earth, and Man in the Book of Changes.* Seattle: University of Washington Press.

Wimsatt, W. K., Jr., and Beardsley M. C. 1946. "The Intentional Fallacy." *Sewanee Review* 54, no. 3 (July–September): 468–88.

Xiang, Shuchen. 2018. "Orientalism and Enlightenment Positivism: A Critique of Anglophone Sinology, Comparative Literature, and Philosophy." *Pluralist* 13, no. 2 (Summer): 22–49.

———. 2019a. "The Symbolic Construction of Reality: The *Xici* and Ernst Cassirer's *Philosophy of Symbolic Forms.*" *Journal of Chinese Humanities* 4, no. 2 (March): 197–224.

———. 2019b. "Why the Confucians Had No Concept of Race (Part I): The Antiessentialist Cultural Understanding of Self." *Philosophy Compass* 14, no. 10 (October): e12628. https://doi.org/10.1111/phc3.12628.

———. 2019c. "Why the Confucians Had No Concept of Race (Part II): Cultural Difference, Environment and Achievement." *Philosophy Compass* 14, no. 10 (October): e12627. https://doi.org/10.1111/phc3.12627.

———. 2020. "The Racism of Philosophy's Fear of Cultural Relativism." *Journal of World Philosophies* 5 (1): 99–120.

Xu Fuguan 徐复观. 1996. "Yuan Renwen 原人文" In *Zhongguo Renwen Jingzhen zhi Chanyang: Xu Fuguan Xinrujia Xuelun Zhujiyao* 中国人文精神之阐扬: 徐复观新儒学论著辑要. Edited by Li Weiwu 李维武. Beijing: Zhongguo Guangbo Dianshi Chubanshe 中国广播电视出版社.

———. 2013a. "Shi Ci de Bixing: Chongxin Dianding Zhongguo Shi de Xinshang Jichu 诗的比兴: 重新奠定中国诗的欣赏基础." In *Zhongguo Wenxue Lunji* 中国文学论集. Beijing: Jiuzhou Chubanshe 九州出版社.

———. 2013b. *Zhongguo Yishu Jingshen: Shitao Zhiyi Yanjiu* 中国艺术精神: 石涛之一研究. Beijing: Jiuzhou Chubanshe 九州出版社.

Ye Lang 叶朗. 2015. *Zhongguo Meixueshi Dagang* 中国美学史大纲. Shanghai: Shanghai Renmin Chubanshe 上海人民出版社.

Yearley, Lee H. 1990. *Mencius and Aquinas: Theories of Virtue and Conceptions of Courage.* Albany: State University of New York Press.

Yeh Chia-ying Florence 叶嘉莹. 1997. *Zhongguo Gudian Shici Jiangyan Ji* 中国古典诗词讲演集. Shijiazhuang: Hubei Jiaoyu Chubanshe 河北教育出版社.

Yu, Pauline. 1987. *The Reading of Imagery in the Chinese Poetic Tradition.* Princeton, NJ: Princeton University Press.

Zammito, John. 2001. "Epigenesis: Concept and Metaphor in J. G. Herder's Ideen." In *Vom Selbstdenken: Aufklaerung und Aufklaerungskritik in Johann Gottfried Herders "Ideen zur Philosophie der Geschichte der Menschheit,"* edited by John Zammito and Regine Otto, 131–45. Heidelberg: Synchron.

Zhu Xi 朱熹. 1983. *Sishu Zhangju Jizhu* 四书章句集注. Beijing: Zhonghua Shuju 中华书局.

———. 1992. *Zhouyi Benyi* 周易本义. Beijing: Beijing Daxue Chubanshe 北京大学出版社.

Ziporyn, Brook. 2012. *Ironies of Oneness and Difference: Coherence in Early Chinese Thought; Prolegomena to the Study of Li.* Albany: State University of New York Press.

Chinese Primary Sources

Chuci 楚辞. 2015. Commentaries by Lin Jiali 林家骊. Beijing: Zhonghua Shuju 中华书局.

Guoyu 国语. 2013. Commentaries by Chen Tongsheng 陈桐生. Beijing: Zhonghua Shuju 中华书局.

He Guanzi Jiaozhu 鹖冠子校注. 2014. Commentaries by Huang Huaixin 黄怀信. Beijing: Zhonghua Shuju 中华书局.

Huangdi Sijing Jinzhu Jinyi 皇帝四今注今译. 2016. Commentaries by Chen Guying 陈鼓应. Beijing: Zhonghua Shuju 中华书局.

Liji Yijie 礼记译解. 1987. Commentaries by Wang Wenjin 王文锦. Beijing: Zhonghua Shuju 中华书局.

Liu Xiang 刘向. 1987. *Shuoyuan Jiaozheng* 说苑校正. Commentaries by Xiang Zonglu 向宗鲁. Beijing: Zhonghua Shuju 中华书局.

Liu Xie 刘勰. 2008. *Wenxin Diaolong* 文心雕龙. Commentaries by Xu Zhengying 徐正英 and Luo Jiaxiang 罗家湘. Zhengzhou: Zhongchuan Guji Chubanshe 中州古籍出版社.

Lunyu Daxue Zhongyong 论语大学中庸. 2015. Commentaries by Chen Xiaofen 陈晓芬 and Xu Ruzong 徐儒宗. Beijing: Zhonghua Shuju 中华书局.

Mengzi 孟子. 2015. *Mengzi* 孟子. Commentaries by Fang Yong 方勇. Beijing: Zhonghua Shuju 中华书局.

Shangshu 尚书. 2012. Commentaries by Wang Shishun 王世舜 and Wang Cuiye 王翠叶. Beijing: Zhonghua Shuju 中华书局.

Shijing 诗经. 2015. Commentaries by Wang Xiumei 王秀梅. Beijing: Zhonghua Shuju 中华书局.

Sima Qian 司马迁. 2011. *Shiji* 史记. Beijing: Zhonghua Shuju 中华书局.

Song Lian 宋濂. 2001. "*Wenyuan*" 文原. In *Zhonguo Lidai Wenlunxuan* 中国历代文论选: 第三册. Edited by Guo Shaoyu 郭绍虞 and Wang Wensheng 王文生, 1–8. Shanghai 上海: Shanghai Guji Chubanshe 上海古籍出版社.

Wang, Bi, and Kong Yingda 王弼 孔颖达. 1999. *Shisanjing Zhushu: Zhouyi Zhengyi*. 十三经注疏: 周易本义. Beijing: Beijing Daxue Chubanshe 北京大学出版社.

Wang Chong 王充. 1993. *Lunheng Quanyi* 论衡全译. Commentaries by Yuan Huazhong 袁华忠 and Fang Jiachang 方家常. Guizhou Renmin Chubanshe 贵州人民出版社.

Xinxu 新序. 2014. Commentaries by Ma Shinian 马世年. Beijing: Zhonghua Shuju 中华书局.

Xunzi 荀子. 2015. *Xunzi* 荀子. Commentaries by Li Bo 李波. Beijing: Zhonghua Shuju 中华书局.

Xushen 许慎. 2013. *Shuowen Jiezi* 说文解字. Beijing: Zhonghu Shuju 中华书局.

Xushen 许慎 and Duan Yucai 段玉裁. 1988. *Shuowen Jiezi Zhu* 说文解字注. Shanghai: ShanghaiGuji Chubanshe: 上海古籍出版社.

Yizhoushu Huijiao 逸周书彙校集注. 2007. Commentaries by Huang Huaixin 黄怀信. Shanghai: Shanghai Guji Chubanshe 上海古籍出版社.

Zhanguoce 战国策. 1985. Shanghai: Shanghai Guji Chubanshe: 上海古籍出版社.

Zhouli 周礼. 2014. Commentaries by Xu Zhengying 徐正英 and Chang Peiyu 常佩雨. Beijing: Zhonghua Shuju 中华书局.

Zhouyi 周易. 2015. Commentaries by Yang Tiancai 杨天才 and Zhang Shanwen 张善文. Beijing: Zhonghua Shuju 中华书局.

Zhuangzi 庄子. 2010. Commentaries by Fang Yong 方勇. Beijing: Zhonghua Shuju 中华书局.

Zuo Zhuan 左传. 2012. Commentaries by Guo Dan 郭丹, Cheng Xiaoqing 程小青, and Li Binyuan 李彬源. Beijing: Zhonghua Shuju 中华书局.

Index

CPSIA information can be obtained
at www.ICGtesting.com
Printed in the USA
LVHW042344220723
753132LV00008B/287